A

BOOK

The Philip E. Lilienthal imprint
honors special books
in commemoration of a man whose work
at University of California Press from 1954 to 1979
was marked by dedication to young authors
and to high standards in the field of Asian Studies.
Friends, family, authors, and foundations have together
endowed the Lilienthal Fund, which enables UC Press
to publish under this imprint selected books
in a way that reflects the taste and judgment
of a great and beloved editor.

The publisher and the University of California Press Foundation gratefully acknowledge the generous support of the Philip E. Lilienthal Imprint in Asian Studies, established by a major gift from Sally Lilienthal.

CANCER AND THE KALI YUGA

# CANCER

# AND THE KALI YUGA

GENDER, INEQUALITY, AND HEALTH IN SOUTH INDIA

Cecilia Coale Van Hollen

UNIVERSITY OF CALIFORNIA PRESS

University of California Press
Oakland, California

© 2022 by Cecilia Coale Van Hollen

Library of Congress Cataloging-in-Publication Data
    Names: Van Hollen, Cecilia Coale, author.
    Title: Cancer and the Kali Yuga : gender, inequality, and
health in South India / Cecilia Coale Van Hollen.
    Identifiers: LCCN 2022004664 (print) | LCCN
2022004665 (ebook) | ISBN 9780520386525 (cloth) | ISBN
9780520386532 (paperback) | ISBN 9780520386556 (epub)
    Subjects: LCSH: Dalit women—Health and hygiene—
India—Tamil Nadu—21st century. | Dalit women—
Cancer—Treatment—India—Tamil Nadu—21st century. |
Equality—India—Tamil Nadu—21st century. | Public
Health—India—Tamil Nadu—21st century. | Dalit
women—India—Tamil Nadu—Social conditions—21st
century. | Dalit women—India—Tamil Nadu—Economic
conditions—21st century.
    Classification: LCC HQ1744.T3 V36 2022 (print) | LCC
HQ1744.T3 (ebook) | DDC 305.5/688095482—dc23/
eng/20220217

LC record available at https://lccn.loc.gov/2022004664
LC ebook record available at https://lccn.loc.gov/2022004665

31  30  29  28  27  26  25  24  23  22

10  9  8  7  6  5  4  3  2  1

*In memory of my mother,*
*Edith Eliza Van Hollen*
*(December 18, 1927–February 21, 2007)*

*and of Dr. V. Shanta, Chairperson,*
*Cancer Institute WIA, Chennai*
*(March 11, 1927–January 19, 2021)*

# CONTENTS

# PREFACE

Seated cross-legged on a soft tan mat made of woven *korai* grass, with my Blossom Special Notebook and pen in hand, a water bottle by my side, and my mini-recorder perched in the middle of a circle of women, I was leaning in to hear a story about a woman from this village who had died of breast cancer. Except for one teenage girl dressed in an indigo *salwar kameez* who was sitting on the edge of our circle, the others were all grown women in worn and faded saris of yellow, orange, purple, and green. The heat was intense on that July morning in 2015. The rains had not yet come to northeastern Tamil Nadu. We were huddled under the shade of a large neem tree next to the Muthumariamman Temple.

The woman had been twenty-five years old with a very young daughter when she noticed the lump in her breast. She had the breast removed during her treatments and seemed to be all clear of the cancer until it returned ten years later. The radiation therapy she received at that time only made her weaker. She succumbed to the cancer within a year after the recurrence at the age of thirty-six, leaving behind a husband and a fourteen-year-old daughter.

At this point in the telling of the story, the girl in the *salwar kameez* stood up abruptly and dashed into her house next to where we were sitting. We could hear her screaming, then sobbing loudly, then softly whimpering. "It was one year ago but she is still so sad," said the woman sitting next to me.

I felt awful for causing the girl to relive the memories. I moved out of the circle and ducked my head to enter the thatched house where she was lying on a mat. I tried to apologize and console her. I wanted her to know that I understood her pain because my mother had also died from breast cancer. I tried to tell her I was still sad about my mother's death even though eight years had passed but that it gets easier with time. But who was I kidding? My mother lived for almost thirty years after her first cancer diagnosis before the disease took her life when she was almost eighty. She remained with me as a supportive and loving mother until I was well into my forties. This girl had lost her mother while she was still so young, before she was even mature enough to wear a sari. Why did I feel compelled to transcend the obvious differences of time and place between the life of this teenage girl from this Dalit "colony" of a rural village in southern India and of myself, a middle-aged white American woman who had led a life of cosmopolitan privilege? It seemed farcical even to try. Was I evoking my own mother's death as a way to emotionally grease the palms of people in this village for the sake of my ethnographic research?

But perhaps we did in fact share something. I remembered visiting my mother in the white and metallic hospital room in Washington, D.C., where she lay frail and wasting away after her breast cancer had metastasized into her spinal fluid. I couldn't hold back my tears then, despite my best efforts, and my mother asked me why I was crying. What could I say? I said I couldn't wait for her to be back in her own bed at home. Then I fed her the hospital vanilla ice cream from a tiny wooden spoon. She loved that. But she didn't go back to her own bed. When my father called me two days later to tell me that my mother had died, a howling scream streamed out of my body like no other scream of mine. One of the last things my mother had uttered was the Buddhist mantra: *om mani padme hum.*

Cancer erupted into my life in 1979 when I was fourteen: my mother was diagnosed with breast cancer at the age of fifty-one. It is not a coincidence that I was drawn to the study of cancer just as I was approaching the same age my mother was when she was first diagnosed. I had begun to wonder if I would face the same fate. Nor is it a coincidence that my research would be based in India, given the trajectory of my parents' lives. My father was a US diplomat, serving first in Delhi and Calcutta (now Kolkata), India, in the early 1950s and eventually in Colombo, Sri Lanka, in the mid-1970s (with stints in Pakistan and Turkey along the way). I studied at an international school—the British Overseas Children's School—for most of our time in Sri Lanka from 1972 to 1976 and briefly attended a boarding school in the small hill town of Kodaikanal in Tamil Nadu, India, before my family was posted back to Washington.

My mother would be diagnosed with cancer two years later, just as she was beginning a new job as an intelligence researcher on the South Asia desk at the US Department of State. I watched as she went through what were routine treatments for breast cancer in America at that time—a radical double mastectomy (to remove both breasts and all her underarm lymph nodes with no breast reconstruction), a hysterectomy (to remove her uterus), an oophorectomy (to remove her ovaries), and an onslaught of chemotherapy and radiation therapy treatments. I tried to care for her in whatever small ways I could, which mostly involved sitting with her on the side of her bed and talking, or preparing frozen Stouffer's dinners for myself and my father when my mother was too sick to cook. At the time, as a young teenager, I didn't comprehend the severity of the situation because my mother was good at shielding me from worrying too much. In later years, she told me that what kept her going was the satisfaction and sense of purpose she got from her new job, where she had been assigned to intelligence research for Afghanistan just one week before the Soviet invasion.

I have continued to return to Tamil Nadu ever since those early childhood days, spending my senior year of college there to learn the Tamil language and returning for my dissertation research and subsequent research projects over the years. I have devoted my career to studying women's health issues in South India, all the while watching my own mother continue to struggle for decades with the breast cancer that eventually took her life shortly after her seventy-ninth birthday.

This is not a book about me or about my mother. But this brief foray into my family's history with cancer and with India is key to understanding the impetus for this book. It serves as a reminder that the personal is political and that the local and the global are deeply and intrinsically intertwined. And it makes me think that that teenage girl in the blue *salwar kameez* and I do share some connection despite the deep divide between us.

# ACKNOWLEDGMENTS

The idea for this project began to percolate during two visits to India in 2013, and I have been working on it ever since in the interstices of much movement and upheaval, including three additional field trips to India, moves from Syracuse to Washington, D.C., to Singapore and back to Washington, D.C., and the global SARS-CoV-2 pandemic. Innumerable people and institutions have inspired, facilitated, and fostered this project from start to finish. I cannot mention each of them but I am grateful to all.

First and foremost, I want to thank the women and men in Tamil Nadu, India, who took the time to share their opinions as well as their stories of their experiences with cancer. Many welcomed me into their homes or cleared a spot on their hospital beds for me to sit with them to bear witness to their struggles with cancer and with their everyday lives. Others graciously gathered with me in small groups on the edges of fields where they worked, or in open-air spaces in their villages and urban neighborhoods, at the threshold of temples, on rooftops, or by the side of dirt roads with motorbikes and water buffalos veering off to avoid us. Doctors, nurses, hospital administrators, social workers, counselors, a spirit medium, and people involved in governmental, multilateral, and nongovernmental public health programs all took time out of their busy schedules to answer my questions, share helpful documents, show me around their places of work, and introduce me to other people in their networks whom they thought could help me with my research. For confidentiality reasons, I cannot name these individuals and have given them pseudonyms in the book.

I obtained Institutional Review Board approval from Syracuse University to conduct interviews and observations for this project.

The fieldwork, library research, and writing for this book were made possible through generous grants and fellowships from the Woodrow Wilson International Center for Scholars, the American Institute of Indian Studies, Syracuse University, and Yale–NUS College, and through my Visiting Researcher affiliation with the Asian Studies Program at Georgetown University. I want to particularly acknowledge the key organizations in Tamil Nadu that provided me with affiliations to carry out this fieldwork: The Cancer Institute WIA, the Rural Women's Social Education Centre, and the Government Arignar Anna Memorial Cancer Hospital. I discuss the history of these institutions and my engagements with each of them in the book. I also thank the Indian Institute of Technology–Madras, especially members of the Department of Humanities and Social Sciences, for providing me with an academic affiliation and fruitful conversations for this project and for accommodating me in a hostel on campus. This book would not have been possible without the enormous help and camaraderie of my research assistants, Shweta Krishnan and Shibani Rathnam, who facilitated every facet of the fieldwork and who became good friends in the process.

Versions of Chapters 5 and 7 were previously published in *Medical Anthropology Quarterly* (Van Hollen 2018) and in *Purushartha* (Van Hollen, Krishnan, and Rathnam 2019) respectively. A version of Chapter 4 will be published (Van Hollen forthcoming 2023) in a volume titled *Cancer and the Politics of Care: Inequalities and Interventions in Global Perspective*. I am grateful to the editors and the anonymous reviewers of each of these publications for their constructive comments, and I thank the publishers for granting permission to include portions of these works in this book.

This book has benefited from feedback on presentations of parts of this research to many audiences. These forums include annual conferences of the Association for Asian Studies, the American Anthropological Association, the Madison South Asia Conference, and the Society for Cultural Anthropology; two workshops ("Cancer in the South: Thinking with Precarity" and "Cartographies of Cancer") organized by the Department of Global Health at King's College London; the Chronic Living Conference organized by the University of Copenhagen; the Gender Cluster Research Seminar at Yale–NUS College; and lectures presented at colloquia for the Woodrow Wilson International Center for Scholars' Maternal Health Initiative, the

Anthropology Department at George Washington University, and the Social Science Division at Yale–NUS College in Singapore.

Insights and suggestions from countless other colleagues and students who have read parts or all of this book manuscript, assisted with the collection of essential books, articles, documents, and affiliations, and provided feedback at conferences and workshops have enriched this project. These people include (but are certainly not limited to) Dwaipayan Banerjee, Carlo Caduff, Subhasri B., V. Shanta, J.S. Maliga, R. Swaminathan, E. Vidhubala, P. Balasubramanian, Sreekumar N., Mathangi Krishnamurthy, V.R. Muraleedharan, Kavita Sivaramakrishnan, Kamala Ganesh, Anandhi S., Aditya Bharadwaj, Ayo Wahlberg, Fabien Provost, Neena Mahadev, Stuart Strange, Gabriele Koch, Darja Djordjevic, Marissa Mika, Lucas Mueller, Mark Nichter, Marcia Inhorn, Joseph Alter, Martha Selby, Ann Gold, Radha Kumar, John Burdick, Shannon Novak, Harris Solomon, Sarah Pinto, Kaushik Sunder Rajan, Lawrence Cohen, Linda Bennet, Lenore Manderson, Belinda Spagnoletti, Sarah Barnes, Neeti Nair, Malin Monjörk, Maria DeJesus, Rachel Sullivan Robinson, Emily Mendenhall, Sarojini N., Mohan Rao, Sunita Reddy, V. Geetha, Purnima Mehta, Aparajita Gogoi, Vineeta Bal, Ravi Verma, Rema Nagarajan, Alisa Weinstein, Madhura Lohokare, Jocelyn Killmer, Laurah Klepinger, Lalit Narayan, Jonathon Jackson, Rahul Bhatia, and Kristian-Marc James Paul.

I am grateful to my editors at the University of California Press: Reed Malcolm, who was enthusiastic about this book when I first pitched the idea to him several years ago and who ushered the book through to the contract, and Kim Robinson, who provided a seamless transition after Reed left the press. The exceptionally thoughtful anonymous peer reviewers of the manuscript have helped me clarify key points through the revision process. LeKeisha Hughes and the editorial team at the press have guided me through the production process to bring this book to print.

Last but not least, I thank my partner, Charles Freeman, and my children, Lila Van Hollen Rodgers and Jasper Van Hollen Rodgers, for keeping me grounded, believing in the value of my work as a medical anthropologist, and inspiring me with their own passionate projects in the midst of so much change in our lives during all the years that I have been working on this book.

## ABBREVIATIONS

| | |
|---|---|
| ACS | American Cancer Society |
| AIADMK | All India Anna Dravida Munnetra Kazhagam |
| AIIMS | All-Indian Institute of Medical Sciences |
| AIWC | All-India Women's Conference |
| BC | Backward Classes |
| BJP | Bharatiya Janata Party |
| CRO | contract research organization |
| DDT | Dichlorodiphenyltrichloroethane |
| DMK | Dravida Munnetra Kazhagam |
| FPS | Fair Price Shops |
| GDP | gross domestic product |
| HCH | Hexachlorocyclohexane |
| HIV/AIDS | Human Imunodeficiency Virus/ Acquired Immunodeficiency Syndrome |
| HPV | human pappilomavirus |
| IARC | International Agency for Research on Cancer |
| IUD | intrauterine device |
| LTTE | Liberation Tigers of Tamil Eelam |
| MBC | Most Backward Classes |

| | |
|---|---|
| MGNREGA | Mahatma Gandhi National Rural Employment Guarantee Act |
| NCI | National Cancer Institute |
| NGO | nongovernmental organization |
| NIH | National Institutes of Health |
| OB/GYN | Obstetrician/Gynecologist |
| OBC | Other Backward Classes |
| PDS | Public Distribution System |
| PHC | Primary Health Centre |
| RUWSEC | Rural Women's Social Education Centre |
| SC | Scheduled Castes |
| ST | Scheduled Tribes |
| UN | United Nations |
| UNICEF | United Nations International Children's Emergency Fund |
| USAID | US Agency for International Development |
| VCK | Viduthalai Chiruthaigal Katchi |
| VIA | visual inspection with acetic acid |
| VILI | visual inspection with Lugol's iodine |
| WHO | World Health Organization |
| WIA | Women's Indian Association |

# NOTE ON TIME OF WRITING
# AND TRANSLITERATION

Most of this book was written while I was on leave from teaching in 2017–18 as a Visiting Researcher in the Asian Studies Program at Georgetown University and a Public Policy Fellow at the Woodrow Wilson Center for International Scholars. I completed writing a draft of the manuscript in mid-2020 and made editorial revisions between June and September 2021.

I have chosen not to use diacritical marks for transliteration on non-English words to facilitate reading.

# INTRODUCTION

Cancer is a process of proliferation. Proliferation of cells, of suffering, of medicine, of technology, of stories. It touches bodies, individuals, families, communities, and nations. It has touched the lives of the women living with cancer in India, whose stories fill this book. It has touched their husbands, daughters, sons, neighbors, doctors, nurses, counselors, and spirit mediums, who also appear in this book. It has touched me. It more than likely has touched you too.

This book is about how women experience and give meaning to cancer in India in the early twenty-first century. How do women think about cancer causality and risk? How do they come to know they have cancer? What measures do they take when they receive a cancer diagnosis? What are their experiences with biomedical and other treatment and healing modalities for cancer? What are their opinions of the recent push for cancer screening and early detection and treatment for women? I am interested in understanding the meaning of cancer in general because, despite the fact that each type of cancer represents a discreet disease, most people worldwide view cancer as a broadly defined disease and have strong feelings and opinions about cancer as an all-encompassing category of disease. At the same time, this book focuses particularly on breast and cervical cancers in India both because these are the two most common cancers among women in India and because the emerging global public health interventions to promote cancer screening for women draw these two reproductive cancers together in their educational programs

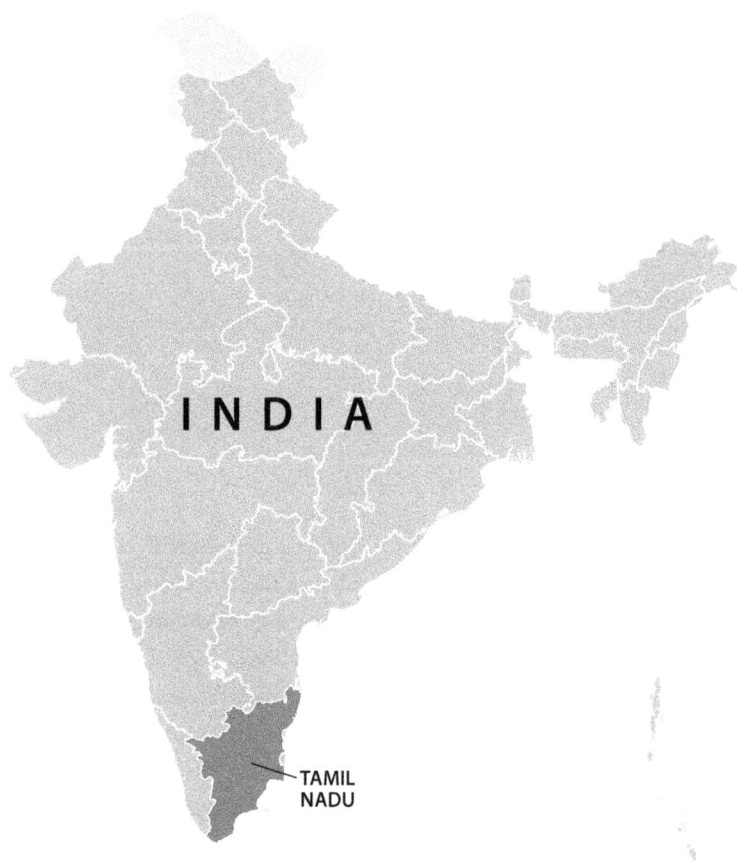

MAP 1. India, with state of Tamil Nadu shaded.

and in their clinical screenings, with consequences for how women view and experience these cancers.

My focus is on the experiences of lower-class, lower-caste (more accurately, oppressed-caste) women who are the targets of these global public health interventions. Throughout this book, I draw from accounts I collected during ethnographic interviews and casual conversations with women in the South Indian state of Tamil Nadu between 2015 and 2016 (see Map 1). By listening carefully to the narratives of the women who generously gave their time and shared their stories and perspectives with me, I came to understand how sociocultural factors (including gender, class, caste, ethnicity, and religion) and political-economic transformations (impacting labor, agriculture and food production, the environment, family structure, and public healthcare) affect women's encounters with cancer. In this book, I present these women's insights so that we can appreciate how sociocultural context shapes the cancer experience.

My goal is twofold. First, I offer this ethnography in the hope that it will prove valuable for global and local public health planners and practitioners seeking to improve health and healthcare for all. Second, while keeping cancer at the center of this study, this ethnography sheds light more broadly on sociocultural dynamics and political-economic changes in India today and on South Indian women's—particularly socioeconomically marginalized women's—perceptions of the social worlds they inhabit. As other anthropologists have noted, borrowing a phrase from Claude Lévi-Strauss,[1] cancer is "good to think with" because the meanings people attribute to it and the ways people respond to and engage with it tell us a great deal about core cultural values and social relationships.[2]

The stories offered by the lower-class and -caste women at the heart of my study make abundantly clear the extent to which their class, caste, and gender positions intersect so as to inform their perceptions of cancer causality and risk and their journeys navigating their cancer diagnosis, treatment, and care. Through their narratives, these women articulated a wide range of critiques about sociocultural and political-economic systems that had marginalized them and that jeopardized their health and well-being. Contrary to the educational messages of public health campaigns, which attributed reproductive cancer risk to individual choices associated with sexual and reproductive practices, diet, and exercise, the women in my study attributed the risk of cancer in their communities to a host of economic, environmental, and social factors beyond their control that had rendered poor women's bodies vulnerable to these cancers. Contrary to doctors who would scold them for being irresponsible by coming to the hospital too late, or for having irrational fears and harmful superstitious beliefs, women cancer patients were quick to point out how the nexus of their class, caste, and gender position constrained their search for cancer treatment and respectful care.

The social stigma of a cervical or breast cancer diagnosis led women to reflect on and assert their integrity as *good* women. Lower-class and -caste women patients recognized that their triply marginalized social status had heightened the stigma of these reproductive cancers and compounded the threat cancer posed to the prestige and honor of themselves and their families.

They also understood that their subaltern status exacerbated the challenges they faced in their search for diagnosis and healing. Their reflections on their own perceptions and experiences with cancer shed light on the everyday precarity of their lives. They felt that their precarity and reliance on the welfare meted out by state and civil society organizations had curtailed their ability to publicly voice their complaints. This ethnography serves as a conduit for a subaltern critique that is already present but too often politically silenced. The experiences and critiques of my interlocutors are intertwined. They commonly described cancer as both a sign and a result of the inhumane, unjust, and amoral contemporary era, resembling the Kali Yuga.[3] The Kali Yuga is a Hindu concept that refers to a dark, unjust era, as I discuss further below. Yet these women's stories also demonstrated how creative and resilient they could be throughout their therapeutic ordeal with cancer as they worked in concert with networks of caregivers to find ways to survive in the face of staggering odds, even while sometimes questioning their will to live in the process.

## POONGODAI'S STORY

I open with the story of a woman I call Poongodai.[4] As with most of my interviews, I conducted this one in Tamil. Tamil speakers often pepper their speech with English words; when they have done so, in the translations I have placed those English words within quotation marks. Unless otherwise indicated, all of the quotes from interviews in this book are translated from Tamil.

Poongodai was fifty years old when I met her at the Rural Women's Social Education Centre (RUWSEC), a small grassroots nongovernmental organization (NGO) run by and for rural Dalit (oppressed, lower-caste) women that has long focused on women's health. I had traveled 60 kilometers south by car from my hostel on the Indian Institute of Technology–Madras campus in Chennai (the capital city of Tamil Nadu), where I was staying for the summer. On the day of our interview in July 2016, Poongodai and her husband had come to RUWSEC from their nearby village for a monthly support group meeting for cancer patients and survivors. She had undergone three months of treatment for cervical cancer at the Cancer Institute in Chennai, where she received fully subsidized care. Because she lived too far away to go home in between her treatments, she had remained in the general ward as an inpatient alongside many other female cancer patients for the full three months. Other women staying with her on the ward had traveled even farther than she had, some from Tirunelveli at the southern tip of the state (twelve hours away by train and much longer by bus) and some from the adjacent state of Andhra Pradesh to the north. Poongodai had received free treatment because her family lived below the poverty line, but her family had had to shell out 1,000 rupees as a bribe to their Village Officer to get the income certificate they needed to prove she was eligible for that subsidy. Poongodai had been discharged from the Cancer Institute and returned to her village three months prior to our meeting, but she was still undergoing cancer treatments on an outpatient basis, traveling almost four hours round-trip by bus to reach the hospital.

A Dalit woman with no formal education who had four grown children (two daughters and two sons) between the ages of twenty-four and twenty-seven, Poongodai had spent her life working as an agricultural daily wage laborer, doing the backbreaking work of transplanting rice paddy in other people's fields in her village. Daily wage labor is locally referred to in Tamil as *kuli* work (often spelled in English as "coolie"). In some contexts this is considered a pejorative term that connotes colonial servitude. Colonists used the term "coolie" to dehumanize migrant laborers by conflating their identity with their mode of payment, calling workers coolies and thereby justifying their exploitation.[5] However, people in contemporary Tamil Nadu who are engaged in daily wage labor use the Tamil term *"kuli"* to refer to work for fixed daily wages; they do not use it to refer to their identity. So I have chosen to use the term to refer to this form of labor in order to remain true to the accounts of my interlocutors.

Poongodai also earned some income working through the government's Mahatma Gandhi National Rural Employment Guarantee Act (MGN-REGA) scheme. She and many other women I met referred to this program as the "100 days" program because, in theory, the rural poor were entitled to paid work for one hundred days. In Tamil Nadu most of this work involved water management-related projects (building ponds, bunds, and irrigation tanks for paddy fields), but in 2016, the state was facing one of the worst droughts on record, so these projects had come to a virtual standstill and my interlocutors reported that that extra income had mostly ended.

Poongodai also owned a goat that she was raising for meat. She had previously owned two cows, which she milked for her family's consumption and for sale. She had recently sold her cows because she had become too weak to take care of them due to her cancer and because she needed the cash from the sale to support herself and her husband, who was suffering from oral cancer, which is the most common form of cancer among men in India and the leading cause of cancer death among Indian men. She and her husband both received cancer treatments free of charge at the Cancer Institute; however, they had to spend a lot on diagnostic tests in private clinics. They had sold their two cows for 8,000 and 9,000 rupees respectively and had pawned Poongodai's only pair of gold earrings to cover the costs of their tests.

Poongodai was diagnosed with Stage I cervical cancer in 2014, just a few weeks after her husband's cancer diagnosis. She had been experiencing heavy white vaginal discharge (leukorrhea), fever, and pain in her pelvic area for a couple of months and had finally gone to see a doctor, fearing she had typhoid. Doctors had recommended immediate treatment following her cancer diagnosis; however, even with her persistent symptoms, she had put off getting medical care for herself for two years in order to take care of her husband, who was already receiving treatments at the Cancer Institute. That women tended to prioritize the health and well-being of other family members before taking care of themselves was a theme that ran through all of my interviews and reflected the gender norms at hand. By the time Poongodai was admitted to the hospital for her own treatment in 2016, her cancer had advanced to Stage III. She began her treatments while at the Cancer Institute but had to curtail them when her white blood cell count became dangerously low due to the radiation and chemotherapy; she was discharged without completing the full course of treatment. She felt that her lifelong hard labor had weakened her body, leaving her not only suseptible to cancer but also unable to withstand her cancer treatments.

When I met Poongodai, she had very short hair that was just beginning to grow back after it had fallen out in clumps during her chemotherapy treatments. The bright pink *pottu* (bindi) on her forehead perfectly matched the color of her sari. But her demeanor was bleak and broken. She spoke softly and with downcast eyes as she described the shame she and her husband felt because of their cancers:

> We feel like it is very disgusting [*asingam*] that we both have cancer. It is so embarrassing for other people to see us like this. Our prestige/honor/respect [*kauravam*] has been diminished. Some people in our village say it is because of our bad intentions [*yennam*] that we are now experiencing this illness.

A few weeks after she returned home from the hospital, her goat had crossed the fence between her property and that of her neighbor and eaten a newly planted sapling in her neighbor's field. Upon seeing this, the neighbor came stumbling out of his house drunk and yelling, saying that her intention to destroy other people's property in this way had given her and her husband cancer. He framed it as a form of karmic justice. She continued to recount this story to me:

> So then I came crying and I yelled at the gods, asking, "What sins have I committed?" Even my husband never wishes ill on anyone. So, why would we get such an illness? I cried, saying that we had become objects of ridicule for others in our village. Ever since then I have been worried about what other people are saying about us in their homes.

Poongodai was not only concerned that people in her village might blame them for their roaming goat. She was also deeply worried that people would question her morality and spread rumors that she was sexually promiscuous and that it was because of such behavior that she had come down with this disease. As she said,

> People say things like, "She must have gone around with everyone she likes. That is why she has the disease." When my husband and I both have this problem, then so many people who see us, think badly about us. There are so many people who do bad and cruel things—rich people who destroy the country. But they are fine. We are good, humble people from lower, humble families [*thazhntha kudumbangal*], so why should *we* get this thing? I think it is because of all the *kuli* work I have done since I was young. We are getting this thing [cancer] while rich people are getting fat. This is the way things are these days in the Kali Yuga.

Poongodai also suspected that her father-in-law's sister's son had used sorcery to inflict cancer on her and her husband, though she did not discuss this openly with others in her village. There had been a land dispute, and when she stood up and protested this man's attempt to claim some of the family property, he had threatened her, saying: "Watch out for what I will do to you. Let us see how you live." Three months later, she and her husband were diagnosed with cancer. Ever since then, Poongodai had tried to avoid this relative at all costs.

On top of all of this, Poongodai was ashamed that her and her husband's cancers were placing an enormous financial burden on their son, who lived with them and who was now supporting them along with his wife and two children while simultaneously pursuing evening studies to get a degree for a better job. During the daytime her son worked for a small company and was earning 10,000 rupees monthly (which was then the equivalent of US$149).[6] This was a respectable income for members of their family and the Dalit community in their village, but it was nearly impossible to make ends meet supporting six people on that income. Her son's wife could no longer earn money because she had to stay home to provide all of the caregiving needed for her young children and now also for her ailing in-laws. The repairs needed to fix their broken roof would have to wait, and meanwhile, water came pouring into their house every time it rained, though thankfully that was rare that year because of the drought. With their reduced household income, they struggled to maintain the healthy diet that had been recommended by Poongodai's doctor. Ironically, one of the things Poongodai's doctors had recommended when she was discharged was that she drink a lot of milk. After selling their cows, they could not afford to purchase milk from others.

Before her illness she and her husband had been financially self-sufficient, even if they lived on a very modest income. She had been earning between 5,000 and 6,000 rupees (US$75–90) each month and was proud that through her hard labor she had been able to raise a son who was on the cusp of moving into the middle class. But because of her illness, she could not even contribute 10 rupees. She could not bear being dependent on her son and lamented that her and her husband's cancers were shattering their dreams for the son to break into the middle class.

Ever since being diagnosed with cancer she had suffered severe pain in her legs and hips and was too weak to continue agricultural wage labor and household chores, such as sweeping and hand-washing the clothes and cooking vessels, all of which require bending, squatting, and stamina. During our interview, she found it uncomfortable to sit still for long and was constantly shifting her position to relieve her pain. She was grateful to her daughter-in-law for doing all of the household work and for not ostracizing her or making her eat from separate plates as some families did when caring for cancer patients due to fears of contagion. Poongodai said that on the advice of the public health counselors at both RUWSEC and the Cancer Institute, she had urged her daughter-in-law and her own daughters to get cervical and breast cancer screenings as soon as they turned thirty and to continue to do so regularly so that they would not have to endure her misery.

Poongodai had prayed to the Hindu goddess Mariamman—a popular goddess among Dalit communities in Tamil Nadu—every day since she could remember by lighting a small oil lamp in the Mariamman temple near her house. Straining hard to hold back the tears gathering in her eyes, she admitted that she felt betrayed by the goddess, for she and her husband were both suffering from cancer at the same time:

> I went to temple and shouted [to Mariamman], "See what days you've made me face! Even if I had nothing more than a rupee in my hand, even if I had to make do with nothing to eat but *kanji* [rice porridge], I always spent money to buy oil for the lamps I lit for you. Every day I came here to pray to you, and now you have put me in this position." I went there and cried loudly.

In her search for some explanation as to why she and her husband faced this grave misfortune, she had consulted a Brahmin astrologer to learn whether it was a result of planetary misalignments and to ask about her future. The astrologer told her that her difficulties should wane by the end of the Tamil lunar month of Aadi (from mid-July to mid-August). That was just a few weeks away from the time of our interview. She had decided that if she continued to suffer physically and to be tormented by the people in her village after Aadi, she would convert to Christianity. She thought perhaps it might help because of advice she had received from of a group of Christian women who sometimes visited to pray for her and other patients on the hospital ward and who brought biscuits and juice and even saris, shirts, and *lungis*.[7] Then she added in a whisper,

> If that also does not work, I will do something to myself. . . . I want to finish my own story. I don't want to live when my body is so very tired. People scolded me, saying, "You have been cured and now you want to die?!" . . . But I am angry with the gods. Praying to them has done nothing but bring me to this.

As I wrapped up our conversation, my research assistants and I urged her to talk to the psychological counselor at RUWSEC to help her cope with these feelings and find a reason to live. While I always maintain the confidentiality of people whom I interview, this time I made an exception and we informed the RUWSEC counselor about the last part of our conversation with Poongodai, before we made the journey back to Chennai at the end of a long and emotionally trying day of fieldwork. The counselor promised to reach out to Poongodai right away. While I thought that psychosocial counseling might help somewhat with the issues of stigma and blame that Poongodai and her husband were experiencing, I had doubts it could do much to address the economic crisis her family faced as a result of cancer.

The story of Poongodai is not representative of all of the women I met. But it does point to the shared experiences of lower-class, lower-caste women on whom cancer wreaks havoc, not only on their bodies but also on the financial and social stability of their families, while shaking their faith to its core. Cancer does not affect only the poor in these ways; it also renders people poor so that these experiences may arise in middle-class families as well, especially in Dalit families that have struggled to gain a foothold in the middle class. A few middle-class, upper-caste women I met claimed that their cancer had been "a blessing" because it had led them to a new appreciation for life and drawn them into social service work to help other women with cancer, thus giving them a newfound sense of purpose. But for the vast majority of the women in my study, cancer was *not* a blessing; it was a curse and a marker of the inhumanity and injustice associated with the Kali Yuga. The narratives presented in this book counter the characterization of marginalized cancer patients in India as passive, ignorant, and noncompliant and demonstrates how they assert their agency in the context of enormous constraints. Poongodai exemplified this. She asserted that it was the hard labor that she endured throughout her life that made her vulnerable to cancer, not her immorality or bad deeds. She explained that she delayed her own treatment and could not follow the dietary recommendations of her doctors not because of ignorance or noncompliance but because she was socially obligated to care for her husband first and because the loss of income and costs of diagnostics and treatment for her and her husband's cancers had drained their family's meager financial resources. She threatened to abandon the gods who had abandoned her and she railed against the injustice of a world that had depleted her body and spirit while rich people get fat. And, morbid as it may be, she asserted her ability to control both her own life and her own narrative when she stated: "I want to finish my own story."

## BREAST AND CERVICAL CANCER AMONG WOMEN IN INDIA

Global public health experts contend that India is facing a mounting cancer crisis in the early twenty-first century. Newly reported cases of cancer are on the rise. It is unclear to what extent this trend can be attributed to an actual increase in cancer incidence and to what extent it is due to the expansion of cancer screening services, educational awareness programs, and treatment options in India. It is most likely a combination of both in India as in other parts of the global South.[8] My ethnography is situated in a moment in history during which cancer has come to be viewed as a public health crisis in India.

Although precise epidemiological data on cancer incidence and mortality rates in India are lacking due to the absence of a long-standing and comprehensive national cancer registry,[9] most reports indicate that the number of newly reported cases of cancer in India was increasing rapidly during the time of my research. In 2014 the World Health Organization's (WHO) International Agency for Research on Cancer's (IARC) GLOBOCAN project predicted that India's cancer burden would rise by almost 70 percent in twenty years (from slightly over 1 million newly reported cases in 2012 to more than 1.7 million by 2035).[10] It is widely assumed that there are vastly more cases of cancer in India than are officially recorded due to underreporting of cancer and of deaths caused by cancer.[11]

Health systems in most parts of India are ill-prepared to respond to this dramatic rise in cancer cases among Indians who cannot afford high-tech privatized cancer screening and treatment. And that is the majority of Indians. Furthermore, because of the terror and stigma of a cancer diagnosis in India, many people delay seeking medical attention. In addition to that, some medical practitioners initially misdiagnose patients and treat them for other problems when they should be treated for cancer. Due to both of these factors, by the time cancer patients *are* correctly diagnosed, they often have late-stage cancers that are much more difficult to treat; moreover, palliative care to ease the pain for patients at the end of their lives is scarce.[12] As a result, India carries a disproportionate share of the world's cancer mortality burden. Fewer than 30 percent of cancer patients in India survive past five years after diagnosis, whereas in North America and Western Europe the five-year survival rate for all cancers is 60 percent.[13]

Unlike in most parts of the world, in India newly reported cancers were higher among women than among men at the time of my research.[14] Breast and cervical cancer are the leading types of cancer among women in India.[15] A 2017 report from the Federation of Indian Chambers of Commerce and Industry's[16] division on women's empowerment stated that in 2015 the reported number of women with cancer in India was 0.7 million. The same study suggested that due to underreporting, the real number of women with cancer in India was more likely between 1 to 1.4 million, and that the incidence of cancer among women in India was growing at a rate between 4.5 and 5 percent per year. It also stated that India has the world's third-highest real (vs. reported) incidence of cancer among women after China and the United States.[17]

Yet the vast majority of Indian women have not had access to a Pap smear or a mammogram for early detection of cervical and breast cancers.[18] The disparity in access to early cancer screening and treatment between low- and middle-income countries, such as India, on the one hand, and high-income countries on the other, is particularly glaring for cervical and breast cancer, given the remarkable progress that has been made in treatment outcomes for these cancers if they are detected at an early stage.[19] One result of this disparity is that more women die from both cervical and breast cancer in India than anywhere else in the world.[20] Breast cancer is now the most common cause of cancer death in India; 13 percent of all deaths from breast cancer worldwide occur in India.[21] A whopping 25 percent of all women who die from cervical cancer in the world are Indian.[22]

In the early twenty-first century, international global health agencies, along with national and state governments and NGOs, have made a major push to promote and provide screening and treatment for cervical and breast cancer in low-income communities in India. With support from the World Bank, Tamil Nadu was the first Indian state to incorporate these screenings into its public primary health program, beginning with some districts in 2010 and reaching state-wide coverage in 2012 through the Tamil Nadu Health Systems Project. In 2016 the Government of India's National Health Mission launched a similar program for all of India. Unlike Pap smears and mammograms, which are routinely used in many countries, recent screening interventions in Tamil Nadu and elsewhere in India have relied heavily on low-cost, low-tech methods of visual screening for cervical cancer that were developed in India,[23] combined with clinical breast exams and instructions for breast self-exams. These new cervical cancer screening technologies—VIA (visual inspection with acetic acid using a vinegar-based swab) and VILI (visual inspection with Lugol's iodine)—use visual examinations with no need for microscopes or laboratory analysis. Although they are not as reliable as Pap smears and require further diagnostic tests to confirm malignancy, many global public health experts consider them economically more sustainable for first-line screening in India and other low- and middle-income countries.

Screening programs can only succeed if there are good treatment options for cervical and breast cancer. Tamil Nadu was selected as the first state to integrate cancer screening into public primary health care because the state government has a long-standing commitment to public health for primary and tertiary healthcare. Public and private medical facilities in Tamil Nadu are among the best in the country.[24] Biomedical treatment for cancer has been included under the state's Chief Minister's Comprehensive Health Insurance Scheme, which provides qualifying low-income families with medical insurance coverage up to one lakh (100,000) rupees per year—more for certain critical conditions and specialized surgeries. This insurance scheme, initially launched under the leadership of Chief Minister Jayalalithaa, issues one insurance card for every family whose income is below 72,000 rupees per year. All members of the family are allowed to benefit from this insurance as long as their names appear on the ration card. That document is used to officially record a family's socioeconomic status and thus its entitlement to subsidies for healthcare, among other things.[25] Launched in 2012, this insurance program covers the costs of basic surgery, chemotherapy, and radiotherapy for cancer patients in public hospitals, or an equivalent sum of money for treatment in a private hospital. Along with these funds, subsidized care in hospitals run by NGOs has encouraged more people in the state to seek cancer screening, diagnosis, and treatment.

In February 2018 the Government of India's budget for 2018–19 included a similar insurance plan—the Ayushman Bharat plan—to provide health insurance coverage for families in poverty throughout India, with up to 5 lakh (500,000) rupees per qualifying family to be used to access healthcare in the private and public healthcare sectors. This is a promising development, particularly considering the fact that India has had one of the world's lowest rates of public health spending per GDP in the world, with a high percentage of government health spending going to the private sector.[26] In response to this national program, Tamil Nadu increased its insurance coverage to 5 lakh in December 2018.[27] Critics argue that the transition from a socialist model of "public health care for all" that was established in the post-independence era to a model of public health insurance coverage after India liberalized the economy in the late twentieth century has undermined the quality of public hospitals by diverting more public funds to private healthcare and health insurance institutions.

Increased access to screening, early detection, and treatment for cervical and breast cancer has the potential to save the lives of countless women in India. Yet social science research to understand Indian women's experiences with these cancers and their views about cancer causality, prevention, screening, and treatment has not kept pace with the public health and biomedical interventions for these cancers. Deeper understanding of the perspectives, opinions, and constraints of the people for whom these health interventions are designed is crucial for the success of the programs. As my colleagues and I have argued, bringing interdisciplinary social science approaches to bear on global public health approaches to oncology can extend "the range of relevant policy agendas beyond a focus on behavior and compliance to the more nuanced, context-specific policy challenges only discernible through long-term empirical research."[28] The ethnographic material presented in this book offers a context-specific portrait of the social contours of cancer as experienced by women who are the targets for global public health cancer programs in South India.

Reflecting on interviews with clinical oncologists in Delhi, the sociologist-anthropologist team of Alex Broom and Assa Doron concluded that "without a greater understanding of social and cultural issues shaping cancer care in India, little progress will be made in coping with a disease that is set to become a major burden within an increasingly aging population."[29] My medical anthropological research helps fill this gap by bringing the voices of women and communities targeted by these public health programs for cancer in India to the table to demand that their concerns be more vigorously addressed by local, national, and global health institutions involved in cancer prevention and treatment.

Public health approaches to stem the tide of cancer in India are premised on assertions that what is needed is more information for poor communities about cancer prevention behavior, as well as the importance of early diagnosis, of seeking biomedical care in a timely fashion, and of following doctors' recommendations. The focus is on individual behavior change. Ignorance, irrational cultural beliefs, and lack of biomedical oncology interventions are viewed as the primary obstacles to the success of public health programs for breast and cervical cancers. Education and biomedical fixes are seen as the primary solutions. The lower-class and -caste women at the heart of my study agreed that more information about cancer causality and better oncological treatments are crucial and would be welcome. However, they attributed the problem of cancer in their communities to a host of sociocultural and political-economic structures that are beyond the scope of individual behavior change, that put them at risk for getting these cancers, and that compromise the biomedical care they receive. Crucially, they explained that the nexus of their class, caste, and gender position in society had rendered them increasingly vulnerable to these reproductive cancers and to the social, economic, and physical suffering they produced.

## CANCER AND THE KALI YUGA

References to the Kali Yuga surfaced repeatedly as Dalit and other lower-caste women framed cancer and its effects. They saw cancer as a modern disease resulting from business greed and government corruption; from rising unemployment and the physical exhaustion of overwork; from drought and poverty; from agricultural chemicals and lack of nutrition; from unequal gender relations and irresponsible husbands; and even from uncaring gods and goddesses. As socioeconomically marginalized women reflected on cancer, they also reflected on the world around them. For them, cancer was a problem that needed explanation on both individual and social levels. They elicited the idiom of the Kali Yuga and its implicit degradation of *dharma* (proper conduct) to make the case that the political, economic, and social structures of contemporary society are shot through with injustice.

The Kali Yuga, as described in ancient Hindu texts, refers to the fourth and final of four eras (*yugas*) the world goes through. It is a period of darkness in which people have lost their way spiritually and are driven by avarice rather than *dharma*. By framing the problems of cancer in their communities as a sign of the Kali Yuga, women found ways to condemn the social, economic, and environmental changes that were impacting their lives. Whereas some may see the discourse of the Kali Yuga as fatalistic and curtailing women's agency, I argue that their use of this trope constituted a powerful act of social and political critique and a call for change. Women in my study were not making millenarian claims that doomsday was at hand. Rather, they were making the case that social, political, and economic injustices had in myriad ways rendered them increasingly vulnerable to cancer and its attendant suffering, and they were pointing to a resemblance between the conditions of their lives and those of the adharmic Kali Yuga. In short, they evoked the Kali Yoga to underscore the magnitude of their daily struggles in an unjust time.

Within the cyclical nature of time in Hindu cosmology described in ancient Sanskrit texts, such as *The Puranas* and *The Mahabharata*, the universe is in a constant cycle of creation and destruction. Each cycle, or *mahayuga*, contains four eras (*yugas*) each of which becomes progressively shorter in time and degenerate in quality. The cycle moves from the first *yuga*, known as the Krta

Yuga (the perfect age), to the Treta Yuga, to the Dvapara Yuga, and finally to the Kali Yuga (the dark age). The Kali Yuga is associated with the demon Kali (not to be confused with the goddess Kālī). With each successive *yuga*, *dharma* diminishes and greed increases. At the beginning of each full *mahayuga* cycle, all beings live well, sustained by "wishing trees abounding in honey," and rains nourish the earth, plants, and trees, which provide food and shelter for all.[30] Over time, virtue diminishes and greed, anger, and violence increase until by the time of the Kali Yuga the world is a desolate and inhospitable place. In their textual extracts from *The Puranas*, Cornelia Dimmitt and J.A.B. van Buitenen write:

> In the Kali there is fatal disease, continuous hunger and fear, awful dread of drought and revolution in the lands.... All kings occupying the earth in the Kali Age will be wanting in tranquility, strong in anger, taking pleasure at all times in lying and dishonesty, inflicting death on women, children, and cows, prone to take paltry possessions of others.... They will be short-lived, ambitious, of little virtue and greedy.... The destruction of the world will occur because of the departure from virtue.... Money alone will confer nobility. Power will be the sole definition of virtue. Pleasure will be the only reason for marriage. Lust will be the only reason for womanhood.... Being dry of water will be the only definition of land.... Oppressed by their excessively greedy ruler, people will hide in valleys between mountains where they will gather honey, vegetables, roots, fruits, birds, flowers and so forth. Suffering from cold, wind, heat and rain, they will put on clothes made of tree-bark and leaves. And no one will live as long as twenty-three years. Thus in the Kali Age humankind will be utterly destroyed.[31]

While this schema may seem deterministic, the concept of the Kali Yuga accounts for human and divine agency in the degeneration or maintenance of the world.

Lower-class Dalit Christians and Hindus alluded to the Kali Yuga when describing the havoc that cancer was wreaking on their communities, as it is a pan-Indian cultural trope. A 2014 special issue of the journal *Nidān* provides ethnographic examples of contemporary uses of the concept of the Kali Yuga among multiple religious communities throughout India, from the southern tip of Tamil Nadu to the Himalayas. Allocco and Ponniah point out that "the Kali Yuga idiom is appropriated and reinterpreted to serve as a dynamic and locally meaningful framework through which actors respond to the myriad social, political, economic and religious changes they witness and experience in contemporary India."[32] Halperin states that the Kali Yuga has "functioned as a sort of Geertzian 'model of reality,' on the basis of which contemporary conditions were put into a meaningful context and thus made sense of" since as far back at the fourteenth century and perhaps long before that.[33] As Dimmitt and van Buitenen wrote, "the most important function of the notion of these four Ages seems to lie in their negative moral judgment levelled on present society."[34]

I chose this emic concept for the book title because it was salient for the women in my study as they tried to make sense of what they believed to be an increasing problem of cancer in their communities in recent times. Applying the concept of the Kali Yuga, they attributed cancer causality and barriers to respectful cancer care to unethical transformations of social, political, and economic values, as well as to practices that benefited some at the expense of others, rather than blaming the individuals suffering from cancer for being ignorant, making bad choices, and behaving improperly. They also used the concept of the Kali Yuga as a critique of modernity, pitting "these days" against "those days." Other ethnographers of India have found that people tend to locate the beginning of the Kali Yuga in the very recent past.[35] Similarly, my interlocutors referred to the Kali Yuga to point to changes that had occurred during their lifetimes or during the lives of their parents or grandparents. Changes to agricultural practices since the 1960s Green Revolution and to the economy as a whole in the wake of India's liberalization were the key reference points for Dalit women, who attributed cancer causality to conditions characteristic of the Kali Yuga.

Women invoked the concept of the Kali Yuga to criticize human greed and selfishness. Additionally, for some, the concern was that gods and goddesses had deserted them despite their proper moral conduct and unwavering devotion. I was struck by how emotional cancer patients and survivors became when I asked whether they found religion to be helpful for them in the face of their cancer diagnosis and treatment. Some responded with a sense of profound joy for a newfound religion or spiritual practice (such as yoga) they had discovered through their brush with cancer. More often, though, they responded with a sense of abject emotional pain caused by the ultimate experience of abandonment by the gods, which they found worse than abandonment by neighbors or family. Pain from feeling abandoned by gods and goddesses led to visceral anger, as I sensed with Poongodai. She was not the only cancer patient who was contemplating religious conversion or who had already converted when her faith was dashed by a cancer diagnosis and its physical, economic, and social fallout.

Tamil Nadu has a long history of social movements promoting visions of egalitarian moral futures that break through power differentials based on caste and gender.[36] One such subaltern, anti-caste movement in Tamil Nadu, known as the Ayya Vazhi movement, envisions a fifth *yuga*, known as the Dharma Yuga, an emancipatory and blissful era that will follow the Kali Yuga in which caste-based discrimination will be eradicated.[37] When the women in my study repeatedly evoked the Kali Yuga to explain why cancer and all of its attendant suffering had laid siege to their communities, they were attributing it to a breach of morality. This was a morality grounded in an ethics of egalitarianism that veered strongly from the individualizing discourse of morality and behavior change promoted through public health campaigns.

## FIELDWORK

Drawing from fieldwork conducted in 2015 and 2016[38]—with enormous support from my research assistants, Shweta Krishnan and Shibani Rathnam—this book presents personal narratives of the extraordinary lives of ordinary women. Most are accounts of forty-two women who had cancer or who defined themselves as cancer survivors. We met them in the Rural Women's Social Education Centre and in the hospital wards of the Government Arignar Anna Memorial Cancer Hospital and Research Institute near Kanchipuram[39] and of the Cancer Institute (WIA) in Chennai or in their homes in villages in Kanchipuram district and in the Chennai metropolitan area (see Map 2). Most, though not all, were from rural communities, even if they received treatment at these urban hospitals. They came from villages in districts all around the state, including Salem, Dharmapuri, Erode, Vellore, Viluppuram, and even Thoothukudi and Tirunelveli districts in the southern reaches of the state. One patient we met came from the state of Andhra Pradesh. Twenty-one of the cancer patients interviewed were breast cancer patients/survivors, and twenty-one were cervical cancer patients/survivors. They agreed to participate in these interviews because they felt it was important to have their stories told so that other people, including policymakers, would know about the problems they had faced with cancer and with caring for people with cancer and might, therefore, make changes to improve the plight of others like them. Some agreed to be interviewed because they wanted other women cancer patients to appreciate that they are not alone, that there are many other women like them who have endured the challenges of living with cancer.

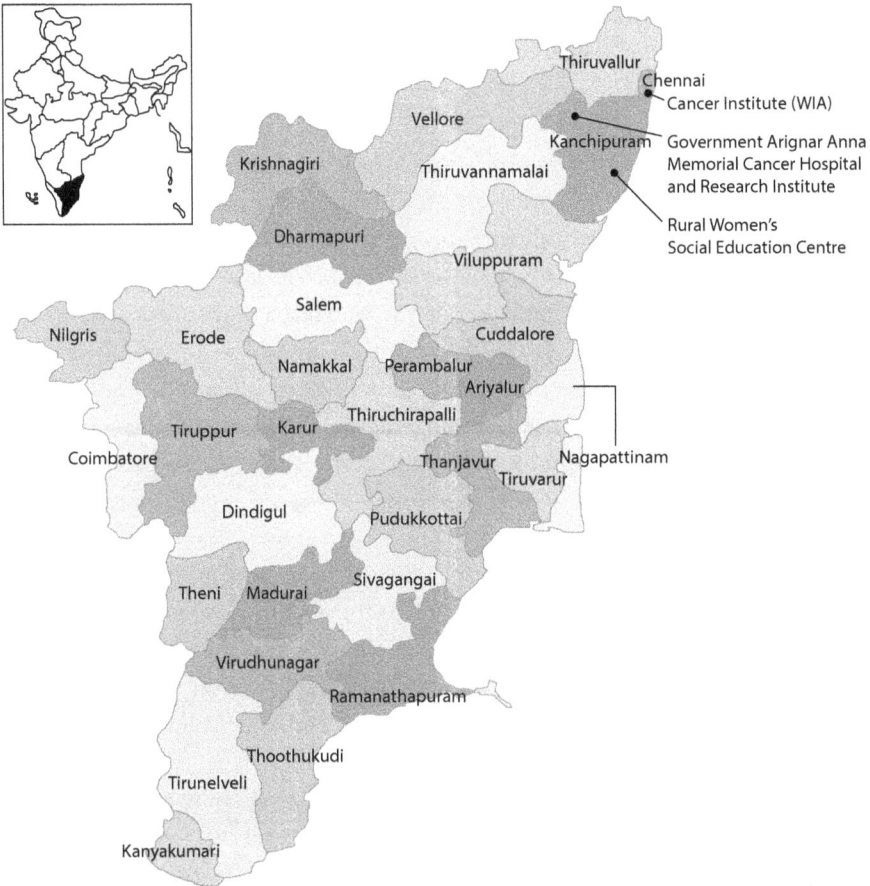

MAP 2. Tamil Nadu and its districts with key field sites: The Cancer Institute (WIA), Government Arignar Anna Memorial Cancer Hospital and Research Institute, Rural Women's Social Education Centre.

The majority of the cancer patients/survivors interviewed were from lower-class, lower-caste communities. A small subset of the cancer survivors interviewed were middle-class and upper-caste women from Chennai. These latter were connected to a network of women cancer survivors who had received treatment at the Cancer Institute and then begun volunteering to provide support to other women undergoing cancer treatments there. Although this study focuses on the experiences of socioeconomically disadvantaged women, my conversations with these highly educated, economically comfortable, and dedicated cancer survivors helped me better appreciate both the commonalities and differences in the cancer experiences for women across class and caste lines in Tamil Nadu.

Some narratives in this book are accounts of family members, oncologists, community health social workers, psychosocial counselors, and a Hindu goddess spirit medium who have cared for women with cancer. Others are of women who participated in eleven focus group discussions (typically consisting of twelve to fifteen women) with lower-income, lower-caste women who had not been diagnosed with cancer themselves, who had a range of experiences with cancer in their families and communities, and who found themselves increasingly contemplating the possibility that cancer would come creeping into their lives. RUWSEC helped arrange most of these group discussions in rural villages, and the Cancer Institute facilitated others in Chennai. Other narratives presented in this book are of women who were interviewed after they had undergone cancer screening through public health cancer screening "camps." Analysis in this book is also informed by my meetings with people involved at various administrative levels of the three key institutions that facilitated my fieldwork—RUWSEC, the Cancer Institute, and the Government Cancer Hospital—as well as by meetings with officials at the Tamil Nadu State National Health Mission and at the WHO office in Delhi involved in cancer projects in India.

The individual and group interviews are foregrounded in narratives presented throughout this book. That said, as an ethnographer, I learned much through observation. The hospital and home settings for interviews allowed me to observe the clinical, family, and community context that informed women's experiences with cancer care. I also learned much from observations in the outdoor spaces that were utilized for the group discussions in rural and urban communities. I sat in on a "tumor board" meeting with doctors and patients and observed five cervical and breast cancer screening "camps" (including educational programs and clinical screening sessions). Observing two cancer support group meetings allowed me to appreciate what kinds of concerns and recommendations cancer survivors shared with one another in a group setting. And in addition to interviewing a *samiyar* (spirit medium) in a village, I sat in on her late-night séances with people who came to see her from nearby villages. I watched as she became possessed by the goddess Muthumariamman, who diagnosed the causes of people's misfortunes, and recommended steps to mitigate their problems.

I took careful notes during my interviews and during and after observations. With permission, I recorded the majority of the interviews, and Shweta and Shibani helped transcribe and translate them. The three of us worked well together as a team and became friends during the fieldwork, decompressing over enormous, crispy "rocket *dosai*" for tiffin at the end of our long, emotionally taxing days.

## GENDER, CLASS, CASTE, AND RELIGION

Breast and cervical cancers do not stand in for all of the cancers that women experience in India (or elsewhere). I focus on these two forms of cancer not only because they are the leading forms of cancer for women in India but also because these cancers are the focus of global public health cancer interventions for women. The preoccupation with these cancers in global public health may be due in part to the fact that they are associated with reproductive parts of women's bodies. Just as women's value in society is often tied to their reproductive abilities, so too women's healthcare has too often been equated with reproductive health at the expense of many other health issues. It is precisely because of these gendered constructions associating womanhood with reproduction that these two reproductive cancers are imbued with the potent moral and cultural meanings explored in this book.

Cancer of course affects men too, both as patients and as caregivers, and men sometimes get breast cancer. This is as true in India as anywhere else in the world. My study focuses on women cancer patients because of my long-standing interest in women's health in India. More studies of men's experiences with cancer are clearly needed. Yet highlighting women's views provides useful insights for policymakers engaged in women's health and sheds light on gender relations in contemporary India from the perspective of women.

"Women" is not a monolithic category, and the views and experiences related to cancer among the women in my study are by no means uniform. Gender identities are inflected and co-produced with numerous other socio-cultural identities (including class, caste, race, ethnicity, nationality, sexuality, religion, age, and urban/rural residence, among others), all of which inform the meanings and experiences of cancer in the lives of the women in my study. My focus is primarily on the views and experiences of lower-class and -caste, cisgender, heteronormative women. This is the same demographic that is the target for the breast and cervical cancer screening and treatment public health interventions. It is also the same demographic that I have studied in my previous research projects on maternity healthcare and HIV/AIDS in Tamil Nadu since the early 1990s.[40] My previous, long-term ethnographic engagement with low-income women's health issues in the region has enriched my understanding and analysis for this project about cancer.

The general correlation between lower-caste and lower-class status on the one hand, and upper-caste and middle- or upper-class status on the other, persists in India today, although class and caste are discreet social phenomena and it is possible for lower-caste individuals to gain wealth and power and for upper-caste individuals to live in poverty. The vast majority of the women in this study were Dalits, who are designated by the government as Scheduled Castes (SC). Others were from the government-designated Most Backward Classes (MBC). The middle-class women whom I interviewed belonged to the government's Forward Castes category. According to ancient Brahminical Hindu texts, Dalits are outside of the fourfold social structure known as the *varna* system and are categorized as people without caste (*avarna*), and those in the MBC group are associated with Sudras, the lowest of the four *varnas*. In practice, Dalits and MBC groups are comprised of numerous, different, largely endogamous castes (*jatis*). Dalits have been viewed by higher-caste groups as occupying the bottom stratum of a caste hierarchy that has been legitimized by a cultural ideology of relative degrees of ritual purity and pollution, with Brahmins at the top. One of the most perverse logics of the caste system is that Dalits are forced to perform degrading and dirty menial work due to their marginalization; the work they do is then used to justify their "untouchable" status. Even when Dalits do not perform "polluting" work, they continue to be stigmatized by it. Furthermore, Tharamangalam notes that the caste system "is maintained not just by ideology and pollution rules but also by considerable violence. It is indeed a system of structural violence manifested by constant threats and periodic outbursts of physical violence"[41] that is enabled by complicit state policies, the police, and the courts.[42] Throughout this book, I have used the common descriptors of "lower-caste" and "upper-caste," but it is crucial to understand that the hierarchy implied by such terms as "lower" and "upper" is a social construction of those at the "top" who serve to benefit from the inequality within the caste system. A more accurate way of describing these social categories today is "oppressed caste" and "oppressor caste."

The term "Dalit" is derived from the Sanskrit root *dal*, meaning "broken" or "crushed." The contemporary use of this term is attributed to the nineteenth-century social reformer Mahatma Jyotiba Phule. It gained popularity within a social justice movement against caste discrimination spearheaded by Dr. B.R. Ambedkar that was founded in the 1920s. It is a self-referential term that activists use to describe people who have been broken by the crushing weight of caste discrimination. It is also the term used by most scholars today in solidarity with this activist movement, and it is the term I use when referring to this category. The Dalit women in my study were not self-described Dalit activists. They used a variety of terms to describe their caste status, including "Dalit," "SC" (Scheduled Caste), "*harijan*" (a Gandhian term meaning "children of god"), and caste-specific names such as Adi Dravida, Paraiyan, and Arunthaitiyar.

As a result of Ambedkar's leadership, since 1950 the government of India has enforced affirmative action "reservation" policies that set aside a certain proportion of spots for students in public higher education institutions, of positions in government jobs, and of seats in some legislative bodies for primarily Hindu Dalits (Scheduled Castes/SC), tribal communities (Scheduled Tribes/ST), and some other communities (Other Backward Classes/OBC) to compensate for the fact that they have historically been marginalized and disadvantaged by the caste system. Tamil Nadu led the way with reservation policies in India both in terms of launching these policies earlier than the country as a whole and in terms of the higher percentage of positions reserved for lower-caste groups. In Tamil Nadu the OBC group is divided into two subsets—the Backward Classes (BC) and the Most Backward Classes (MBC)—with more preferential reservations for the latter than for the former. The official category of SC only includes Dalits who are Hindu, Buddhist, or Sikh, whereas Christian and Muslim Dalits are placed in the OBC category. The term Dalit, therefore, is more inclusive of all of the most oppressed, "untouchable" groups.

Despite the reservation policies, Dalits and most MBC communities have remained socially, politically, and economically marginalized, even if some specific castes (*jatis*) have benefited from the reservation policies. In the wake of India's move to liberalize its ecomony in 1991, the effects of the reservation policies have diminished. Structural adjustments to privatize the economy were implemented by the Indian government when the International Monetary Fund made them a precondition for a large loan at a time when the country was facing an economic crisis. Since that time, India has shifted increasingly toward a privatized economic model. The disinvestment of public education and proliferation of private higher education institutions, in tandem with a shrinking pool of government jobs and the growth of the private sector (which now offers higher wages than the public sector), has meant that reservation policies are no longer as effective at leveling the caste playing field as they once were. Liberalization resulted in a burgeoning middle class, but it also heightened economic inequality, further impoverishing poor Dalits.[43] The plight of Dalits in India has worsened under the Bharatiya Janata Party (BJP) government. Since its inception, the base supporters of the BJP have been middle-class, upper-caste Hindus.[44] Emboldened under Prime Minster Modi's BJP administration, this base has pushed back against the political and economic gains of lower-caste communities, and atrocities against Dalits and religious minorities are on the rise across India, particularly in rural areas, where most Dalits live (including the majority of my interlocutors).[45]

Dalit and MBC women face triple discrimination and exploitation due to their caste, class, and gender. As Karin Kapadia notes, "castism and patriarchy strengthen each other."[46] Because caste purity depends on endogamy, the control of women's sexuality—and by extension their unsupervised movement—is a cornerstone of caste honor. That control has also become a hallmark of middle-class respectability in India since the British colonial Victorian era and is vigorously promoted as a core value of Indian/Hindu culture and morality in Hindutva nationalist ideology. Dalit women bear the brunt of caste-based violence as victims of rape, which upper-caste men inflict on them to assert their caste dominance. They are also faced with domestic violence at the hands of Dalit men, who feel emasculated when they cannot defend their wives in the face of upper-caste rape or when their wives become the family breadwinners.[47] Within this gendered respectability politics, "the charge of promiscuity is used very widely against Dalit women, *both by Dalit men and by non-Dalits*, as a weapon with which to control their freedom of movement."[48] The policing of women's movements in public often becomes more pronounced as families move into the middle class, both because it is a symbol of middle-class prestige and because it is only with more financial resources that it becomes possible for women to cease working outside the home and become self-described "housewives."[49]

Among the lower-class and -caste women in my study, there was widespread consensus that women's workloads and "tension" (stress) had increased substantially over the past twenty-five years or so, following the shift in India's economy after economic liberalization. Lower-class and -caste rural and urban women noted that liberalization had led to an intensification of consumerism and that a family's prestige was now increasingly tied to the capacity to purchase expensive consumer items such as motorbikes and modern electric cooking gadgets for dowries and to spend lavishly on marriages and other life-cycle rituals. Women were being called upon to earn more money so that their families would be able to afford these consumer items, and this added to their workloads. Dalit women were increasingly engaging in agricultural wage labor as lower-caste men began to abstain from such work, viewing it as demeaning once more nonfarm industrial work opportunities emerged in urban and peri-urban areas. Dalit men in Tamil Nadu had begun refusing to do agricultural wage labor even if they were unable to secure other employment, placing an even greater burden on women to provide financially for the family.[50] Women reported that under such conditions, many husbands began drinking heavily and taking their frustration out on their wives through violence or even deserting the family (sometimes by committing suicide), leaving women to fend for themselves and their children.

The liberalization policies also had an impact on the agricultural economy in Tamil Nadu as real estate developers bought up land from small landowners for new business initiatives. This resulted in less agricultural daily wage work for people in lower-class and -caste communities. Recent chronic droughts resulting from climate change have further weakened the agricultural sector and propelled more people into nonagricultural work. Thus, rural Dalit women in Tamil Nadu have also taken up more nonagricultural "company" work with eight-hour work shifts sandwiched between all of their unpaid domestic labor. The loss of land has also led to the breakup of joint and extended families and a shift toward nuclear families. Although women said they appreciated some of the independence they found in these new family arrangements, there was no question in their minds that it had resulted in more work for individual members of the family. The added work in these smaller family units was particularly hard for women, who were now expected not only to earn more money for the family but also to hold the domestic unit together on their own. In these new family structures, the responsibility for upholding the prestige of the family fell heavily on women's shoulders, not only in terms of respectability politics and control of women's sexuality, but also in terms of women's role as earners for their families.

The triple discrimination faced by lower-class Dalit women is often compounded by their religious affiliations and practices. This is true for Dalit

Hindus in Tamil Nadu, who are more likely to participate in worship and rituals associated with non-Sanskritic Tamil deities—particularly in forms of Amman goddess worship—that are viewed as "backward" by many upper-caste people, just as they were by colonial-era European and American Christian missionaries. Moreover, Dalit Christians face discrimination in India in the context of Hindu majoritarianism, though Hindu nationalist recriminations against Christians are rarer in South India than in the North. Many Dalits in Tamil Nadu have converted to Christianity to escape caste discrimination associated with Hinduism, yet paradoxically, their Christian identity marks them as Dalit, thus reinforcing their caste stigma.

I did not seek out a particular religious demographic in my study, but the religious makeup of the women who participated in my study was generally representative of the Tamil Nadu context. Thus, 85.7 percent of the cancer patients interviewed were Hindu, which is reflective of the large Hindu majority in Tamil Nadu. According to the 2011 Indian Census, 87.6 percent of the population in Tamil Nadu was Hindu (versus 79.8 percent for India as a whole).[51] Also, 14.3 percent of the cancer patients in my study were Christian. This was not surprising, in part because Christianity is the second-largest religion in the state. The 2011 census reported that 6.1 percent of the population in Tamil Nadu was Christian (compared to 2.3 percent for India as a whole). It is even less surprising given that the majority of the Christians in Tamil Nadu are Dalits who have converted to Christianity or whose parents or ancestors had converted, sometimes in the hope of escaping caste-based forms of discrimination that many attribute to Brahminical Hindu ideology. Since the 1990s most of the Dalit conversions in Tamil Nadu have been to Pentecostalism; these conversions are most prevalent among Dalit women.[52] It is not uncommon for Dalit women in Tamil Nadu to convert to Pentecostal Christianity during times of calamity. This was the case for some of the Christian women in my study, who said they had converted to Christianity to help cope with the negative impact of cancer in their lives when they felt that the Hindu gods to whom they had previously prayed did not help them enough.

There were no Muslim cancer patients in my study. The 2011 Census reported that 5.9 percent of the population in Tamil Nadu was Muslim. That is a small percentage relative to India as a whole, where 14.2 percent of the population was Muslim in 2011. Nevertheless, this is a limitation of my study, and it would be interesting to have a better understanding of Muslim women's experiences with cancer in Tamil Nadu and in India more broadly to appreciate the role that Islam and a Muslim identity may play as women cope with cancer.

While much of India has witnessed a hardening of boundaries between religious identities with the rise of Hindu nationalism and the BJP over the past two decades, Tamil Nadu has largely bucked this trend. This is due to the unique regional cultural politics of Tamil Dravidian nationalism, which celebrates and seeks to preserve Tamil language and a South Indian cultural identity—not a pan-Indian Hindu identity—in response to perceived threats of North Indian, Brahminical, Hindi-language hegemony. Nonetheless, Hindu nationalists have made inroads in Tamil Nadu as well.

It was common for lower-class, lower-caste women who were suffering from cancer to pray to and receive advice from Hindu, Christian, and Muslim religious figures alike. They defined their religious affiliation less as Hindu or Christian and more in terms of the divine being to whom they prayed, such as the Tamil goddess Mariamman or Jesus. Some sought advice from a mix of lower-caste Hindu *samiyars* and Muslim *bhais* (both of whom could mediate if sorcery or spirit possession were involved in an illness episode), from Hindu Brahmin astrologers, and from Pentecostal Christian priests and self-help groups in their neighborhoods. Some made the rounds to Hindu temples, to Christian churches, and to the tombs of Muslin Sufi saints in their search for healing. They did so while simultaneously receiving treatment from the two premier biomedical hospitals providing cancer treatment for the poor in Tamil Nadu—the Cancer Institute and the Government Cancer Hospital.

## "THIS THING" THAT IS CANCER

One of the challenges to conducting ethnographic research on cancer in India is to figure out what to call a disease that typically goes unnamed. The fact that cancer is not named tells us a great deal about its cultural meaning in India. Public health workers and medical practitioners in Tamil Nadu often use the Tamil word *puttrunoi* instead of "cancer" out of concern that the English word "cancer" is associated with danger and stigma. I began my interviews using the Tamil word but would sometimes switch to the English word "cancer" if people were not familiar with the word *puttrunoi* or if they themselves used the word cancer more than *puttrunoi*.

The stigma of cancer is intense in India for several reasons: fears that it is a death sentence; fears that it is contagious; fears that it is a disgusting (*asingam*) disease because it disfigures and putrefies bodies when left untreated or when treatment fails; and fears that others will assume that the cancer patient and her/his family have done something to bring this disease upon themselves. In this last instance, the concern is with the assumption that cancer is a result of bad karma for misdeeds and immoral behavior or that it is caused by vengeful forms of sorcery employed to wreak havoc through the manipulation of evil spirits. A cancer diagnosis could lead to the loss of prestige and respect for the individual afflicted with cancer and for the family of that person.

Public health educators hoped that by using the term *"puttrunoi"* they could avoid some of the stigma of cancer and thereby encourage people to undergo cancer screening and to seek treatment for cancer. This placed them in a bind as they tried to destigmatize cancer and bring it out of the closet, while simultaneously working within the parameters of its stigma in order to encourage people to get screened or tested and to accept treatment. In practice, I found that people often use the two terms—*"puttrunoi"* and "cancer"—interchangeably and that the word *"puttrunoi"* also carried stigma. People often avoid using either word. Instead, they refer to cancer elliptically, using terms such as "this thing," "this problem," or "this disease," as is evident in many of the quotes throughout this book.

Silence surrounding the naming of cancer is not unique to India. Maren Klawiter documented the sociocultural attitudes and practices related to breast cancer in the United States from the early twentieth century up through to the early twenty-first century.[53] She notes that since the 1970s, cancer has gradually come out of the closet due to concerted efforts among activists and patient advocates and of pharmaceutical and medical industries engaged in cancer screening and treatment. Even so, it is still often mentioned in hushed tones. By pointing to similarities and differences between the US and India, I am not suggesting that there is, or should be, an inevitable progression from concealment to the open naming and disclosure of cancer. As I show in this book, the meanings and practices of acts of concealment are highly complex and may be interpreted in a positive or negative light depending on the interpersonal contexts in India. Nevertheless, the silence around naming this disease is primarily due to its stigma.

The problem is not simply with the stigma that accrues to one who has cancer. It is also that words have effects beyond mere communication. In Tamil Nadu one of those effects may be to bring uttered words into being. As I was wrapping up a long afternoon group discussion on the edge of some paddy fields, a young woman spoke up quietly:

> They say that you should not say these words "cancer" and "*puttrunoi*" because it will make bad things happen. Now you have just made us say this so many times, we are afraid we will get a *pey pisasu* [ghosts and evil spirits] and will get this disease [cancer]. We need to protect ourselves now!

She proceeded to snap her fingers a few times quickly in front of her wide-open mouth, which is common way to ward *pey pisasu* off from entering a person through the mouth. Openings into the body leave one vulnerable to penetration by *pey pisasu* and diseases, and opening the mouth is viewed as rendering one particularly vulnerable. Because of this, it is common to see someone snap their finger in front of their mouth when they yawn. This young woman laughed as she told me this. Her laughter seemed to be a way of publicly saying how silly such superstitious beliefs are, but it also registered as nervous laughter. The other women around her all laughed heartily in response, but they too joined her in loudly snapping their fingers in front of their open mouths, as did I.

## WOMEN'S REPRODUCTIVE CANCERS AND GENDERED MORALITY

Although all cancers are stigmatized to some degree, breast and cervical cancers carry a unique kind of stigma because they affect reproductive parts of women's bodies that are associated with sexuality—a taboo and censored topic in India and in many parts of the world—and lead to speculation about women's morality. That is why I use the term "reproductive cancers" to refer to both cervical and breast cancer together. Some reserve the term "reproductive cancers" for cancers of the reproductive tract, such as cervical, uterine, and ovarian cancer, but not to breast cancer. Yet women's breasts are biologically central to the reproduction of humans as mammals. Furthermore, women's breasts carry powerful cultural meanings associated with reproduction and sexuality. These cultural meanings associated with reproduction and sexuality shape the contours of what it means to be a good, moral woman and play a critical role in women's experiences with both breast cancer and cervical cancer. Cervical cancer is more stigmatized than breast cancer because of cultural ideas about the impuritiy of vaginas and because women who carry the sexually transmitted human pappilomavirus (HPV) are at increased risk for cervical cancer, leading to suspicions of promiscuity. Yet women with breast cancer also expressed concerns about stigma, worrying that others would assume they had not breastfed their children according to expected cultural and public health norms for good mothers and thus brought this disease upon themselves.

Cervical and breast cancer diagnoses raise existential questions about causality that are infused with concerns about morality as women ponder the question: How could I have gotten cancer when I have always been such a good woman? Social and cultural constructions of gender inform what women think it means for them to be a good woman. Breast and cervical cancer diagnoses raise serious concerns for women that they will be deemed to be bad women who have not lived moral lives according to the gender norms of Tamil society. They worry that they will be held individually responsible and be blamed for their own illness and suffering. Their narratives, presented in this ethnography, serve as powerful rebuttals against such assumptions as Tamil women seek to heal and to maintain a sense of dignity in the face of cancer. Their struggles with the duel challenges of disease and stigma parallel experiences of cancer described by other anthropologists working around the world.

## AN ANTHROPOLOGY OF CANCER

Until recently, anthropologists did not pay much attention to cancer, even within the field of medical anthropology. Several ethnographic monographs, edited volumes, and special journal issues published since the end of the twentieth century and proliferating in the twenty-first feature research on cancer by anthropologists working around the globe.[54] Impetus for much of this new work comes from the attention to cancer within the global health agenda. *Cancer and the Kali Yuga* contributes to this burgeoning field of the anthropology of cancer.

As critical medical anthropologists, our collective ethnographic work illuminates the increasingly common human reality of living and dying with cancer while highlighting the diversity of this human experience across time and space and within communities. We investigate the cultural politics of cancer reflected in competing discourses of cancer causality and about appropriate steps for cancer prevention and treatment. We document how biomedical and public health discourses typically frame cancer causality in ways that hold individuals and individual behavior "choices" responsible for health outcomes in terms of cancer prevention as well as treatment. Some of us describe the moralizing gendered nature of this discourse as it is applied to women and cancer. Many of us point out that individualizing discourses are not universally accepted and that members of communities targeted by public health interventions often hold different views about cancer causality and treatment modalities, sometimes identifying structural social and political-economic factors as more important than individual will. While most ethnographic research on cancer focuses either on perceptions of cancer causality or on experiences of cancer treatment and care, my book gives equal weight to both. I contend that they are intertwined; you cannot understand one without understanding the other.

Ever since Broom and Doron's 2011 call for research on the sociocultural dynamics of cancer care in India, a handful of ethnographers have responded with careful and empathic attention to the lives of patients suffering from cancer and to the travails of people caring for others with cancer in India.[55] Banerjee's ethnography, *Enduring Cancer: Life, Death, and Diagnosis in Delhi*, is the first monograph by an anthropologist studying cancer in India. His book centers on the lives of the urban poor—particularly men—in Delhi, North India, as they navigate a public health system that is ill-equipped to handle the mounting need for cancer treatment. *Cancer and the Kali Yuga* complements Banerjee's work and extends it by elucidating the distinctiveness of the social, cultural, and political context of Tamil Nadu, South India, and by focusing on women's experiences with cancer.

In addition to the regional specificity of my study—in the global South, in India, and in Tamil Nadu—what sets it apart from other ethnographies of cancer is my analysis of how the nexus of gender, class, and caste affects women's encounters with cancer from the moment they experience symptoms, to their diagnosis, to their medical and personal care in hospitals, to their management of invasive and disfiguring cancer treatments, to their search for spiritual explanations and healing. This book provides a unique perspective by bringing to light the views of the most marginalized—rural Dalit women—whose experiences and social critiques are too often systematically ignored. I present the voices of these marginalized interlocutors, not only for the sake of listening but also because they reveal crucial subaltern critiques. Through their engagements with this ethnographic research project, they articulated their understanding of how the intersection of their class, caste, and gender status made them vulnerable to cancer and its consequences in the twenty-first century. Other ethnographers have focused on their interlocutors' lived experience of cancer or their interlocutors' use of metaphor to describe cancer, often separately making their own anthropological critique of public health and social inequality. My aim is to link my interlocutors' experiences and critique together—to present their critiques from the point of view of their experience. Experience and critique are interwoven in a way that makes my role as an ethnographer a conduit for what is present but often politically silenced. As Kapadia writes, we need to take the discourses of Dalit women seriously as everyday forms of subaltern political practice that challenges hegemonic caste, class, and gender norms.[56] My book does this through the lens of cancer because thinking about cancer—particularly reproductive cancers—provokes this response.

*Cancer and the Kali Yuga* explores the everyday pragmatics of ordinary women in search of oncological treatments in the face of an extraordinary disease that wreaks havoc on bodies, social relationships, family finances, psyches, and entanglements with the spirit world. In some instances, women are remarkably resilient in the face of great odds, while in other cases, their lives unravel through no fault of their own. Women's accounts of their journeys through diagnosis and treatment for cancer reveal their critiques about sociocultural and political-economic structures that complicate their ability to heal even while demonstrating their creative resilience and ability to navigate such constraints in order to endure. Banerjee rightly argues that the discourse of resilience is often used to praise heroic individuals for having the determination and fortitude to not only overcome but also ultimately transcend obstacles in order to survive. Such heroic, sometimes self-congratulatory narratives were absent among the patients and their caretakers whom he met in Delhi. Instead, he finds the concept of endurance to better capture his interlocutors' struggle to "make the present livable" and their "inventiveness required to survive, persist, and retain form under impress of slow and chronic duress."[57] Many of the women's stories presented in my book epitomize this endurance as they work hard to maintain health and survive—sometimes even to thrive—in the face of incredible odds. Yet not all are lucky enough to survive this devastating disease. Those who do not survive or who can no longer find the strength to live should not be regarded as lacking in faith, will, knowledge, wits, or grit. For some lower-class women, like Poongodai, whose lives are already precarious, a cancer diagnosis in the family can lead quickly to economic disaster and social ostracism and can be unbearable.

Whether we characterize the ability to live with or survive cancer as resilience or endurance, it is important to recognize that it requires so much more than information, individual will, or technological medical breakthroughs. It is only possible through establishing and maintaining social systems that can provide opportunities for all members of society to thrive with equal access to health, healthcare, and dignity. The views presented by the women in my study stood in stark contrast to the underlying assumptions of the public health paradigm regarding the root causes—and thus the possible solutions—to what many see as a growing reproductive cancer crisis in India. By listening to women's critiques about the social determinants of cancer in their communities and the social determinants of the suffering and indignities they encounter as they navigate their cancer care, we gain insight into their aspirations for change. The stories of the women that fill the pages of this book make it abundantly clear that although they appreciate some aspects of the systems in place for them to access healthcare in Tamil Nadu, there is much about their social and political worlds that they find to be lacking and detrimental to their health and well-being. They evoke the idiom of the Kali Yuga to articulate these critiques.

# CHAPTER I

# History and Hospitals

Although cancer has only recently come to be seen as a major public health concern in India, it has long afflicted Indians. This chapter provides a brief overview of the history of cancer care in India from the late-colonial period to the postcolonial independence era and up to the early twenty-first century. This historical snapshot allows us to recognize that the current global public health discourse of a mounting cancer crisis as part of an "epidemiological transition" in India (and the global South more generally) obscures the on-the-ground realities of the past and the present. Epidemiology transition theory suggests there has been a shift from a higher burden of disease associated with communicable, maternal, neonatal, and nutritional diseases to a higher burden of noncommunicable diseases, including cancer, and attributes this to longer life spans and modern, urban, middle- and upper-class lifestyles. This chapter reminds us that cancer has in fact long disrupted the lives of many Indians—rich and poor, urban and rural—even if it has not been prioritized by the global public health sector until recently. Banerjee reveals two harmful effects of the discourses of epidemiological transition and of cancer as a newly emerging crisis resulting from urban, middle-class, "westernized" lifestyle changes in post-liberalization India. First, it conceals the prevalence of cancer among the economically marginalized in India. Second, it "places blame on patients rather than on a failed health care system."[1]

This chapter focuses on cancer prevention and treatment programs in Tamil Nadu, paying particular attention to the development of the institutional sites where I conducted my fieldwork: the Cancer Institute WIA, the Government

Arignar Anna Memorial Cancer Hospital and Research Institute, and the Rural Women's Social Education Centre. Given its prominence in the historical and contemporary landscape of cancer care and research in India, I devote particular attention to the Cancer Institute, which was designated India's first Regional Cancer Centre in 1975 and continues to play a central role in cancer care and cancer research in India.

In tracing this history, I demonstrate that the prevention and treatment of cancer among women—particularly among lower-class women—has been an important component of cancer care programs in Tamil Nadu from the late-colonial period up to the present. This attention to cancer care among low-income women is apparent at each of the three institutions with which I was affiliated, although these institutions vary in terms of age, size, and political agenda.

## BIOMEDICAL CANCER CARE IN LATE-COLONIAL AND EARLY INDEPENDENCE INDIA

We know very little about cancer care in pre-colonial India. Martha Selby's work on translations of Sanskrit Vedic Ayurvedic texts—*The Caraka Samhita* and *The Susruta Samhita*—suggests that cancer existed in India at the beginning of the Common Era when those texts were written. Sections of *The Susruta Samhita* describe various kinds of bumps, lumps, and swellings, and procedures to remove them, including procedures to scoop out breast lumps with tools made of horns.[2] However, whereas biomedical science understands cancer to be a particular disease entity (which manifests itself in multiple ways), this is not the case in either Ayurveda or Siddha.[3] These traditional Indian medical systems do not conceptualize any disease as a discreet phenomenon the way biomedicine does. Jean Langford quotes an Ayurvedic doctor to demonstrate this point: "If it is one symptom, one disease, and one treatment, then it is not Ayurveda." That doctor explained that cancer is not a "definite entity"; rather, it is "a manifestation of things going on."[4] This epistemological difference in conceptualizing the body, illness, health, and healing makes it difficult to trace how cancer—as biomedical science understands it—was treated in India prior to the development of biomedicine in the colonial era. By the end of the colonial era and moving into the period after India's independence in 1947, biomedical treatments and technologies had emerged as the dominant and authoritative modality of medical care for cancer, even if such care was unequally distributed in the population.

During the late colonial and early independence eras, biomedical interventions for cancer were entangled in nationalist projects and debates. India's first prime minister, Jawaharlal Nehru, and the leaders of his political party, the Indian National Congress (aka the Congress Party), placed a premium on developing scientific, medical, and technological institutions and infrastructure to further their vision of a modern India. As Banerjee wrote, Nehru "famously suggested that if newly independent India was to shake off the shackles of colonialism and its stultifying religious traditions, a revolution had to be engineered and led by a scientific, medical and bureaucratic elite."[5] One such Nehruvian project was the All-Indian Institute of Medical Sciences (AIIMS), India's premier public medical institute, founded in Delhi in the 1950s. On the eve of India's independence, the 1946 Bhore Committee report that laid the groundwork for India's public health system noted that cancer was a problem for India and recommended the establishment of specialty cancer care services as a public good.[6] Yet although AIIMS has been treating cancer patients since its early days, the specialty cancer hospital within AIIMS—the Dr. Ambedkar Institute Rotary Cancer Hospital—did not start functioning until 1983. Even then, it had only thirty-five beds. Since that time, this hospital has grown in leaps and bounds; in 2003 it was expanded to two hundred beds in a seven-story building.[7]

Cancer treatment and research was not a priority for public hospitals and medical research institutes in Nehru's time. Nonetheless, the government provided financial and political support to private, philanthropic cancer institutes founded around the time of independence. Most noteworthy were three institutes established in India's principal colonial cities: the Tata Memorial Hospital, founded in 1941 in Bombay (now Mumbai); the Chittaranjan Cancer Hospital, founded in 1950 in Calcutta (now Kolkata); and the Cancer Institute (WIA) founded in 1954 in Adyar, Madras (now Chennai).

Indian central and state governments have played important roles in the development of these private/public cancer institutions over the years. Donations by foreign governments and collaborations with foreign medical research institutions and researchers have also been a crucial source of support since the early days of these institutions. Professor Irène Joliot-Curie of France—a Nobel laureate for her research on radioactivity, and a daughter of Marie Curie—formally inaugurated the Chittaranjan Cancer Hospital in 1950.[8]

And Atomic Energy of Canada partly gifted Asia's first radiotherapy machine, a Cobalt-60 beam generator (dubbed the "Cobalt Bomb"), to the Cancer Institute in 1957.[9] Although the prevention and treatment of cancer may not have played a central role in India's public health system or in the international global health sector in the past, the Indian government, state governments, and the international community have long been engaged in founding cancer hospitals and developing biomedical technologies for cancer in India.

## THE CANCER INSTITUTE (WIA)

Nehru traveled to Madras (now Chennai) in 1952 to lay the foundation stone for the Cancer Institute, South India's first cancer hospital, which opened two years later. I would regularly pass this black stone when I went to check in with the nurse matron before preceding to the wards to interview patients. It was embedded in the wall in an out-of-the-way corner of the institute's older campus in Gandhi Nagar, usually with a wheelchair or two stashed in front of it. The Cancer Institute was the brainchild of Dr. Muthulakshmi Reddy. The legacy of her mission and vision, which focused on providing cancer services for women from the lower socioeconomic ranks of society, lives on today within the Cancer Institute and in the approaches to cancer prevention and care taken by the public health sector and NGOs in Tamil Nadu.

Born in 1886, Muthulakshmi was the daughter of a Brahmin middle-class father and her mother was a member of the *devadasi* community.[10] Such an inter-caste marriage between a Brahmin and a *devadasi* was highly unconventional. Muthulakshmi would rise to become the first female member of a British Indian legislature, serving as the Deputy President of the Madras Legislative Council in 1926. The Women's Indian Association (WIA) had lobbied hard to get Muthulakshmi onto the council. WIA was founded in Madras in 1917 by three British and Irish women members of the Theosophical Society in Adyar who were women's suffragists as well as supporters of the Indian self-rule movement. It became a branch of the All-India Women's Conference (AIWC) in 1927. These women's organizations fought for women's rights and for Gandhi's independence movement. In 1930, Muthulakshmi resigned from the Legislative Council in protest against the imprisonment of Gandhi. She became the AIWC leader in 1931.[11]

Muthulakshmi's social and political reform initiatives for women and children were at the center of her legislative efforts and her civic work. Inspired by Gandhi's call for the "uplift" of women and "untouchables," Muthulakshmi fought for "social purity" and "moral hygiene" issues to improve the lives of socioeconomically marginalized women and children.[12] She worked to pass legislation to prevent child marriage, to eradicate the *devadasi* system, to end what she called the "immoral traffic" of women and children through prostitution, to promote equal access to education for girls and young women, and to gain equal voting rights for women. She also founded a home for orphans and destitute women who had been "rescued" from prostitution and campaigned to provide latrines for all, particularly for women.[13]

Muthulakshmi was one of India's first woman doctors and was the first woman to receive a medical degree from Madras Medical College, in 1912. Her sister's untimely death from a misdiagnosed and mistreated cancer of the rectum in 1923 motivated Muthulakshmi to improve medical care for cancer patients in India.[14] After years of fundraising for this cause, she founded the Cancer Institute (WIA) for clinical care and research, which opened its doors in 1954. Muthulakshmi's vision of the Cancer Institute must be understood in the context of her broader social reform agenda. This impetus continues to reverberate in the mission of the institute, which still includes the WIA acronym in its name.

Nehru and Muthulakshmi had different rationales for committing resources to cancer care in the early days of India's independence.[15] Nehru argued that cancer was a disease that warranted attention in India because it was likely to emerge as a growing problem as he predicted that India would become increasingly prosperous and urban. This assumption supports Margaret Trawick's observation that in India, cancer has often been viewed as a "Western disease" that only afflicts the westernized, urban, upper- and middle-class sector of Indian society. Trawick's work reveals Indian critiques of the deleterious effects of westernization which posit that "cancer is associated with unchecked consumption of the kinds of expensive poisons Westerners are thought to favor, most notably cigarettes and hard liquor."[16] Nehru viewed cancer as unavoidable collateral damage inflicted by the benefits of the urban, modern India he sought to build. In his estimation, modern technological science and medicine would be an antidote to the inevitable rise in cancer in India.

Muthulakshmi, by contrast, saw cancer as a more immediate and pressing problem for *all* Indians, rich and poor, rural and urban. She argued that cancer affected people from all social strata in the prime of their lives in

India (whereas it tended to affect older people in the West) and that it was therefore a threat to the productivity of society just at a time when India was trying to emerge as an independent nation. Drawing from her work with Gandhian movements, she stressed the plight of poor women with cancer. For Muthulakshmi, cancer awareness campaigns and the provision of cancer treatment for all were forms of social uplift from backwardness, and she placed women at the center of her campaign. Muthulakshmi's campaigns to educate women about cancer prevention highlighted practices that were associated with the social backwardness of Indian women, such as repeated childbirth, which could lead to uterine cancers.[17] Her work with WIA on campaigns against child marriage for girls dovetailed with her uplift and awareness programs for the prevention of cancer among lower-income communities, in that she linked early marriage to increased cancer risk for women. In her vision of the Cancer Institute, rural areas were to be sites of cancer screening and the hospital in Madras would draw people from rural and urban areas for advanced treatments. The Cancer Institute was established primarily to serve poor patients by providing subsidized medical care; simultaneously, it would treat wealthier patients who could pay their way. In her fundraising efforts among Madras's elite, Muthulakshmi underscored that cancer also affected the educated, middle classes and that ultimately everybody was vulnerable. Her original goals for the Cancer Institute remain in place today.

According to Trawick, in the 1970s, cancer was deemed a "Western disease" in India because of its association with the physiological effects of adopting a westernized lifestyle. But cancer also came to serve as a metaphor for the invasive, destructive, extractive, and imperialistic interests of Western governments and Western-owned companies in the Third World.[18] For Congress Party leaders who were trying to create national unity in the initial days of India's independence, the metaphorical allusions to cancer and the body politic revealed fears of political dangers lurking *within* the nation more than from without, just as cancer itself grows within the body. When the Cancer Institute opened its doors to patients in 1954, Nehru's finance minister came to Madras for the function, where he stated,

> What is true of this disease of the human body is perhaps true of the body politic also. If one allows small irritations to remain unattended, then the result will be anarchy and I am certain that there will be a very grave lesson for us responsible for the governance of the country—that all irritations when they are found should be recognized and dealt with very early.[19]

In the newly emerging nation, the campaign to raise awareness of cancer symptoms and for early detection and treatment served as a potent metaphor for the need for vigilance in governance.

When it opened, the Cancer Institute had twelve beds and two medical officers (physicians). One of those medical officers was Dr. S. Krishnamurthy, the son of Muthulakshmi, who, after receiving training in cancer management and treatment in the United States, Sweden, and the United Kingdom, returned to Madras to become the institute's founding director. I often found myself sitting alongside patients and their families, waiting on hard wooden benches in the main lobby of the older campus in Gandhi Nagar, staring up at large portraits of Dr. Muthulakshmi and Dr. Krishnamurthy above opposing doors that led down the two main hospital hallways. In Muthulakshmi's portrait, she was sitting upright in a chair, wearing a white sari to match her white hair and horn-rimmed glasses. The portrait of Krishnamurthy was a close-up of his warm face with combed-back, silvering hair and a coat and tie. Krishnamurthy remained engaged with the institute until his death at the age of ninety in 2010. The other original medical officer was Dr. V. Shanta, who took over as the director of the institute in 1980 (at which point Krishnamurthy became the chairman). Dr. Shanta then became chairman in 2000, a position that she still held at the time of my research.[20] She used the designation "chairman" (instead of chairwoman or chair) because she had to make her way "in the male world of oncology, becoming in some ways an 'honorary male.'"[21] She did not simply get by in a male-dominated profession; she excelled and went on to receive the Government of India's Padma Shri award in 1986, the Padma Bhushan award in 2006, and the Padma Vibhushan award—the second highest civilian award granted by the Government of India—in 2016. Despite the acclaim she enjoyed and her intensely busy schedule, Dr. Shanta graciously agreed to meet with me on several occasions. I was struck by her sharp intellect, the excited tone of her voice as she enthusiastically recalled the projects she had worked on across her career, and her gentle, caring demeanor.

Raised in a family of highly distinguished male scientists—an uncle and great-uncle were both Nobel laureates in physics—Dr. Shanta was the first woman in her family to pursue a professional education.[22] She received her medical degree from Madras University in 1949, her Diploma of Obstetrics and Gynecology in 1952, and her MD in 1955. After traveling to Canada for postgraduate research, she returned to set up India's first radiation oncology unit at the institute in 1957 with an Eldorado Cobalt-60 beam radiotherapy unit provided by Atomic Energy of Canada.[23] This was the first of many international technological transfers to arrive at the Cancer Institute. Over the years, the institute has received radiotherapy units from foreign governments and civil society organizations in Canada, Germany, Denmark, the Netherlands, and Japan. In 2008 the Cancer Institute installed the Siddharth, the first radiotherapy linear accelerator unit designed and manufactured in India, built by the Indian company Sameer.

The Cancer Institute has a research division that includes the Tamil Nadu Cancer Registry, one of the best cancer registries in the country. Researchers there have also been involved in international studies, including research collaborations with the US National Institutes of Health's National Cancer Institute (NIH/NCI) to improve treatment outcomes for children with leukemia in India. Through an affiliation with MGR University, the institute's Dr. Muthulakshmi College of Oncological Sciences provides postgraduate medical education and grants medical degrees in oncology and preventive oncology.

In 1975, India's Ministry of Health and Family Welfare declared the institute India's first Regional Cancer Centre for research and treatment. In 2013, Tamil Nadu's Chief Minister Jayalalithaa wrote a letter to the prime minister urging the central government to recognize the Cancer Institute as a National Centre of Excellence. In her letter, she noted that WHO had rated the institute as "the top ranking centre for cancer in the country."[24]

The Cancer Institute has grown into a globally recognized and technologically sophisticated clinical and research center, yet the original vision and spirit of Muthulakshmi prevail to this day in Dr. Shanta's "six C's" mission for the institute: it strives for Commitment, Compassion, Care, Cure, Challenge, and Change.[25] Ganesh aptly describes the Cancer Institute as "an institution built brick-by-brick with an amalgam of Gandhian austerity and Nehruvian science."[26] Those core impulses continue to inform the institute's values. It has resisted the neoliberal turn toward the corporate model of privatized healthcare best symbolized by the gleaming Apollo hospitals that have sprung up in Chennai (and elsewhere in India) and by the mushrooming "medical tourism" industry, which draws patients from all over the world to receive top-notch medical care in India at significantly reduced prices compared to many other countries but far out of reach of the average Indian's budget.

The difference between private hospitals and the Cancer Institute's hospital is apparent in the latter's fee structure. By 2018, the institute had 535 beds and each year was providing care for more than 15,672 new patients from all over India as well as 140,935 follow-up cases. In 2018, 60 percent of the patients received free medical care and room and board.[27] There was a multitiered fee structure for the remaining 40 percent. The quality of the biomedical care was the same for all patients, but the amenities differed: fully subsidized patients roomed together in large general wards without air-conditioning, whereas fully paying patients in the A-Class were given private rooms with an attached bathroom, an extra bed for visitors, air-conditioning, and a television. The majority of patients I met who had received treatment at the Cancer Institute were in the general wards; the middle-class women in my study enjoyed the extra amenities in the higher-"class" rooms. Some of my middle-class interlocutors told me they could have afforded to go to the prestigious Apollo cancer hospital in Chennai but they had heard that the Cancer Institute provided better treatment than most of the private hospitals for a more reasonable price. Some said they preferred the humble atmosphere and social service mission of the Cancer Institute to that of the newer private hospitals in Chennai.

During my research in 2015 and 2016, the institute had two separate campuses. There was the older, smaller campus in the quiet, tree-lined neighborhood of Gandhi Nagar, where I spent more time because that was where long-term breast and cervical cancer inpatients receiving fully subsidized care stayed and where the preventive oncology screening program was housed. The newer, larger main campus was at a major intersection where the fast-growing Guindy and Adyar neighborhoods of south Chennai meet. The sprawling main Adyar campus was the site of numerous buildings for patient care and research. I spent time on that campus for meetings and research in the epidemiology division, the Tamil Nadu cancer registry, and the psychosocial educational and counseling department that facilitated the Dr. Muthulakshmi Reddy Women's Cancer Support group meetings. Patients and family members coming to the hospital for the first time would come to the Adyar campus. They would pass a small Hindu temple just inside the entrance gate and walk through open dusty courtyards with lots of people sitting and milling around to reach the main building, where they would jostle for a place in line to check in and then wait in rows of plastic chairs in a large hall before seeing a doctor. Paying patients could wait in smaller, less crowded rooms. The two campuses were close as the crow flies. With no traffic, you could travel from one to the other in five minutes, but the constantly clogged traffic meant it could sometimes take twenty minutes to get from one campus to the other.

Among the institute's many initiatives undertaken by Dr. Shanta in the early 1960s was community-based screening for early detection of common cancers in rural parts of the state.[28] She and her team conducted a survey of towns and villages in what was then called Chengelput district (now part of Kanchipuram district), which revealed that the most common form of cancer was cervical cancer, followed by oral cancer. Their goal was to establish a cancer control project using screening and early detection and treatment of these cancers for people from low-income communities in villages and towns surrounding the city of Kanchipuram. In 1969, WHO approved the project; later, though, it had to revoke its funds for procedural reasons, for the Cancer Institute was an NGO and not a government hospital—WHO was not allowed to fund NGOs. The Cancer Institute later developed rural preventive oncology screening projects elsewhere in the state, including some that I attended.

## THE GOVERNMENT ARIGNAR ANNA MEMORIAL CANCER HOSPITAL AND RESEARCH INSTITUTE

The Cancer Institute's efforts in Kanchipuram did not go to waste. That same year, 1969, the Tamil Nadu state government took over this project. With funding from WHO, the government established a specialty cancer hospital and research center in Kanchipuram, which engaged in community-based cancer screening. Also that same year, C.N. Annadurai, the enormously popular Tamil film star and Chief Minister of Tamil Nadu, died of cancer. Annadurai was the last chief minister to serve in Madras Province (from 1967 until 1969) before it was renamed the state of Tamil Nadu. He was also the first Chief Minister of Tamil Nadu elected on a Dravidian[29] party ticket. Every Chief Minister of Tamil Nadu since then has been a member of one of the Dravidian political parties, celebrating pride in ethno-linguistic Tamil identity and opposition to North Indian, Hindi, and Brahminical hegemony. Praised for his Tamil oratory and his writing skills, Annadurai's supporters affectionately called him Arignar Anna ("the scholarly older brother"). Given the coincidence of the timing of Annadurai's death to cancer and the fact that he hailed from Kanchipuram, it was fitting that this new government cancer hospital was named the Government Arignar Anna Memorial Cancer Hospital and Research Institute.

In 2019 the hospital celebrated its fiftieth anniversary. During the time of my research, most people in Tamil Nadu referred to this hospital simply as the Government Cancer Hospital because it was the only tertiary specialty cancer hospital in Tamil Nadu. Initially built in the city of Kanchipuram, in the early 1980s the hospital was relocated to its current spacious grounds in Karapettai on the outskirts of that city.

When we visited the hospital, we traveled by rental car round-trip from Chennai on the highway connecting Chennai to Bengaluru. On this journey, we would pass the Rajiv Gandhi Memorial in Sriperumbudur, where Prime Minister Rajiv Gandhi was assassinated in 1991 by a Sri Lankan woman who was a member of the Liberation Tigers of Tamil Eelam (LTTE), a political organization fighting for autonomy in Sri Lanka that had branches in Tamil Nadu. During rush hour, this highway was densely congested leaving and approaching Chennai, making our journey sometimes as long as three hours one way. I used the travel time to write up field notes, talk to Shweta and Shibani about our research or about Rajinikanth's blockbuster film, *Kabali*, that we saw in 2016, and catch up on sleep.

As patients entered the walled compound of the Government Cancer Hospital, they encountered a large open sandy area with built-in stone benches and stools under shady trees, where patients and families would gather in small groups. The main building, where patients checked in to see doctors on an outpatient basis, housed the core departments—medical oncology, surgical oncology, gynecological oncology, radiological oncology, and pathology. The surrounding buildings, all interconnected, were for the inpatient wards. There was also a small, separate building that held stacks and stacks of dusty brown folders full of patient medical records, which were being digitized at the time of my study. Unlike in government maternity hospitals in Chennai where I had conducted my previous research projects, this hospital was not crowded; there was a quiet, calm atmosphere in the hospital wards and corridors and on the grounds outside.

At the time of its founding, the short-term goals of the Government Cancer Hospital were to organize cancer screening and treatment programs for cervical and oral cancers, to develop a research platform for cancer demographics in and around Kanchipuram, and to train personnel. Its long-term objectives were to achieve cancer control, to record incidence and prevalence rates and causative factors of cancer in Kanchipuram, and to establish training centers for medical and paramedical workers in the field of cancer control.[30] From its inception, the founders of this hospital saw the need to develop educational programs to inform the public about the importance of screening and early diagnosis of cancer. They were interested in understanding the sociocultural and psychosocial factors, particularly among women, that were contributing to people's reluctance to be screened for cancer in the absence of symptoms.[31]

According to the hospital's website, between 1969 and 1989 it ran a public health project in which "the Female Hospital Workers were sent to the Govt. Head Quarters Hospital, Kanchipuram to bring the suspicious women for screening programmes. This was not accepted by most of the women."[32] It is not clear what exactly they meant by "suspicious women." Presumably, they meant women whom they considered to be at risk for cervical cancer. The word "suspicious," however, carries a moral connotation and seems to allude to moral assumptions about cervical cancer risk—and thus about women with cervical cancer—that were prevalent during the time of my research. Muthulakshmi's mission to improve the "social purity" and "moral hygiene" of women from lower-caste communities may have been passed along through these emergent government-sponsored public health programs for cervical cancer when the government stepped in to take over the Kanchipuram program that Dr. Shanta envisioned.

By the 1990s the cancer control program for Kanchipuram district (then known as the Chengleput MGR district) included cancer screening "camps" at select Taluk district hospitals and Primary Health Centres. These camps served as satellite centers that would refer patients to the Government Cancer Hospital for further diagnosis and treatment as needed. After 2006, this satellite screening camp model was ramped up in district headquarters hospitals, Taluk hospitals, nonspecialty tertiary care government hospitals, and Primary Health Centres throughout the northeast part of the state, all of which referred patients to the Government Cancer Hospital.[33]

The Indian government designated the Government Arignar Anna Memorial Cancer Hospital as a Regional Cancer Centre in 2005, after which patients from all around Tamil Nadu and from other states in South India began to flock there.[34] It was the first and only public government hospital to receive this designation in Tamil Nadu. There was a hospital-based cancer registry with patient records dating back to 1981. According to these records, in 2014 (the year prior to the start of my research), there were 33,086 patients receiving treatment from the hospital, including outpatients and inpatients.[35] Among the inpatients who were newly admitted for the first time in 2014, around 50 percent were women with either cervical or breast cancer.

The Director of Medical Records at the Government Cancer Hospital told me that the vast majority of patients there were living below the poverty line and were receiving fully subsidized care, using the state insurance program. He noted that even very poor patients who found their way to the Government Cancer Hospital had usually been to several private medical practitioners and private clinics first. They would come to the public hospital only when they had run out of money while seeking care in the private sector. His observation resonated with the narratives of many of the patients whom I met, who tried to avoid government hospitals because of the perception that private medical care must be better than subsidized government medical care and because they felt they were treated with disrespect by the staff in government hospitals due to their class and caste status. Some patients assumed that the Cancer Institute was a public hospital because they could receive free medical care there; sometimes this was a deterrent to seeking care there initially.

This raises an important question about the oft-repeated refrain that the biggest problem related to cancer in India is that patients do not seek care as soon as they begin to have symptoms so that by the time they present at the hospital, they have late-stage cancers that are difficult to cure. I heard this argument expressed by doctors and administrators wherever I went. Women cancer patients or their family members told me that doctors scolded them about this when they went for diagnostic testing. Yet most women whom I interviewed told me they had gone from doctor to doctor to doctor seeking explanations and treatment for their ills. They had done so because doctors had either misdiagnosed their problem or charged more than they could afford. So it is not surprising that statistics show that by the time patients in India present at specialty cancer hospitals, such as the Cancer Institute and the Government Cancer Hospital, they have advanced-stage cancers. The records from the Government Cancer Hospital showed that of the 378 new cervical cancer patients admitted in 2014, the majority[36] were either Stage IIB or Stage IIIB. We need to interpret these statistics in light of the fact that for many patients, being admitted to the Government Cancer Hospital is the endpoint of a long and winding journey seeking explanations and care for their ills from a wide array of healers, including biomedical doctors. This suggests there is a need to improve the cancer diagnostic and referral skills of doctors in public and private clinical care and for more respectful care of socioeconomically marginalized patients in government hospitals.

The Government Cancer Hospital's satellite screening camp model in the 2000s had relied on Pap smears. This changed in the early 2010s, following the discovery of visual technologies—VIA and VILI—for cervical cancer screening. Between 2000 and 2003 a team of researchers led by Dr. Rengaswamy Sankaranarayanan (with support from French-based IARC) conducted a randomized clinical trial in Dindigul district in Tamil Nadu to test the efficacy of VIA. These researchers concluded that "VIA screening, in the presence of good training and sustained quality assurance, is an effective method to prevent cervical cancer in developing countries."[37] The efficacy of VIA technology for cervical cancer screening was further established in 2013 by Dr. Surendra Shastri and his team of researchers from Mumbai's Tata Memorial Centre (with funding from the US National Cancer Institute), following a twelve-year randomized clinical trial. This study established that the VIA test "curbed deaths caused by cancer by 31 percent in a group of 1.5 lakh women." The researchers also projected that the "VIA test can prevent 22,000 cervical cancer deaths in India and 72,600 death[s] in 'resource-poor' countries worldwide annually."[38]

Although the Mumbai study was hailed as positive news in that it indicated the public health benefits of VIA screening, critics cried foul on ethical grounds. They condemned the fact that there was a control group that had not been provided with *any* screening, even though the Dindigul study had already demonstrated the efficacy of VIA testing and Pap smears were known to save lives. The Mumbai-based research team justified their decision to have such a control group on the grounds that the pre-existing "standard of care" in the low-income communities of Mumbai where the tests were conducted was no screening at all.[39]

This logic is exemplary of what Adriana Petryna refers to as "ethical variability" in the domain of globalized clinical trials carried out by contract research organizations (CROs) working for multinational pharmaceutical companies. Petryna provides a pointed critique of CROs and drug companies that exploit the international ethical standards for clinical trials established by the International Conference on Harmonisation. Such trials make room for variability in ethical standards based on the pre-existing standard of care for the particular populations in which the trial is being conducted. She noted that "ethical variability" enables CROs to "achieve recruitment success" by recruiting the bodies of people in resource-poor communities for clinical trials.[40] There is, however, an important distinction between the clinical trials described in Petryna's work and VIA trials conducted by the Tata Memorial

Centre team. Petryna's study focuses on CRO trials for medical interventions intended for markets in the global North that ultimately will not be made available in the low-income communities where they were tested. By contrast, the potential positive results of VIA clinical trials in low-income communities in Mumbai were intended to be made available to these communities in the absence of affordable cervical cancer screening for the majority of women in India and the global South more generally.

With VIA, acetic acid is dabbed onto the cervix using a swab. If the reaction results in pearl-white uniform coloration, it is an indication for cancer. In clinical trials in India, VILI was also found to be effective. With VILI, it is a mustard-color reaction that indicates cancer. The VIA and VILI tests can be conducted by trained nurses or paramedics. Often both tests are performed simultaneously for diagnostic verification. These methods detect both cancerous and precancerous cells. If cancer is suspected using these methods, a colposcopy[41] and biopsy are performed to ascertain whether cancer is present. When the biopsy is positive, the patient is referred for treatment. The VIA/VILI kits cost as little as 5 rupees when they were first developed for the market in the late 2000s; a Pap smear cost ten times that amount.[42] VIA/VILI methods have higher rates of false positives than Pap smears, and some have criticized these methods for causing undue stress and because of the costs associated with follow-up tests. Proponents of these methods argue that the benefits of cheaper tests, which require less medical training and less technology, outweigh the risks associated with false positives because these methods make cervical cancer screening available to many more women who would otherwise be unable to access Pap smears due to cost and to the dearth of trained physicians and diagnostic technologies in rural India.

As a result of the Dindigul study, the Tamil Nadu Health Systems Project,[43] part of the Government of Tamil Nadu's Department of Health and Family Welfare, began integrating cervical cancer screening with VIA and VILI, along with manual clinical breast cancer screening, on a voluntary basis for any patient visiting a Primary Health Centre (PHC) for any medical reason. Once this became an integral part of primary healthcare services in the state, the Government Cancer Hospital scaled back its programs to provide cancer screening camps, although it continued to occasionally work with NGOs to conduct educational programs about cervical and breast cancer screening in nearby rural communities.

With the development of the VIA/VILI technologies, NGOs got involved in providing this low-cost, low-tech screening to women who had not yet had access to cervical cancer screening. RUWSEC was one of the first NGOs in the state to initiate these screening programs, beginning in 2010, the same year the Tamil Nadu Health Systems Project rolled out its screening programs in PHCs in some districts in the state.

The government program in the PHCs offered cancer screening to people who were already coming to the hospital for other medical needs. The PHCs also organized occasional large educational and health screening camps in nearby communities that covered information on a wide range of medical problems, and they would refer people coming to those camps to various tertiary care hospitals for whichever medical problem was detected. RUWSEC, by contrast, developed targeted education and screening programs for cervical and breast cancer among rural Dalit women.

## RURAL WOMEN'S SOCIAL EDUCATION CENTRE

Just over 50 kilometers southwest of the Kanchipuram Government Cancer Hospital and 60 kilometers south of the Cancer Institute in Chennai sits an unassuming, small, rural clinic in the middle of open farmland. It is managed by the Rural Women's Social Education Centre (RUWSEC), an NGO run by and for rural Dalit women from the surrounding villages on the outskirts of the town of Thirukazhukundram, in Kanchipuram district. This clinic— which offers biomedical, Siddha, and homeopathic medical care as well as psychological counseling services—is one among many programs organized by RUWSEC. As was the case for our trips to Kanchipuram, when we visited RUWSEC and the surrounding villages where RUWSEC worked, we would travel by rental car from Chennai. This journey would often take two hours each way with traffic but was much more relaxing than the drive to Kanchipuram, for we came by the scenic, coconut- and palmyra-tree-lined East Coast Road along the Bay of Bengal toward Mahabalipuram, before turning inland to reach RUWSEC. RUWSEC's single-story red building with white trim sits under the shade of a giant almond tree. The clinic is at the entrance to the building. As you pass through the clinic, you come to an empty meeting room, with walls covered by open shelves and glass cabinets crammed full of books and reports, where groups gather to sit on the brown-painted stone floors to participate in RUWSEC programs, including the educational programs for cancer screening and the cancer support programs that I attended.

RUWSEC was founded in 1981 by T.K. Sundari Ravindran (a renowned scholar of health systems in India) and twelve Dalit women activists from towns and villages surrounding the city of Chengalpattu in Tamil Nadu. Drawing inspiration from Paulo Freire's model of education as a liberatory form of consciousness-raising and engaged problem-solving, they established RUWSEC to address social justice issues for rural Dalit women, such as the prevention of violence against women, particularly domestic violence. From its inception, RUWSEC has been engaged in raising consciousness about healthcare rights and the social determinants of health, and providing rural Dalit women with the tools to demand rights to equitable and respectful sexual and reproductive healthcare.[44]

In the early 1990s, women in communities where RUWSEC was working were critical of the condescending and sometimes abusive behavior of the medical practitioners in public hospitals and urged RUWSEC to establish its own clinic. The RUWSEC clinic opened in 1995 to provide subsidized "women-centered, gender-sensitive care" and "technically good-quality care." The clinic was led and managed by rural Dalit women.[45]

Tensions flared between the rural Dalit women who led RUWSEC and the professional-class and higher-caste doctors and nurses from Chengalpattu who had been hired to provide medical care in the clinic. The latter resented being managed by members of RUWSEC, whom they regarded as "illiterate, ignorant women."[46] This fraught relationship ultimately led RUWSEC to shift operations from the city of Chengalpattu to a rural site closer to the village communities it served. In 2001, they opened a new, scaled-back clinic and made a concerted effort to only hire medical practitioners who shared the values of RUWSEC and were committed to its goals. Dr. Subha Sri was serving as an obstetrician-gynecologist for outpatients during the time of my research and provided clinical screenings for cervical and breast cancer to Dalit women from fifty surrounding villages. This model of clinical care is difficult to sustain and cannot be a substitute for comprehensive public healthcare because it relies on a combination of political commitment and time from a unique breed of qualified healthcare providers, most of whom, like Subha Sri, commute four hours round-trip from Chennai and can only be present in the clinic one or two days each week.

Since the opening of RUWSEC's clinic in 1995, the rural public health system in Tamil Nadu has improved dramatically. I interviewed an OB/GYN doctor who had joined RUWSEC in 2006 after it relocated to its current rural facility. She said at that time that the closest Primary Health Centre, in Nerumbur, was "pretty much dysfunctional; there was nothing there." Over the next three or four years, the National Rural Health Mission[47] began pumping money into the primary healthcare system throughout Tamil Nadu, and with the help of dedicated women medical officers, the Nerumbur PHC became a highly functional primary care hospital, improving its reputation in the eyes of the community. This was also the time when the Tamil Nadu government's Muthulakshmi Reddy scheme was introduced, which provided monetary incentives to encourage women to deliver their babies in public hospitals, including PHCs. According to this RUWSEC doctor, that project succeeded, and lower-class and some middle-class women from the surrounding villages began to go the Nerumbur PHC for their deliveries, something that had been rare up until then.[48]

As the local PHC became a viable option for women's maternity healthcare, RUWSEC decided to move into other arenas of women's healthcare. The same OB/GYN explained, "The RUWSEC clinic was never intended to be competing with the public health system. The idea was always to use it as a model to push for better services in the public health system." After consulting with women and men in communities where RUWSEC was working, they decided to focus on women's health concerns that were not being adequately addressed at the PHC, including reproductive tract infections, prolapsed uterus, gynecological urology problems, and cancer (particularly cervical cancer). The new VIA and VILI screening technologies were particularly suitable for resource-poor settings such as RUWSEC's clinic.

In 2010, RUWSEC began conducting educational programs and clinical screening for cervical cancer using VIA and VILI technologies as well as manual clinical breast cancer exams. It also began educating women about breast self-exams. Women with a positive test result for cancer through such screenings would be referred to both the Cancer Institute and the Government Cancer Hospital, leaving it up to patients to choose which hospital they preferred. Initially RUWSEC provided these services within villages, making use of public schoolhouses to set up mobile screening clinics. Over time, as women from the villages started to seek out cervical and breast cancer screening on their own initiative, RUWSEC began offering these services at its clinic. RUWSEC's community health workers, who were also members of the rural Dalit communities in which they worked, served as resources for information about cancer prevention, screening, and treatment, encouraging women to undergo regular cancer screening at the RUWSEC clinic or the PHC in Nerumbur. RUWSEC also organized educational and clinical cervical and breast cancer screening "camps" twice each month at the clinic and held monthly support group meetings for cancer survivors in the RUWSEC building. I was able to observe these programs and visit the surrounding villages with RUWSEC healthcare social workers during my fieldwork.

Like many other NGOs in India, RUWSEC was struggling from funding cuts, for the Government of India had restricted international funding for NGOs. Also, the success of Tamil Nadu's public health system had brought about a retrenchment of funding from both philanthropic organizations and the central government for healthcare projects in Tamil Nadu. These funds were now being directed toward states with weaker health systems and poorer health indicators. In this climate of diminishing funding, RUWSEC relied on the interest earned from a corpus fund received from the Ford Foundation in 2000.

This brief overview of the history, missions, and programs of these three institutions—the Cancer Institute in Chennai, the Government Cancer Hospital in Kanchipuram, and RUWSEC in a village near Thirukazhukundram—demonstrates that a concern for the prevention, early diagnosis, and treatment of women's reproductive cancers in low-income communities has long been a cornerstone of cancer care in Tamil Nadu. These institutions were established at different moments in history, were grounded in varying political philosophies and mandates, and differ today with respect to their funding structure and size.

The Cancer Institute was founded in 1952 by a Gandhian women's rights advocate who was committed to the social uplift of lower-class, lower-caste women. It has grown into a major NGO hospital, serving low-income and some middle-class patients, not only from Chennai but also from communities throughout the state and from other South Indian states. The Government Arignar Anna Memorial Cancer Hospital and Research Centre, founded in 1969 as the first and only public tertiary hospital for cancer care in the state, took up the Cancer Institute's initiative for cervical cancer screening and treatment in rural villages in Tamil Nadu. This hospital, named after Chief Minister Annadurai, is a testament to the political commitment to the provision of public healthcare that has been a hallmark of Dravidian parties' political platforms in Tamil Nadu.[49] It too has grown into a large hospital, serving low-income patients from all over the state (and beyond); over half of its new patients are women with cervical or breast cancer. The RUWSEC clinic, founded in 1995, is part of an NGO inspired by a mixture of liberation theology and feminist Dalit grassroots social movements. It is a much smaller operation, focusing exclusively on women, that provides education and screening for cervical and breast cancer and refers patients to the Cancer Institute and the Government Cancer Hospital for treatment. Despite their differences, the one thing these three organizations have in common is a commitment to improving educational outreach and access to cancer screening and treatment for lower-class, lower-caste women in South India.

Shweta, Shibani, and I circulated in and through the interstices of these three institutions and along the pathways that connected them to the women they served. For lower-income women in Tamil Nadu, the journeys leading them to a cancer diagnosis and eventually to treatment were complex and never linear. That said, a significant portion of the cervical and breast cancer patients from the northeastern corner of Tamil Nadu and even many from farther afield ended up receiving subsidized care at either the Cancer Institute or the Government Cancer Hospital.

# CHAPTER 2

# Poverty and Chemicals

The summer of 2015 was one of the hottest on record at that time, with temperatures consistently above 40°C (104°F) every day, sometimes well above that. The rains, which should have begun to arrive, had not come by mid-July. Under the narrow shade of our umbrellas, Shweta, Shibani, and I followed one of the RUWSEC community health workers, walking along a dirt path to the edge of some paddy fields in a village in Kanchipuram district. There we met a group of about thirty Dalit women, ranging in age from twenty to seventy. Wearing multicolored but worn-out saris, they were squeezed together under a clump of trees on a small strip of raised land between two fields. They had taken refuge under the shade while they waited, hoping to be called for *kuli* work in the fields. They had been waiting all morning with no work available; it had been the same for several days because there was a drought and the crops were failing.

The women knew the RUWSEC health worker and greeted her warmly. She explained that we had come to learn about their views on and experiences with cancer and cancer screening and treatment programs in their communities, and they agreed to discuss these things with us, perhaps to help pass the time while they waited indefinitely for work. People of little means in Tamil Nadu often rush to find chairs for visitors in their home while they would sit on the floor; here, in the middle of the fields, they handed us the large metal concave pans they used to collect weeds, dirt, and stones from the fields. They turned the pans upside down and insisted that we sit perched on the rounded tops. It was quintessential Tamil hospitality. There was a resounding consensus among these women that cancer was on the rise largely because of changes in agricultural practices, conditions of labor, lack of work, and increasingly frequent droughts and that these phenomena were poisoning, weakening, and sickening bodies in modern times. One elderly, white-haired woman was having difficulty getting her raspy voice heard among the din of the other voices. She stood up and came to sit beside me and spoke right into my ear, saying:

> "Cancer" is a sign of the Kali Yuga. It has come because of the way we live, because of agricultural chemicals [*vivasaya marundu*] in our food, and lack of work. It was not like this when I was a young girl. This is the Kali Yuga.

This woman elicited the Kali Yuga to describe changes she had seen in her lifetime, and the other women in the group concurred as they described the economic, social, and environmental transformations of recent times, which were driven by greed and had given rise to this disease. These factors were consistently the most common—and the most vehemently expressed—causal explanations for cancer offered by women from rural, lower-caste communities. This chapter presents these pointed and poignant political and economic explanations for cancer, which were noticeably absent from public health cancer campaigns.

Listening to these women's explanations, we can gain insight into lower-class and -caste women's profound experience of precarity and their awareness that their vulnerability to cancer stems from their marginalization. This is most dramatically exemplified by one ethnographic vignette at the heart of this chapter: the women mentioned above were convinced that cancer was on the rise because of the agricultural chemicals used to grow the white rice they received as a government subsidy provided to people living below the poverty line. Yet they did not want to say so publicly for fear of having the subsidy withheld. They felt caught in a Hobson's choice—compelled to eat that which might poison them in order to survive.

In this chapter, I draw primarily from group discussions in rural villages in Tamil Nadu to provide insights into people's perceptions of the causes of various cancers, including reproductive cancers. Chapter 3 will present views specifically on cervical and breast cancer causality, drawing from interviews with cancer patients and survivors and from group discussions.

Typically, in our group discussions, the first response to my question about what people thought caused cancer was that they did not know. It was a mystery, and they wanted more information. As one woman said,

> We want to know where cancer comes from. We know how to get treatment but we don't know what causes it right now. If we know, then we ourselves could do things to prevent it.

The mystery of cancer's causality was what made it particularly frightening. Due to the long-running public health campaigns in India about the dangers of smoking and chewing tobacco and betel *paan* (a combination of betel leaf, areca nut, and lime), people knew that those substances could increase the risk of cancer. Yet they were witnessing a rise in cancer among members of their communities who did not use those products, and they did not know why. They were left feeling fearful of everything and wondering if each and every symptom they had might be a sign of cancer. One woman stated,

> When we think of "cancer" we feel fear. People with "cancer" will get frequent headaches, and stomachaches. When we have headaches and stomachaches now we fear that it might be "cancer." Since we don't know what causes "cancer," any time we feel any kind of symptoms, we wonder if it might be "cancer."

Many sensed that they did not know what causes cancer because they were too poor to access information and education about it. As one woman put it,

> When it comes to how you can save yourself, only the educated ones will have the access to that sort of information, right? They can easily go on the "net" [Internet] and find out how they can protect themselves from this disease. We don't have that so we don't really know much about it at all.

These initial curt replies about the need for more information in order to prevent cancer echoed the emphasis on education in public health campaigns. Yet as our conversations unfolded, I found that rural Dalit and MBC women in fact had many theories about cancer causality that differed sharply from the messages about cancer causality presented by public health educators. The overarching theory voiced was that poverty and labor and environmental changes brought about by modernization and economic liberalism were driving the increase in cancer rates.

I will address three aspects of this critique, moving from the most general to the more specific. First, women argued that water shortages, both natural and anthropogenic, were leading to loss of work and consequently to increased poverty, which in turn was contributing to an upsurge in all types of disease, including cancer. Second, there was widespread criticism of the increasing use of chemicals in agricultural production. Women felt that cancer was on the rise as a result of the consumption of food and water tainted by these chemicals, and to some extent by exposure to hazardous chemicals through agricultural work. Furthermore, women expressed concerns that foods produced using these chemicals were less nutritious and were leading to weaker bodies that were more prone to getting cancer than in the past. Anxieties about exposure to agricultural chemicals were paramount. Most of this chapter is devoted to elucidating these concerns and the profound sense of powerlessness and perceived inability to protest that women in my study felt in the face of the onslaught of these chemicals. Third, women reaffirmed public health messages that cancer was caused by chewing tobacco and betel *paan*. However, unlike the public health messages, which framed these practices as bad habits that individuals could kick, women who used these products asserted that they did so to calm excruciating pain from toothaches in the absence of access to dental care. What links these three factors—water, chemicals, and *paan*—together is that they demonstrate that lower-class and -caste women understand cancer to be something that materializes in the midst of poverty and economic and political inequality.

## RURAL DALIT WOMEN'S WORK IN TAMIL NADU

To appreciate the discourses of cancer causality presented in this chapter, we must first examine the working lives of most rural Dalit women in Tamil Nadu. Like Poongodai, they depended on two main sources of employment. First, they did agricultural daily wage labor (*vivasaya kuli*) for landowners (who were from higher-class and higher-caste groups). This work involved plowing, planting, transplanting, and weeding rice paddy and other crops such as sugarcane, groundnuts, okra, *brinjal* (eggplant), and watermelon. Nowadays much of the harvesting is done by machines, so there is less *kuli* work associated with harvesting than there used to be. The *kuli* agricultural labor was backbreaking and exhausting and often meant long hours under the hot sun. Women and men would sometimes do this work in exchange for a share of paddy but more often for a daily wage.

Women typically earned 120 rupees per day (around US$1.90)[1] for agricultural *kuli* work, whereas men received around 400 rupees per day (around US$6.30).[2] Some women were critical of the discrepancy between men's and women's wages, while others accepted it as fair given that men did work that required heavier manual labor, such as plowing by hand, whereas women were mostly involved in transplanting and weeding paddy, which was still a backbreaking task requiring women to bend over for hours on end. More significantly, men were expected to work longer hours than women. Men's *kuli* work began between 5:00 or 6:00 a.m. and went until 6:00 p.m., or even as late as 8:00 p.m., because they were not responsible for unpaid household and childcare work. Women's *kuli* work typically began between 9:30 and 10:00 a.m. after they had prepared both breakfast and lunch (to be taken to work in tiffin carriers) for the family and after the children had left for school. Women's *kuli* labor usually ended around 3:00 or 4:00 p.m., when children were returning home from school and women needed to begin preparing dinner for the family. Sometimes women would stop work at 2:00 p.m.; other times they would work in the fields until as late as 8:00 p.m. The length of time they worked and amount they would be paid depended on the availability of work. During my research in 2015 and 2016, I found that neither men nor women were working as much as they would have liked because there was little work available as a result of droughts, increased mechanization, and a general economic crisis that Indian farmers were facing in the early part of the twenty-first century. Women were more concerned about the lack of work available to both men and women in their families than about the gender disparities in pay, although some women did complain about the gender wage gap.

The second type of work on which rural Dalit women depended was provided through the MGNREGA program. The Government of India's MGNREGA Act was passed in 2005 and has been implemented in all districts of Tamil Nadu. The Tamil Nadu Rural Development and Panchayat Raj Department's website states that this Act

> guarantees 100 days of employment in a financial year to any rural household whose adult members are willing to do unskilled manual work. This Act is an important step towards the realization of the right to work. It is also expected to enhance people's livelihoods on a sustained basis, by developing the economic and social infrastructure in rural areas. The Village Panchayat will issue job cards to every registered individual. Payment of the statutory minimum wage and equal wages for men and women are the notable features of the scheme.[3]

People who turn to this scheme do so because they are unable to find gainful employment and are living in poverty. They are typically undereducated, underemployed Dalits or members of designated tribal communities.

The central government covers 90 percent of the costs of this program, the states 10 percent. Tamil Nadu prioritized water management-related projects for this work, including creating and renovating ponds and channels, desilting the bunds of irrigation tanks, and other water conservation and flood protection measures.[4] In Tamil Nadu people referred to this as "one hundred days work" (*nooru naal pani*) or pond work (*ezhi velai*), since most of the work was on water projects. This proved to be a problem in times of water scarcity. In 2015, women reported that because of the drought, MGNREGA work was only available for two or three days each month, and they were concerned that it would not reach the one hundred days per year as intended. When they did get MGNREGA work, both men and women earned 150 rupees per day (around US$2.40) to work from 10:00 a.m. to 3:00 p.m. Because men could earn more through *kuli* work than from MGNREGA work, women were more likely than men to claim the right to MGNREGA work for the household.

## CANCER AND "THE WATER PROBLEM"

A woman from the Dalit section of a village that I visited several times in the summer of 2015 summed up the source of the cancer problem succinctly as she eyed the water bottle I always carried with me to quench my thirst on those hot summer days. She said, "To understand the problem of cancer in our village, there is only one thing you need to understand—the water problem." Others in the group agreed and went on to explain the myriad ways that the water problem affected their health and contributed to the mounting cancer problem.

The water problem to which she was referring was that summer's drought. Without rain, the crops would not grow. Without crops, there was no *kuli* wage labor for them in the fallow fields. Without water, there was virtually no work on water-related MGNREGA projects. Without work, there was no money. Without money, they could not buy food or medicine or pay the bus fare to the hospital. Without money, they could not even afford to go to the public government hospitals, where, while they could get medical care free of cost, they would have to pay for scans and tests and for small bribes to the hospital staff for various services provided.

The bore well that had been built to raise drinking water from the bottom of the riverbed into the large water tank in the middle of the village was not reaching enough water to supply the village with adequate drinking water. Water was so scarce in their village that they had resorted to illegally cutting the pipes that irrigated the fields to siphon off some water that trickled out for drinking and for washing their bodies and dishes. I watched women collecting water in colorful plastic jugs where they had cut the pipes and young children playing gleefully in this contraband water. That water was intended for irrigating fields and was making them sick when they used it for drinking. They also took their clothes into the fields under the cover of the night to use the irrigation water to wash their clothes, leaving suds in the fields, thus damaging the crops.

Most of the households in the Dalit section of this village did not have their own latrines. There was a pit latrine for collective use, but most people went to the surrounding fields to go to the bathroom. The government was encouraging them to build and use latrines to improve hygiene and health. But there was not enough water to clean themselves in the latrines (as is customary in India, where people use water instead of toilet paper) or to keep the latrines themselves clean. The result was that the public latrine was a stench pit, attracting flies that spread diseases, which weakened people's bodies and made them vulnerable to cancer. People usually steered clear of the public latrine and went back to using the fields.

The situation was dire. Women in this Dalit section of the village saw cancer as just one symptom of their poverty that had been exacerbated by the water shortage. I heard the same complex cluster of explanations in every village that I visited.

Water scarcity was particularly acute in this village and others like it in northeastern Tamil Nadu along the banks of the Palar River. The headwaters of the Palar are in the state of Karnataka. The river then winds its way through Andhra Pradesh before entering Tamil Nadu, flowing through Kanchipuram district, and ultimately emptying into the Bay of Bengal south of Chennai. That is, when the river flowed at all. When giving us directions to visit her, one RUWSEC community health worker instructed us to cross the Palar River to reach her village. Upon arriving in the village, I was confused because we had not crossed a river. I thought perhaps we had come by a different route and asked her if we had come the wrong way. She laughed, saying that we *had* crossed the river and that we could in fact see it from the Muthumariamman temple in the middle of the "SC Colony" where we were standing. She pointed just past the statue of Ambedkar toward the river. I looked back and realized that we had indeed crossed the river. In fact, we had driven right *through* it on a rutted-out dirt road! The river was wide but completely dried out, with scraggly bushes taking root in the sand across the full span of the riverbed.

Men and machines were working on one side of the riverbed, erecting large pillars to build a high concrete bridge and a road for vehicles to cross the river. It was an anomalous sight: a bridge being built where there was not a drop of water to be seen. It seemed like an example of either extreme government waste or supreme optimism.

I took out my camera and snapped a photograph of Dalit women laborers from this village walking across the Palar River on the dirt road, carrying plastic water jugs under the beating hot sun. I have used this photo as the cover image for this book because it is evocative of Dalit women's assertions that the cycle of increased droughts, exacerbated poverty, overuse of agricultural chemicals, and the gendered intensification of the labor, heat, and stress they face in the current era are leading to eruptions of cancer in their communities.

The lack of water in the Palar River was not simply a problem caused by that summer's drought: the river had been dry for several years. That was partly because of dams across the river in Karnataka (and there were plans to build still more dams in Andhra Pradesh). People in Tamil Nadu applauded their then Chief Minister Jayalalithaa's hard-fought battle to stop the dam projects in Karnataka; she had declared them to be a breach of inter-state agreements dating back to 1892, during the colonial era. This was also a concern for the city of Chennai, because the Palar River was an important source of water for the city, especially during droughts. Andhra Pradesh has since proceeded to build new check dams and raise the height of existing ones across the Palar, further angering the people of northeastern Tamil Nadu, who have depended on the river for irrigation and drinking water, and spurring the government of Tamil Nadu to file a suit with the Supreme Court.[5]

Nevertheless, villagers whom I met along the banks of the Palar primarily blamed the Tamil Nadu government for taking bribes and turning a blind eye to the "sand mafia," thus allowing companies to mine sand out of the river in order to sell it to concrete companies. Sand mining—legal or illicit—has become a lucrative industry in India, generating more than $50 billion a year in revenue.[6] Sand mining had contributed to the drying up of the Palar River and had created an acute scarcity of water for these villagers, who depended on that river for their livelihood. It was a cruel irony that the same industries that had caused the Palar to dry up, leaving a desert in its place, were now benefiting from constructing a concrete bridge across the wasteland that was once a river.

Activists from the Social Action Movement and the Water Rights

Protection Group in Chengalpattu protested to block the Palar dam and mining projects and to prevent problems with industrial waste pollution in the river.[7] But the projects continued. Activists, villagers, and government officials who have spoken out against the illegal sand-mining operations in the state have faced violent reprisals; there are allegations that people who stood up to the sand-mining companies have been killed, with the cause of death going unreported.[8] These activists have raised alarms about the inequities of the political economy of water and the environmental harm inflicted by these economic pursuits. In the same vein, rural women whom I met considered the political economy of water scarcity and the toxic effects of chemicals in their food and in the water they drank to be causal factors of cancer in their communities.

## CANCER AND CHEMICALS

Although women in my study placed cancer within broader structural problems of water scarcity, lack of employment, and poverty, they also pointed to what they saw as the most proximate cause and primary offender for rising rates of cancer: agricultural chemicals. Anxieties about the negative health impacts of agricultural chemicals were widespread. This was the most pervasive and dominant view of cancer causality in my study. People did not link these chemicals to specific forms of cancer; they were implicated in *all* cancers.

The Tamil word typically used to refer to all these substances—chemicals used in plant agriculture (including pesticides, herbicides, fungicides, and chemical fertilizers), chemical hormones and antibiotics used for livestock, and chemical food preservatives—was *marundu*. Initially I was confused when people said it was the over-use of *marundu* that was causing people to get cancer because the most common use of the term *"marundu"* refers to medicine. Similarly, Akhil Gupta's study of agricultural development shows that the Hindi word for medicine (*davaa*) was employed by farmers in North India to refer to herbicides that kill weeds.[9] It would be interesting to know how and why these terms came to be used for chemicals. Perhaps it was a strategy among policy planners and agro-chemical companies to encourage farmers to use these substances to enhance crop production in the early days of India's Green Revolution. The use of the word "medicine" to refer to these chemicals was jarring because people overwhelmingly felt that these "medicines" were killing members of their communities by causing cancer.

The irony becomes tragedy given that India has been witnessing an epidemic of farmer suicides through direct pesticide consumption as India's farmers face an economic crisis.[10]

### Agricultural Chemicals, Food, and Cancer

People felt intense anxiety about the food they were eating because of the risks of thereby ingesting agricultural chemicals, as is clear from this excerpt from a group meeting with rural Dalit women:

> *Shweta:* If you compare it to events ten or twenty or thirty years ago, do you think cancer rates have increased since then or do you think it is just the same?
>
> *Woman 1:* It is only now that cancer has become so prevalent. In those days there was no such disease.
>
> *Woman 2:* It is being caused by the *vivasaya marundu* [agricultural chemicals] they put in the fields to get rid of the bugs [*poochi*] when they are growing the food.
>
> *Woman 3* (older woman): Yes! In farming they put a lot *marundu* for fertilizer. When I was young, there was no *marundu*; we only used manure and naturally prepared nitrogen with decomposed leaves and we did all the weeding by hand. No one used to get sick. Now the use of *marundu* is too high. *The amount of marundu we put in the food we eat is directly proportional to the amount of money we spend at the doctor's office* [emphasis added].
>
> *Woman 4:* In those days they used natural fertilizers [*uram*]. Now they use *marundu* everywhere. It isn't just a little *marundu* they use, they use a lot of it! They also put *marundu* to make the rice paddy grow very quickly. Before it would take six months, now they are ready for harvest in just three months.
>
> *Woman 5:* Yes, they use too much *marundu* to grow the rice and we eat that "ration" rice.
>
> *Woman 6* (another older woman): Before we used natural fertilizers. We used the dung of farm animals—cows, goats, and pigs—and the leaves from trees and the shells of groundnuts to make natural manure. We did not apply *marundu* to remove the bugs. Now everything has *marundu*. It is only now that cancer has come. This is a problem now because they put *marundu* in the "ration" rice.
>
> *Woman 2:* It is not only the rice, it also comes from the vegetables.
>
> *Woman 4:* That is true. Sometimes it comes through the vegetables. But the main problem is with the rice.
>
> *Many women together:* Yes! The main problem is definitely with the "ration" rice.

Across all of my conversations with lower-class Dalit women there was agreement that the greatest risk factor for cancer was the consumption of the white rice they received as a subsidy from the government of Tamil Nadu when they presented their "ration cards" to prove that they lived below the poverty line. This is not surprising given that rice is the staple of the South Indian diet; people typically eat rice with every meal. Similarly, Gupta found widespread concerns about the use chemical fertilizer in wheat production among rural communities in North India, where wheat is the staple food.[11] In Tamil Nadu, middle- and upper-class people typically eat rice along with a lentil-based soup (*sambhar*), vegetables, and sometimes meat (among non-Brahmins) for their main meal at lunchtime, and rice-based tiffin foods such as *idli* or *dosai* for breakfast and dinner. For those living in extreme poverty, it is not uncommon to eat rice alone, with little else to accompany it for some meals.

The Tamil Nadu Civil Supplies Corporation is a state-owned public sector company, established in 1956 to provide "essential commodities" such as rice, wheat, sugar, and kerosene at subsidized prices at Fair Price Shops (FPSs) to ration card holders who are permanent residents of the state. This is part of the central government's Public Distribution System (PDS), which dates back to the 1940s, prior to independence. In 2013, under the leadership of Prime Minister Singh and the Congress Party, the Government of India passed the National Food Security Act, which brought this food subsidy program under the jurisdiction of the Department of Food and Public Distribution. In 2011 the Tamil Nadu state government launched an initiative to provide rice free of cost to those living below the poverty line who held ration cards. These government programs are enormously popular in Tamil Nadu and are lifelines for people living in poverty.

As I was wrapping up my conversation with the group whose comments about the agricultural chemicals used to produce rice are provided in the excerpt above, I reiterated that one of the aims of my research was to learn about healthcare concerns among communities like theirs in order to relay these messages to the public by writing a book so that people involved in policymaking and public health programs could improve healthcare in the region. Upon hearing this, the woman who had been the first to speak up about the problem with the rice came to my side and quietly mumbled, "Can you cross off what I told you before about the rice 'ration'? If the government finds out, then they will take away our 'ration.'" Another woman next to her chimed in, saying, "We all get our rice through the Amma scheme. If we say anything bad about it, Amma might get angry and stop this scheme in our village. We need this rice to live so please do not say that we said anything bad about the rice we get from the Amma program." A third woman who had also said that cancer was linked to chemicals used to grow this rice blurted out, "Cancer does *not* come through the rice! It only comes through the vegetables which are grown with chemicals. It has nothing to do with the rice!" *"Amma"* means mother in Tamil. It is the term of affection, respect, and even devotion, and supporters of then Chief Minister Jayalalithaa used it to refer to her.[12] It is also the term that Jayalalithaa and her All India Anna Dravida Munnetra Kazhagam (AIADMK) political party used to promote her administration and its populist welfare schemes.

One woman in the group began looking at my notebook and my recorder and asked me to cross out whatever I had written and to delete whatever was recorded about what they had said about the rice. I explained again, as I had at the very beginning of the discussion, that I would not identify the name of their village or the names of anyone present but rather would write that this was a concern among some rural communities in Tamil Nadu. I said I thought this was an important concern to report but that I did not want to put anyone as risk by presenting their views to the public. They agreed that it was important to report as long as their particular village was not identified. One woman said, "If Amma finds out that *we* are the ones who said this, she will take away our 'ration' and then we will face grave difficulties. Please do not mention the name of our village in your report."

This whole discussion was a stark and painful commentary on the profound sense of precarity harbored by the women in my study, who felt that their survival depended on this welfare scheme that provided them with free rice. Yet at the same time, they thought that very same rice was killing them. Their precarity curtailed their ability to speak out publicly about their fear that the heavy use of agricultural chemicals was giving them cancer.

In 2017, facing strong pressure from the central government to cut costs, the Tamil Nadu state government made sweeping changes to its subsidies program for ration card holders, barring many from that program who had once been entitled to those subsidies, including households with at least one tax-paying member and any household owning an air conditioner. An *India Today* reporter stated that "the new guidelines for availing ration supplies have caught people off-guard who since years have been dependent on public welfare distribution systems encouraged by both AIADMK and DMK[13] governments. Tamil Nadu's public distribution system is often referred to as a model system across India."[14]

The government's announcement came shortly after Jayalalithaa's death. Some criticized the plan for rolling back populist programs that Jayalalithaa had championed, though she had been involved in this decision prior to her death.[15] These changes would cause greater hardship for middle-class people, who also received some subsidies, but they would not impact the more destitute people who participated in my research. This policy change demonstrates the vulnerability of this highly popular welfare scheme under a neoliberal agenda and underscores why the women I met were hesitant to publicize their criticism of this government subsidy.

It was clear from my discussions with women in Tamil Nadu that people had grown fearful that virtually anything they consumed could cause cancer due to the increased use of chemicals in food production. It was not only chemical pesticides, herbicides, fungicides, and fertilizers that concerned them. They were also suspicious of chemicals used as preservatives for lengthening the shelf life of food. People have become more dependent on processed foods with preservatives for convenience's sake and are eating less fresh food. They also considered hormone- and antibiotic-treated livestock to be potentially carcinogenic.

Women from these low-income communities held all of these substances responsible for the growing problem of cancer in their communities. I present this conversation from another group discussion at length because it folds together many of these themes:

> *Cecilia:* Is cancer increasing or decreasing in villages in this region?
>
> *Woman 1* (older woman): There was nothing like this in the past; it is only now.
>
> *Woman 2:* Back then, they couldn't find it [i.e., couldn't screen and/or diagnose cancer], so they didn't know. And it [cancer] was not there so much back then.
>
> *Woman 1:* The use of agricultural chemicals has also increased. They never used *marundu* on plants before. These *marundu* are causing this disease.
>
> *Woman 3:* They have started using so much *marundu* now and we harvest those with our own hands and eat that food!
>
> *Woman 4:* It's not just the crops, even the store-bought goods are not safe. They use *marundu* to ripen fruits. And they use *marundu* to raise and fatten the "broiler" chickens that are packaged and sold in stores. And they give *marundu* to cows to produce more milk.
>
> *Woman 2:* When we buy a food item, it doesn't immediately reach the shop. It is stored in multiple places before reaching the shop so it is not fresh. The *marundu* used to store it on shelves soaks and absorbs into the item. So, when we cook and eat it, this disease [cancer] happens.

*Woman 3:* If everything we eat has *marundu*, what is a person to do?! Rich people can buy naturally grown [organic] food from special shops in the city but no one is bothered that *we* have to eat all this *marundu*. This is the Kali Yuga.

*Woman 5:* From rice to water, everything has *marundu* these days!

*Woman 1:* Yes, it's even in the water! What are we to do?!

This discussion is jam-packed with disquieting sentiment and anger: Dalit women attributed their increased exposure to agricultural chemicals and the disproportionate risk this poses to the rural poor to a lack of concern about their well-being. They saw this as a reflection of the Kali Yuga. I will address some of the issues they raised, beginning with the water. The groundwater from bore-wells and open wells in rural Tamil Nadu is contaminated by agricultural chemicals such as DDT, HCH, and Endosulfan, which enter the soil and groundwater directly when they are applied to crops and indirectly when the rain washes them off treated crops. These chemicals are restricted in India because they have been proven to cause a range of health problems (especially neurological disorders), yet they continue to be used due to their low cost, which makes them popular among farmers.[16] In her book on India's environmental crisis, Meera Subramanian notes that "a study of three thousand village wells around India revealed that a fifth of them contained nitrates in excess of WHO limits."[17] Nitrates are found naturally in water and do not always cause health problems; however, an excess of nitrates in drinking water can have serious health consequences, including cancer, and such excess is typically due to heavy use of artificial fertilizers, which then enter the water.[18]

Women in group discussions and cancer patients alike frequently evoked concerns about "broiler *kozhi*" (broiler chickens), which are bred on large-scale corporate farms and then plucked, skinned, cut, and sold in packages in stores. They said that these chickens cause cancer because of the artificial *marundu* they are fed. News reports have revealed that chickens raised on corporate chicken farms in India are dosed with some of the world's strongest antibiotics, including "antibiotics of last resort" (i.e., intended to be kept in reserve, to be used on humans only in the most extreme medical cases when more commonly administered antibiotics fail to work).[19] Widespread routine use of these antibiotics can lead to health problems for those who consume the chicken; it can also cause resistance to antibiotics for people who need them. Women contrasted this broiler chicken with "country chicken" (*naattu kozhi*). These latter birds are purchased while still alive, are *marundu*-free, and are considered to be natural and healthy. The contrast between broiler and country chicken was articulated within the twin discourses of tradition versus modernity on the one hand, and village versus city on the other. Broiler chicken was associated with modern convenience (i.e., the growing presence of supermarkets in urban centers throughout India). By contrast, country chicken, which was bought whole and processed at home, was nostalgically reflective of an earlier era when people worked harder but lived simpler, healthier, and less stressful lives.

Finally, as one woman noted, organic grocery stores have sprung up in cities like Chennai, offering chemical-free alternatives but at prices the poor cannot afford. Middle-class women from Chennai in my study said they did try to buy fresh produce from these organic shops if they could afford it. Yet they were skeptical about whether it was genuinely chemical-free, given the lack of government oversight.

### Agricultural Chemicals as an Occupational Hazard

One woman in the above group stated, "They have started using so much *marundu* now and we harvest those with our own hands and eat that food!" This raises the issue of occupational hazards associated with agricultural labor where these chemicals are applied. A few other women from rural areas who were wage laborers on farms also raised concerns about exposure to these agricultural chemicals through their work. Some explained that when women transplant paddy in fields that are filled with agricultural chemicals, they "inhale" (*svasithal*) these chemicals into their vaginal tracts because they do not typically wear underpants. They thought these chemicals were causing cervical cancer. However, most reported that such worries were mitigated by the fact that farm owners and work supervisors informed laborers when they were going to apply chemicals and did not allow them to work in the fields for a certain length of time after the chemical application. The following was a common reply to my question about whether people thought there were links between cancer and exposure to these chemicals through agricultural labor:

> We don't go to work the fields immediately after they put the *marundu*. They [the farm owners/supervisors] don't let us return to the fields until three days after they put *marundu* so that doesn't harm us. But the *marundu* gets absorbed into the food that we eat and that is harmful.

This line of inquiry did not generate much discussion, but more ethnographic research would be helpful to appreciate people's thoughts on this issue and to better understand what measures are or are not taken to protect agricultural workers from potentially harmful exposure to such chemicals through agricultural labor.

Seth Holmes's ethnography[20] about the plight of indigenous Mexican migrant farm workers in the United States demonstrates that people sometimes buy into stereotypes and ideologies that support their marginalization and undermine their health. Holmes found that indigenous Triqui berry pickers working in the US believed they did not have to worry about the negative effects of pesticides as much as white people because their bodies were stronger and tougher (a reflection of the "brutish" quality that white Americans attributed to them), so they could, therefore, tolerate the pesticides. They thought white people had weaker bodies and could not tolerate them as well as they could and, therefore, white workers needed to take more extreme measures to avoid exposure to agricultural chemicals in the workplace. Triqui workers said this with a sense of ethnic pride. Holmes presents this as an example of how inequality comes to be "naturalized" by all parties involved, including those at the bottom of the social hierarchy, thus demonstrating the process of misrecognition in what Bourdieu calls "symbolic violence."[21] Yet lower-class Dalit agricultural workers in Tamil Nadu whom I met did *not* uncritically naturalize the logic of their marginalization. In fact, in contrast to the public health discourse of cancer and individual responsibility for lifestyle choices, they saw cancer as directly linked to their conditions of economic marginalization. Furthermore, whereas the Triqui laborers in Holmes's study saw themselves as immune to environmental hazards because of their stronger bodies, women in my study lamented that their bodies had become progressively weaker.

### Agricultural Chemicals, Machines, and Weaker Bodies

Women were worried about more than the carcinogenic effects of chemicals used in food production. They also believed that foods produced using such chemicals were less nutritious, resulting in weaker bodies that were more vulnerable to cancer than they had been in the past, before the use of these chemicals, when people's bodies were stronger. Furthermore, they felt that bodies have become weakened as a result of increased mechanization in agricultural production. This combination of factors was thought to be leading to an increase in cancer and other diseases associated with development. The following conversation from a group discussion in the Dalit section of one village reveals these concerns:

*Woman 1:* It is only nowadays that we have cancer.

*Shweta:* In earlier times there was no cancer?

*Woman 2 (older woman):* No there was not. When I first got married and came here we used to do everything manually. Now they have vehicles to do all the work and use *marundu* when they grow the crops. Because of this, "cancer" and other diseases like "BP" ["blood pressure"/hypertension] and "sugar" [diabetes] have come up.

*Cecilia:* Are you saying that the lack of manual labor can cause cancer?

*Woman 2 (elderly woman):* Yes, that is definitely true because our bodies have become weak.

*Woman 3:* Now they put *marundu* to kill insects, right? That is why this is happening. In those days the rice used to be thick and big, now it is very fragile [*mellisu*] and small. The rice those days gave you strength [*balam*]. The rice now does not give you strength because of the *marundu* they use. The rice is weaker so our bodies are weaker.

*Shweta:* Is it because our bodies are weaker from eating weaker rice that these diseases are happening more frequently? Or is it that these diseases are happening more because our bodies are weaker from not working as hard in the fields now that the machines have come?

*Woman 2 and 3 together:* It is because of both these things.

Older women spoke with pride about the manual labor they performed in the past, and they were nostalgic about the healthier foods they ate. Middle-aged and younger women spoke with admiration about the older ways and the strength of the bodies of older women. Some feared what the future would hold for generations to come: they expected bodies to become progressively weaker over time. This concern was greater among lower-class women who had migrated from rural villages to suburban and urban areas for new work opportunities that were physically less strenuous than agricultural work. The following discussion between two women in a suburb of Chennai captures this intergenerational perspective well:

*Older woman:* When we were young, we had to do a lot of hard labor. We worked in the fields. We ate *ragi* [millet] and maize and items like that. Now it is not like that. Now we eat only rice. We grow our crops using *marundu*. When we eat that kind of food, we get this disease [cancer]. But when I was younger, from the moment we woke up in the morning, we would draw water from the wells, and then we would use the grindstone and the mortar to grind the grains. But now, we don't do it like that. All we have to do is turn a switch on. So there is no exercise. That in itself causes the disease. That is the biggest reason for cancer and all these things.

*Middle-aged woman:* She is right. That is the difference between us and older women. This makes us question whether we will be as healthy as that generation. They ate well and had healthy foods. At least we know about these things, but our children do not even know of the grains that she is talking about. We still work a lot, but our children work even less. The risk of illness is only going to increase. I don't see how it will decrease. Normally, healthy foods are grown using natural fertilizers. I have seen that in my village when I was a child. People would take cow dung and use that as a fertilizer and then they would transplant the crops and wait for it to grow. Now they use *marundu,* and in only three months' time, they harvest the land twice. The landowners who do this want to sell it to make money. But they think twice about eating such food themselves. We also feel suspicious about this kind of food but we don't have any choice. This is how it is in the Kali Yuga. What can we do?!

This discursive contrast between weaker bodies in the present compared to stronger bodies in the past is a common trope in critiques of modernity, which can conjure up highly romanticized visions of a traditional past in which life was simpler and people were physically and morally stronger. It was not specific historical dates for these changes in agricultural practices that mattered most. People referred to various time periods to account for the changes they were experiencing. Typically, the reference point was generational. Grandmothers in their sixties and older would regale younger women with nostalgic tales about how strong they had once been and how tasty and fortifying the food once was compared to now. Middle-aged and younger women would speak wistfully about a time when their parents and grandparents were growing up in healthier environments. Sometimes middle-aged women in their forties and fifties noted changes for the worse during their own lifetimes. Even women in their twenties sometimes spoke of the glory days of their early childhoods when the world was a healthier place. Gupta encountered the same slipperiness when it came to pinning down specific dates to understand farmers' views about changes in agricultural practices in North India. He found that what was significant was not the dates per se but the concept of "the past." As he noted, "What made a period 'the past' in their discourse was not its distance on a linear time line. 'The past,' instead, was a *time of difference.* That is what *made* it 'the past,' and that is what was significant about it."[22] The same was true for how my interlocutors conceptualized the idea of the past and its relation to the present when referencing the concept of the Kali Yuga.

Setting aside the apparent historical fuzziness, the generational references do in fact align with major changes in agricultural practices in India. Women who were grandmothers during my research had witnessed the early years of the most significant transformation in Indian agriculture: the Green Revolution, which began in the mid-1960s as a joint project of the Government of India and international development institutions. It sought to provide a technocratic solution to poverty and hunger in India. The plan involved the introduction of hybrid, high-yielding seeds, which were distributed by multinational seed corporations, as well as the heavy use of biochemicals produced by multinational corporations. The result was increased crop production with each harvest as well as an increase in the number of harvests per year. However the Green Revolution also brought about increased dependency on these imported agricultural inputs and led to a widening income gap between those farmers who could afford these new inputs and who acquired more and more land with their profits, and those who could not compete, who eventually had to sell their land, often migrating to cities when they did.[23] The agricultural techniques introduced by the Green Revolution also required much more water than was previously needed. This has contributed to India's water shortage. As water levels fall, farmers and others need to dig deeper wells. The water may then become contaminated by naturally occurring uranium, which releases radon gas and arsenic, both of which have been linked to cancer.[24]

Tamil Nadu was one of the states selected for early implementation of the Green Revolution because of its relative abundance of water. The success of these interventions in Tamil Nadu in terms of increasing rice production during the early phase of the Green Revolution was variable and dependent on the vagaries of nature. All but the wealthiest farmers at that time were hesitant to invest heavily in agricultural chemicals in the early phase of the Green Revolution. This contributed to the rise of leftist peasant resistance movements, which themselves were a response to increased wealth inequalities that had been exacerbated by the Green Revolution.[25] These early interventions transformed agricultural production in the state; since that time, farmers in Tamil Nadu have become increasingly reliant on hybrid seeds and chemical fertilizers, pesticides, and herbicides for the production of rice and other crops.[26] The rural Dalit women in my study, who represented three different generations, perceived increasing toxicity in agricultural production and in the food they have been eating in the decades since the Green Revolution.

*Possibilities for Protest*

If the lower-class and -caste women I met were so alarmed about the link between cancer and the use of chemicals in food production, did they feel there was anything they could do to change the situation? Could they demand an end to the use of chemicals? Could they demand food grown without these chemicals? In my study, the answer to these questions was a resounding "No."

I am not suggesting that subaltern women in Tamil Nadu or India more broadly do not have agency to engage in protest. On the contrary, Dalit and tribal women have been a driving force in many activist movements in India—including movements against environmental health degradation—such as the 1970s Chipko movement against deforestation by logging companies in the Himalayan regions of Uttar Pradesh and the Narmada Bachao Andolan movement during the 1980s and 1990s against the damming of the Narmada River in Gujarat. More recently, in 2018 Dalit women in Thoothukudi, Tamil Nadu, galvanized a protest against environmental violations at the Sterlite copper smelting plant (owned by London-based Vendanta Resources).[27]

Nevertheless, the women I met during my fieldwork reported a sense of powerlessness when it came to demanding changes to the chemically intensive modes of agricultural production that are the norm in Tamil Nadu (and around the world). Based on their experience, they felt their low social status made it futile for them to even try to demand such changes.

It is important to counter global stereotypes of powerless Indian women.[28] Nonetheless, I agree with feminist anthropologist Lila Abu-Lughod that we should be careful not to get carried away by the "romance of resistance." As she wrote,

> the problem has been that those of us who have sensed that there is something admirable about resistance have tended to look to it for hopeful confirmation of the failure—or partial failure—of systems of oppression. Yet it seems to me that we respect everyday resistance not just by arguing for the dignity or heroism of the resistors but by letting their practices teach us about the complex interworkings of historically changing structures of power.[29]

Abu-Lughod provides insights into the everyday resistance of Bedouin women in Egypt. She does so not to rejoice at the power they gain through these forms of resistance but rather to point to the changing forms of power against which they resist. In their conversations with me, the Tamil women in my study were enacting narrative resistance through their critiques of the dangers of agricultural chemicals. Yet they were also aware of the limits of their power to resist in more transformative ways. Sharing their sense of powerlessness and futility as articulated in their own words does not deny them of agency but rather illuminates the structures of power within which they live as identified by them.

Here are some typical responses by rural Dalit women to my queries about their capacity to demand changes to the methods of agricultural production they considered harmful to their health:

> If we thought we could do that, we would have done it already.

> If we want change, we need to go address the people responsible for agriculture. We need to go to people who own the shops where they sell the food. We need to go to the "high level" in the government. But if we go, we will not be taken seriously. There is no use in that.

> See, we should go to the government and complain. But will they take us seriously and take steps? No, they won't. There is really nothing that comes out of it. So, people will just get frustrated if they take such steps. If you come from lower, humble families [*thazhntha kudumbangal*] like ours, we don't know where to go.

It was not simply that women felt that nothing would come of complaining about these issues to "high level" people in the government or in the agricultural business; they were also fearful of repercussions for speaking out. Recall the desperation women felt as they tried to retract what they had told me about their fears that the ration rice was causing cancer when it suddenly occurred to them that Jayalalithaa might deny them their rice rations as punishment for their criticism. A cancer survivor from a Dalit community in rural Kanchipuram district expressed similar fears of governmental retribution against those who protested. At the age of sixty, she was still engaged in agricultural *kuli* wage labor and in MGNREGA work. She told me that cancer had increased significantly due to the proliferation of agricultural chemicals. When I asked her if people like her could organize to ask for reduced use of these agricultural chemicals, she said that

> to do that, we would have to talk to the landowners and businesspeople who own the farms where we work. Or we would have to go talk to those people in charge of making the chemicals. But we are just *kuli* workers. We will all say, "What can we do about that? We cannot do that." Those are all big people [*periya manushanga*] and all they think about is money. The government itself is involved. The government people and the "business" people work together. If we go and try to do anything like that, then the government will take the one hundred days'

work [MGNREGA work] away from us. So, we cannot ask. This is how it is now. It is like the Kali Yuga.

There have been highly publicized protests against the use of agricultural chemicals in India. In 2013 there was public outcry following the deaths of schoolchildren in Bihar who had been poisoned by toxic levels of agricultural pesticides in their free midday meals.[30] In 2004, Indian Members of Parliament called foul after it was revealed that Coca-Cola and PepsiCo soft drinks sold in India contained higher levels of pesticide residues than were found in drinks marketed by these companies in the US and Europe.[31] In 2018, countries that are major importers of Indian basmati rice, including Saudi Arabia and several European countries, refused to accept basmati rice that had traces of the carcinogenic fungicide tricyclazole. This led major rice-exporting states such as Punjab and Haryana to try to enforce a ban on the use of tricyclazole and a host of other hazardous chemicals often used in rice production.[32] Nevertheless, my interlocutors felt disenfranchised when it came to protesting against the prevalence of agricultural chemicals and being able to affect change.

When I relayed rampant fears about the possible connection between agricultural chemicals and cancer to people at governmental and NGO institutions involved in cancer care, prevention, and research in Tamil Nadu, I found that most were aware of these general concerns within society. But I was also told that the government and the major NGOs engaged in cancer prevention work there were not investigating this connection and that not enough data were available to draw any conclusions. Both the Director and the Resident Medical Officer at the Government Arignar Anna Memorial Cancer Hospital and Research Institute thought there might be a connection between chemical fertilizers and cancer. Yet both also said that the research institute attached to that hospital was not delving into this issue and that there were no plans for it to do so. Similarly, the chair of the Cancer Institute (WIA), the director of the research division, and some of the leading oncologists whom I interviewed at the institute all said they were aware of suspicions about the carcinogenic effects of chemicals used in food production. But they also explained that to date there had not been any thorough scientific studies to test these theories in Tamil Nadu and that this was not the focus of their research agenda.

Lack of attention to such research in Tamil Nadu should come as no surprise, given that the same is true in the US and elsewhere. S. Lochlann Jain's 2013 auto-ethnography, *Malignant: How Cancer Becomes Us*, provides a seething critique of how cancer causality has been depoliticized in the US.

She demonstrates that links between chemical exposures and cancer are chronically ignored in the US despite compelling evidence of a connection, first chronicled long ago in Rachel Carson's 1962 book *Silent Spring*.[33] Jain notes that instead of conducting targeted studies to test the potential carcinogenic effects of specific chemicals that infuse our daily lives in order to potentially prevent cancer, the focus of cancer research has been on high-tech screening and treatment, or only on certain aspects of causality, such as genetics. She argues that this research focus is no accident, given that the companies producing these potentially carcinogenic chemicals are the very same companies that also produce the techno-medical responses to cancer. As these companies' profits surge through this synergetic process, so too does their political power to direct the research agenda in the battle against cancer. Julie Livingston provides a similar critique in her 2012 ethnography about oncology care in Botswana. She writes that "industry commands resources, including access to data, and therefore can produce doubt about causation through preemptive science, whereas workers and community members are often ill-positioned to seek research that serves their interests."[34] The rural Dalit women in Tamil Nadu who would say "What can we do about that? We cannot do that," were neither apathetic nor ignorant. Rather, they were keenly aware that they were "ill-positioned" to set the research agenda and demand fundamental changes to agricultural production methods that would better serve their interests.

## CHEWING TOBACCO, *PAAN*, AND TOOTHACHES

I have shown how Dalit women understood all kinds of cancer to be caused by their condition of poverty exacerbated by chronic droughts and their exposure to biochemicals. These explanations differ fundamentally from the public health educators' individual behavior explanations of cancer causality, and the solutions to the problems identified by these women are more complex than the public health recommendations for behavior change to prevent cancer. One area where public health messages about cancer causality seemed to converge with ideas of the women in my study targeted chewing tobacco and chewing *paan* as culprits. Yet even in this instance, women's explanations often shifted the blame away from individual choice and situated the problem in the context of the socioeconomic constraints they faced.

Campaigns to get people to stop smoking or using other tobacco products have been a hallmark of public health behavior change initiatives for cancer prevention worldwide. Such campaigns were only able to succeed after a long-fought battle to expose the tobacco industry's attempts to cover up the carcinogenic effects of smoking. In India, one way to get people to stop using tobacco and *paan* has been to have cancer warning signs flash on the big screen whenever a character in a movie—usually a morally suspect character—uses these products.[35] Given the immense popularity of the cinema in India, these messages reach wide swaths of the population. While smoking tobacco, smokeless tobacco, and *paan* are widely used among lower-income men in India, women from this socioeconomic sector rarely smoke, though they may use smokeless products. This tends to be the case more so among rural rather than urban women and older rather than younger women.[36]

Women I met considered the use of tobacco and *paan* to be a "bad habit" (*ketta pazhakkam*) when talking about people other than themselves. In particular, women complained about their husbands' bad habit of smoking (along with heavy use of alcohol) and used this to point out the flawed "character" (always using the English word) of their husbands. When I spoke with Dalit and MBC women who used *paan* or chewing tobacco themselves, they represented this practice in a very different light. In such cases, they explained this was not a bad habit resulting from a weak character. Rather, they used these products out of necessity to manage extreme pain in the absence of access to dental care. These women's explanations of the causal connection between cancer and the use of chewing tobacco and *paan* demonstrates their understandings of how their marginalized life circumstances put them at risk for cancer.

We met Parimala in the cervical cancer ward of the Cancer Institute in 2016. She was a forty-five-year-old woman from a village near Dharmapuri who did *kuli* work in cotton fields and also worked through the MGNREGA scheme when such jobs were available. She said her husband was unemployed because he was an alcoholic and could not hold down a job. She was a member of an MBC caste and had never attended school. She discussed her ideas about the connection between chewing tobacco and *paan* and her cervical cancer:

> Shweta: We have heard that sometimes people think the cancer is a result of some mistake [*tappu*] they made. Do people near Dharmapuri have similar beliefs?
>
> Parimala: They say it comes from using tobacco leaves [*pogailai*] and betel-nut *paan* [*vethalapakku*]. I used tobacco leaves and *paan* because I had a terrible toothache. Even then, when I started using it, people would say "Don't use

it; it causes cancer. If the cancer germs [*puttrunoi kirumi*][37] in the tobacco and the betel-nut go in through your mouth, then they will cause that person to get cancer inside the body." They told me not to use it. But I had such a bad toothache and I felt good only when I was using it. So, I would use it continuously. But when I went to the hospital and they told me I had this [cervical cancer], I stopped it. I stopped immediately and they have given me some tablets for the tooth pain here in the hospital. I think that is why I got this [cervical cancer].

Parimala's comments highlight two common ideas that I heard about both the mode by which tobacco and *paan* lead to cancer and the reasons why women used these substances. First, we see the idea that chewing tobacco and *paan* bring "cancer germs" (*puttrunoi kirumi*) into the body and that these germs then spread throughout the body and cause cancer. As I will discuss in Chapter 3, I encountered widely held views that cancer can enter into the body by various means and that tobacco and *paan* were conduits for cancer to come into the body. Second, Parimala stated that she began and continued to use these products, despite the warnings of people in her community, in order to numb the intense pain from her toothache. Medical anthropologist Mark Nichter heard the same explanation from rural people in the south Indian state of Karnataka.[38] Research in poor communities in the US has also pointed to the use of chewing tobacco to numb tooth pain in the absence of access to dental care.[39]

These points were reinforced in another interview, with Vallamma immediately after she attended the Cancer Institute screening camp in Gumminipoondi district. Her VIA/VILI test results from the screening were negative. Like Parimala, she was in her forties and had never attended school. She worked as a domestic servant while her husband, who had been an agricultural laborer, was unemployed because he had had his thumb amputated after a snakebite, leaving him unable to perform manual labor. Vallamma reflected on the links between tobacco and *paan* and cancer:

> *Cecilia:* Can you tell me about what you think causes cancer?
>
> *Vallamma:* It forms because of using tobacco powder [*podi*], tobacco leaves [*pogailai*], *Hans* [a brand of chewing tobacco in India], betel *paan*, and *beedis* [Indian cigarettes]. It [cancer] forms in the mouth, in the neck and even in the head. Once it forms, the cancer germs [*puttrunoi kirumi*] come into the body. We don't use tobacco powder and leaves and all of these things simply to be happy. It is because of dental cavities. A lot of people start using these things because of cavities, because of all of the pain from the cavities. So

many people in my village have this problem of dental pain, especially when we get old. But even young people can have this problem. When we use these things [tobacco, *paan*, etc.], it helps to lessen the pain. How else will we be able to manage that pain? It can also prevent tooth decay from getting worse.

*Shweta:* So that is the reason people use these things?

*Vallamma:* That is the only reason people use it. Even I used to use tobacco powder. See this cavity. [She points to one of her teeth that is blackened from tooth decay.] I have one. When I came here after my marriage, I used to see people using chewing tobacco while working in the mango orchard. I wanted to do it too. When you see someone, you feel like doing it too. So, I would take a lot. My mother-in-law uses this powder. She told me to put some on the damaged tooth to stop the decay and the pain. So, I used to do that. The first two days it made me nauseous. But from the third day onward, I got used to it, and the pain stopped. Then I began using it regularly a little at a time. Then I had my two children, and during my delivery, the doctors in the hospital told me about the risk of cancer from chewing tobacco and powders. So, at that time I gave up the powder. And now too, I remain like that.

*Shweta:* You don't use it now?

*Vallamma:* No, not much. I use just a little bit when I have a bad toothache.

It is possible that women who use chewing tobacco, tobacco powders, and *paan* may be inclined to deflect moral condemnation for this practice by suggesting that they only use these things to deal with their problems of tooth decay and pain. However, it is also important to point out that lack of access to dental care is closely correlated with poverty in India, as it is in the US.[40] Even people who may be able to get basic medical care through the primary public health care system, or access cancer treatments through larger government hospitals in Tamil Nadu, complain about the dearth of services to address their dental problems. This problem is particularly acute in poorer, more rural communities, where toothless elderly men and women are a common sight.

## CONCLUSION

When Merrill Singer sought to establish a road map for the newly emerging field of critical medical anthropology in 1986, he wrote:

There is an emergent perspective within medical anthropology that is closely aligned with the contributions of researchers from several other disciplines who work in the political economy of health tradition. This perspective, referred to as "critical medical anthropology"... understands health issues in light of the larger political and economic forces that pattern human relationships, shape social behavior, and condition collective experience, including forces of institutional, national, and global scale.[41]

Since then, critical medical anthropology has grown to be one of the most robust analytical approaches within the social sciences for understanding and ethnographically documenting the relationship between health and society and for shedding light on the human condition in local and global contexts. Critical medical anthropologists contend that disease is not caused simply by biological phenomena. It is often the outcome of profound social and political inequalities that predispose certain groups to disease and death at greater rates than others and that deny people the political power to alter the social conditions that put their health at risk. Today this idea is commonly referred to as "structural violence," "structural vulnerability," or "precarity." Paul Farmer, a medical anthropologist, doctor, and global health activist, defined structural violence thus: "Their sickness is a result of structural violence: neither culture nor pure individual will is at fault; rather, historically given (and often economically driven) processes and forces conspire to constrain individual agency. Structural violence is visited upon all those whose social status denies them access to the fruits of scientific and social progress."[42]

Other medical anthropologists suggest that the concept of "structural vulnerability" more aptly captures the broader structural system of inequality produced by capitalism, within which all perceive themselves as vulnerable but the consequences of the unequal structure produce worse health outcomes as one goes down the social hierarchy.[43] The concept of structural vulnerability encompasses multiple forms of sociocultural inequality, as noted by Quesada, Hart, and Bourgois, who contend that such socially "patterned" suffering is a result of "class-based economic exploitation and cultural, gender/sexual, and racialized discrimination."[44] They used the concept of structural vulnerability to explain poor health outcomes among undocumented immigrants in the US. Other anthropologists have found it useful for describing patterned inequalities in cancer prevalence and cancer care around the globe.[45] Medical anthropologists Carolyn Sargent and Peter Benson suggest that the term "precarity" more accurately describes the cancer care experiences of the West African immigrants in France whom they study. They argue that precarity is a broader concept than structural vulnerability because it "underscores uncertainty across domains of everyday life without prioritizing structures.

It helpfully links structural forces and the consequences of these for certain populations."[46]

The lower-class Dalit and MBC women in Tamil Nadu whom I met did not draw from these theories of critical medical anthropology to make sense of what they viewed as a rising problem of cancer in their communities. For them, such theories were self-evident. They understood that for them the risk of getting all kinds of cancer was rooted in their condition of poverty and political marginalization; in the pursuit of profit by industries engaged in sand-mining, agricultural chemical production, and farming that endanger the health of humans and the natural environment; and in their lack of access to medical care for dental pain.

Lower-class rural Dalit women's discursive use of the concept of the Kali Yuga as articulated during their ethnographic encounters with me served to crystalize their critiques of an amoral political economy that has led to increased suffering from cancer in their communities. Although they felt that their marginalized class and caste social status rendered them unable to publicly protest and make demands, they were clear-eyed about their critique in their conversations with me and my research assistants when we offered to anonymously present their views in this book.

# CHAPTER 3

# Women and Work

When people spoke about links between cancer and chemicals or lack of water, employment, and money, they ascribed all kinds of cancer to these factors. When I elicited causal explanations for cervical and breast cancers specifically, lower-class and -caste women linked these cancers to gendered factors impacting their work or gendered understandings of women's bodies, or both. They attributed cervical cancer to excessive, overheating, physical work and to mounting stress from juggling paid work with unpaid childcare and domestic labor. They ascribed breast cancer to lack of breastfeeding due to women's work away from home and their stressed, worn-out, anemic bodies. In the previous chapter, we saw that some women felt that their bodies were weaker in recent times as a result of less nutritious food and more mechanized agricultural labor and that their weaker bodies made them vulnerable to cancer. In this chapter, the focus is on *excessive* labor—that is, labor so intense and stressful that it weakens women's bodies, thus putting them at risk of cancer. This discursive connection between hard labor and cancer resonates with the findings of other medical anthropologists working in China[1] and Mexico.[2] These discourses on the etiology of both cervical and breast cancer revealed rural and urban, lower-class, lower-caste Tamil women's critiques of the challenges they face in the early twenty-first century and their need to assert their moral integrity as it is called into question by a diagnosis of reproductive cancer.

In addition to thinking that overwork, heat, stress and malnutrition put them at risk for cervical and breast cancer, women worried about the movement of "cancer germs" and "cancer bugs" into, through, and among open, porous bodies. Because women's bodies were considered to be more "open" than men's bodies, women thought they were particularly vulnerable to cervical and breast cancer as contagion. Even if they did not believe their cancers were contagious, cervical and breast cancer patients worried that other people would think so and would ostracize them. Concerns about stigma associated with ideas about cancer contagion and heredity weighed heavily on cervical and breast cancer patients, who feared that their cancer could lead to the collapse of the prestige of the extended family lineage. They tried to mitigate this by regulating the flow of information about their cancer diagnoses.

## GENDERED WORK, GENDERED BODIES—CERVICAL CANCER RISK

Women frequently remarked that there is a connection between overheated bodies and cancer and that women are prone to get cervical cancer because women's bodies are particularly "hot." These comments refer to the importance of balance between hot and cold properties in the body to maintain health. The principle of the hot/cold balance is important within traditional South Asian systems of medicine such as Ayurveda, Siddha, and Unani. Even people who do not use those formal systems of medicine often seek remedies for hot/cold imbalances. Several factors can influence the hot/cold balance in a person's body, including diet, season, ecological locality, type of work, sex, age, personality, and sometimes caste.[3] Throughout much of South Asia, people monitor their activities to achieve a hot/cold balance in order to maintain their health. More commonly, if someone becomes ill, their illness may be attributed to an excess of either heat or cold in the body, and people will try to counteract the imbalance. Foods are considered to be hot or cold based on the effects they have on the body when consumed, and diet is the primary mechanism used to counteract a hot/cold imbalance. Work and sexual activity may also be adjusted to correct a hot/cold imbalance.

Women's bodies are generally thought to be hotter than men's bodies, particularly during the reproductive years from puberty to menopause.[4] Menstruation is viewed as an indicator that the heat in women's bodies is so intense that it must be naturally released each month to restore the hot/cold balance.[5] Sexual intercourse is considered to be heating, and women are thought to have a stronger sexual drive than men, rendering them hotter than men.[6] This idea is used as a patriarchal justification for the need for tight controls over women's sexuality and over women's movement in public. Furthermore, because women's bodies are hotter than men's, women are said to be at higher risk for illnesses associated with overheating. Also, overheated bodies are perceived to cause more illnesses than overly cool bodies.[7]

Lower-class Dalit and MBC women asserted that nowadays women are suffering more from ailments associated with overheating than in the past due to their intensified workloads and the physical and mental stresses associated with overwork. They noted that cervical cancer was on the rise due to increased labor and added "tension" in women's lives, both of which overheat the body. Women frequently stated that excessive labor for women led to overheated bodies, which led to white vaginal discharge (*vellaipadudal*, i.e., leukorrhea) and vaginal bleeding (*rattapokku*), which in turn led to cervical cancer.

When they first experienced symptoms of vaginal discharge or unusual vaginal bleeding, most cervical cancer patients I met thought these were normal symptoms associated with menopause. They experienced these symptoms when they were already in menopause or were perimenopausal. Others who were younger sometimes thought they were entering into menopause early when they experienced these symptoms. Their first response in these situations was to treat these symptoms using *nattu marundu* (country medicine) and herbal remedies (*mooligai/pacchai ilai*). If the symptoms persisted, women would consult a biomedical doctor. Even then, cervical cancer patients reported that biomedical doctors frequently told them they were experiencing normal aspects of menopause and sent them home. It was only when the symptoms persisted and grew more severe and women repeatedly went to the doctor to complain about the symptoms that they would finally be sent for cancer testing, at which point they would be scolded by oncologists for not having come sooner, when they first experienced their symptoms.

That is what happened to Parimala. When she first experienced heavy white discharge in her early forties, she went to a private clinic near Dharmapuri to get it checked. They told her there was a chance it might be cancer and that she would need to pay 30,000 rupees for the diagnostic tests and that if the tests came back positive, it would cost 50,000 to 60,000 rupees for them to treat her. Since she did not have that kind of money, she went to the PHC near her village instead. There the doctors told her the discharge was normal for women entering menopause and that there was nothing they could do to treat it. This was *after* Tamil Nadu implemented its cervical cancer screening program in PHCs. As the discharge grew progressively worse, Parimala kept returning to the PHC, and each time they told her the same thing. A year went by during which she went to the PHC five or six times. Finally, feeling desperate, she traveled to a larger government hospital in Dharmapuri. The physicians at that hospital suspected cancer and ordered a biopsy, which came back positive for cervical cancer. She was admitted for treatment at that hospital, but after eight days and another biopsy they said her case was too complicated and referred her to the Cancer Institute in Chennai, where she was receiving care for free when we met her. She could not afford the bus fare to travel to Chennai; her son-in-law took out a loan to travel by bus with her to get her admitted to the hospital. While she was getting admitted, the doctors scolded her for not coming sooner because there was a chance that the cancer had now spread to other parts of her body.

Public health messages about cervical cancer mention that white discharge and vaginal bleeding are both possible symptoms of cervical cancer and that women who are experiencing these symptoms should immediately see a doctor to get checked for cancer. Yet many people said they thought white discharge and vaginal bleeding *caused* cervical cancer, and sometimes they interpreted the doctors' scolding about delaying cancer testing in this way. Here is a comment by a cervical cancer patient in response to my question about what she thought was the cause of her cervical cancer:

> This disease comes because of the white discharge. They tell you that at the hospital. If you have white discharge and you do not go to the hospital for a long time, it will get very bad. They scold us if we do not go to the hospital as soon as we have the white discharge. This discharge causes this disease. If we wait too long with the discharge, this disease will come and it will be very serious.

Although women pointed to white discharge as the proximate cause of cervical cancer, they thought the underlying cause of the white discharge was overheating from excessive work. This was apparent in my conversations with lower-class women from both rural and urban communities. The following three themes emerged about the relationship between excessive work, overheating, and cervical cancer: (1) excessive work under hot sun, (2) excessive work near a hot stove, and (3) excessive work, "tension," and poor eating habits. I discuss each of these themes and consider how women's narratives addressing these connections may be understood as a critique of the plight of women today, who must endure extreme hardships to make ends meet for themselves and their children.

When I met Selvi at home in her village in Kanchipuram district, she thought she was around sixty years old, though she did not know the exact year of her birth. She had been treated for cervical cancer when she was around forty-five and it had been in remission ever since. She lived in one of the nicer houses in the MBC section of her village. It was a two-story cement house, freshly painted in bright-green hues with a blue-faced, red-tongued mask to ward off the evil eye hanging on the front wall of the house. She described her life as one of extreme toil in the hot sun, and she and her friends and family speculated that this was the reason she had excessive bleeding and white discharge that led to her cancer.

Selvi was one of four siblings—three girls and a boy. Her parents died when they were all young. Her brother was sent to school after their death, but she and her sisters could not go to school, because "who would send *us* to school?!" Instead, the sisters worked to provide income for the extended family. For most of her childhood she worked on construction sites, breaking stones and carrying stones in baskets on her head—both jobs that are typically done by female daily wage laborers in Tamil Nadu. She said she performed this work in the intense hot sun until she got married. At the age of eighteen, she was married to a man who was ten years older whose family owned some land. After her marriage, she continued a life of labor, transplanting paddy in the fields under the sun, and giving birth to and taking care of four children of her own.

Selvi felt that hard, physical labor under the beating hot sun had overheated her body, which led to vaginal sores with white discharge, which led to her cancer. When I asked her if the doctors had told her this, she replied,

> No, this is our own way of understanding it. When we discuss it among ourselves here in the village, this is how we think about it. The doctors don't say this; they don't want people to panic, thinking they too will get this cancer from hard work.

Selvi further explained that although the doctors do not directly say that cervical cancer is caused by heating, patients infer this, in part because doctors and counselors tell them to take only "cooling" foods (*kulirchiyanna unavu*) after they are discharged from the hospital.

I also heard women connect excessive work, overheating, and cervical cancer by focusing on long hours spent working over open-air hot, smoky wood stoves. Vijaya, a fifty-two-year-old woman from an MBC caste, was an inpatient on the cervical cancer ward of the Government Cancer Hospital, not far from her home in a nearby town. She explained:

I think it [cervical cancer] comes from being too close to the stove. I don't go out to work in the heat so much. But I do spend time near the stove. My daughter goes to work in the morning so I have to wake at 4:00 a.m. to prepare a meal for her. I wash my face at dawn and then stay at the stove for one or one-and-a-half hours. After that there is not much work near the stove during the day because I work doing block-printing on saris. At the end of the day I have to start all over again cooking over the hot stove. As soon as I wake up, I feel "tension" and I go stand near the stove. I have been thinking that I could have gotten this [cervical cancer] from that practice.

I have a hot body [*soodana udal*]. I have always had a hot body. So, I have always eaten cooling foods. When I say cooling, I don't mean things from a "fridge." I mean things that are cool like spinach. But in spite of that, I got this [cervical cancer]. Along with that I have hemorrhoids [*moolam*, usually referred to as "piles" in English in India] and that is a nuisance. That is also a problem for people who have a hot body. I went to the hospital to get checked out because the hemorrhoids were bleeding and then I discovered this [the cancer]. This was huge. It was an earthquake. What was it? It was an earthquake! The other thing [hemorrhoids] paled compared to this [cancer]. I thought I was just having the hemorrhoids checked, and then it turned into an earthquake. I went to check out a small tide, and then this tsunami struck.

I think these things have come from all of that work at the stove and the heat from the "tension" from waking up at 4:00 a.m. every morning. I had white discharge for twenty days before I went to the hospital. I thought that was just from being heated. I didn't think it was a problem. But when I went to the hospital I learned that the white discharge had become this thing [cervical cancer].

In a similar vein, Shantamani, a forty-four-year-old cervical cancer survivor whom I met in her home in Chennai, attributed her cancer to the strenuous task of juggling childcare with her cooking jobs and underscored the toils of long hours of work over a wood stove. She had a son and two daughters, and her mother moved in with her to help after her husband committed suicide by hanging when her youngest child was a year-and-a-half old and her oldest child was in the fourth standard. She complained that her husband was drinking a lot around the time he died. She explained her views on the connection between the struggles of her life and her cancer:

I used to work right at the stove in the kitchen all the time, making *idlis* [steamed rice and lentil cakes] and other foods for sale. I got married very young and I would work in the kitchen all the time. The stove let out a lot of smoke. After my husband died, it became very difficult to manage everything. He left me alone with three children to raise and I didn't know anything. We women have so many difficulties these days. It is like the Kali Yuga. My husband died fourteen years ago so my parents and I managed everything. My daughter was in the fourth standard but I had to take her out of school to help with work. I would work at the stove where there was a lot of heat and smoke. That is why I got this [cervical cancer]. I wouldn't eat well either. I became a "workaholic." I focused so much on working to get money to pay rent and take care of the family that I didn't eat properly. I would eat lunch in the early evening and have dinner very late in the night. Or I would miss meals all together. I would go to bed at 1:00 a.m. and wake up by 4:00 a.m. so I didn't get much sleep.

The doctor told me that I got this because I was married when I was seventeen. She said that was too young. But I have heard that smoke from the cooking stove can cause cancer. People I knew used to say that breathing excessive smoke from the fire can be overheating and that will cause white discharge. I also had excessive white discharge because of that and the discharge became this thing [cervical cancer]. I had a lot of bleeding which we get when our bodies have too much heat. I had so much "tension" so my body was always hot from that.

There are several points to make about this narrative. First, we see a parallel between Shantamani's story and that of Selvi. In both cases, girls in the family were taken out of school to begin working for the family at a young age, following a tragedy in the family. Second, Shantamani notes that smoke from the cooking stove could have caused her cancer. According to a 2016 WHO report, "approximately 17% of annual premature lung cancer deaths in adults are attributable to exposure to carcinogens from household air pollution caused by cooking with solid fuels like wood, charcoal or coal. The risk for women is higher, due to their role in food preparation."[8] Yet the WHO report attributes cooking smoke to lung cancer and not cervical cancer. Shantamani considers the smoke from the fire as well as the fire itself and the physical exhaustion from her cooking work near the fire to all be factors causing her body to become overheated, leading to white discharge and vaginal bleeding and bringing about her cervical cancer. Shantamani's doctor told her that she most likely got cervical cancer because she was married when she was "too young." As I discuss in the next chapter, public health educators in Tamil Nadu consider early marriage to be a key risk factor for cervical cancer. Yet Shantamani is dismissive of this doctor's explanation. She attributes her cancer to arduous labor performed over a hot stove that was exacerbated by the death by suicide of her husband and the subsequent burdens she faced as a single mother who became a "workaholic" to support and care for her three children. She likened this situation to the Kali Yuga.

The English word "tension" is a catch-all term for talking about mental and physical stress that has found its way into the everyday parlance of people in India, even for those who do not speak English. It is a condition that people—especially women—claim to experience with more frequency in the increasingly fast-paced, competitive world of twenty-first-century India.[9] Vijaya says she experienced tension from her long hours working over a hot stove. According to her, the strenuous work, the stove, and the tension she experienced from juggling her responsibilities all conspired to make her body overheat and put her at risk for cancer. Shantamani's narrative also highlights the extraordinary stress she experienced as she juggled the domestic work for her children with her responsibility to work and provide for them financially. She felt that this led her to become a "workaholic," which contributed to her "tension," and that the tension, along with work over the stove, caused her body to overheat, making her vulnerable to cervical cancer. Tension is viewed as both a cause and a result of overheating and poor eating habits, compromising women's health and putting them at risk for cervical cancer.

Kalaa also reported that excessive work and physical and emotional tension led her to have very poor eating habits and that stress was a significant risk factor for her cervical cancer. She framed this not in terms of overheating but rather in terms of anxieties that impeded her from eating properly. She was a destitute forty-two-year-old woman from an MBC caste community in a village near Salem who eked out a living by gathering firewood in the forest and through the MGNREGA program. She reported earning around 120 rupees per day (less than US$2) and that she had had to support herself and her two sons on her income when they were young because her husband had deserted her to live with another woman. Her younger son, who went on to receive a degree in computer science and was working for a private company when I met her, helped support her financially and assisted her with the process of getting admitted to the Cancer Institute for her treatment, which is where she was when I spoke with her. She explained her thoughts about the etiology of her cervical cancer:

> When I think about why I have cancer I think that it must be because I work a lot so I don't eat on time. My husband left ten years ago and he won't come to me. I just think of my children and work. I made everything about my children. And whatever food I could buy and cook, I would give to my sons. I did not eat on time because I was always working under the sun's heat and in the forest. And I couldn't eat because I am always worried, ever since my husband left. If I could leave my worries behind, I could eat. These are the times we live in today. Some people say it must be the Kali Yuga and I agree.

Vijaya and Kalaa both criticized their husbands for abandoning them with small children to raise and suggest that this is the plight of other women like them in the contemporary era that resembles the Kali Yuga.

Public health campaigns point to poor diet as a risk factor for cervical cancer and encourage women to eat a healthy diet. Such messages make it sound as if a healthy diet is an individual lifestyle choice, yet these cervical cancer patients attribute their poor diet to socioeconomic factors beyond their control. Furthermore, women point to some tragic event—the premature death of their parents, the death of their husband, their husband's suicide or abandonment for another woman—that forced them into a life of excessive labor. In each case, they present themselves as sacrificing their health and well-being for the sake of their children.

Susan Sontag[10] showed us how metaphors used to describe cancer in America in the late twentieth century obscured more than they illuminated and did more damage than good to people like herself who were suffering from cancer. She argued that breast cancer patients in the US were metaphorically perceived as having been struck with this disease because of their repressed emotions; that is, they had brought this condition on themselves because of their failure to feel and experience passion, whether it be funneled into sexual or capitalistic drives. But metaphors are not monolithically applied to all cancers the same way, nor are they the same across cultures. For example, anthropologists Jessica Gregg and Rebecca Martínez show that patients with cervical cancer in Brazil and Venezuela may be accused of bringing cancer upon themselves, but often this blame is laced with accusations of sexual promiscuity, not repression, because of the role that sexually transmitted HPV plays in cervical cancer causality.[11] The cervical cancer patients whom I met in South India similarly worried that others might accuse them of sexual promiscuity. They counter that moralistic narrative not by turning it on its head and claiming that it was in fact their sexual repression that caused their cancer, but rather by reclaiming their virtue as hard-working mothers who had no choice but to sacrifice their bodies through hard labor for the sake of their children.

There are parallels between the metaphor of repression and that of self-sacrifice, but in South India, sacrifice is highly valued and toil is a virtue. Anand Pandian's ethnography underscores the extent to which toil—particularly agricultural toil under the beating sun—is valued as a virtue for both men and women in Tamil Nadu.[12] This was evident in the previous chapter, when women from older generations expressed pride that the hard physical agricultural labor they performed in the past had given them stronger bodies. The discourses of cervical cancer patients' overwork, tension, undereating, and overheating to provide for their children may have consciously or unconsciously served to deflect the moral blame associated with cervical cancer and sexuality by allowing these women to represent themselves as virtuous.

Yet, although toil is a virtue in the Tamil sociocultural context, excessive toil is *not* something to which people aspire. I contend that these discourses provide a platform for women to articulate their grievances about the excessive labor they must perform as lower-income, lower-caste women making ends meet to provide financially for their families while simultaneously being the primary caregivers for their children. This is starkly evident when we consider the highly gendered forms of labor they discuss when reflecting on why they got cancer: cooking, childbirth, childcare, child labor, breaking stones, transplanting paddy, and collecting firewood. These are all unpaid or underpaid forms of labor that are disproportionately performed by women (and girls).

As we will see in the next chapter, public health educators attributed cervical cancer risk to behaviors associated with marriage, reproduction, and sexuality. In their own narratives of cancer causality, lower-class and -caste cervical cancer patients did not point to bad individual lifestyle choices they had made. Rather, they described work that had been thrust upon them as women living in difficult circumstances. They suggested that it was excessive and overly heating gendered forms of labor under conditions of poverty, often with little or no financial support from husbands, that compromised women's bodies by overheating them, thus rendering them vulnerable to cervical cancer.

## GENDERED WORK, GENDERED BODIES—BREAST CANCER RISK

Like cervical cancer patients, as breast cancer patients reflected on why they got cancer, their narratives emphasized their virtuous behavior, counteracting moralizing public health discourses that focus on improper individual behaviors. In doing so, they deflected what might otherwise be negative assumptions about their past behavior. Breastfeeding was the preeminent issue for these women and was of greatest concern to those who grappled with the existential question about why it was they who had gotten breast cancer. All said they had heard through public health announcements on television and other media sources and from doctors that women who do not breastfeed at all, who do not breastfeed for a long enough period, or who do not breastfeed properly, are at risk for breast cancer.

Women's narratives about breastfeeding and virtue differed across class and caste lines. Middle-class, upper-caste breast cancer patients were baffled as to why they got breast cancer when they had followed the proscribed cultural and public health norms for women to breastfeed for at least one year. As they reflected on this, they presented an image of themselves as ideal mothers and good women. The comments by Jayanthi were typical of these middle-class views:

> At that stage when I first learned I had cancer, it caused me to have a lot of emotional disturbances. A lot of questions came into my mind. I kept thinking to myself: "I breastfed my children and I did not have any bad habits." I knew that nothing was bad about me. You know, I was brought up to be a very good girl and a good housewife, taking care of the children and taking care of the family. And I breastfed my children for a long time. Those were the values ingrained in me by my parents to create a very, very good household atmosphere. So, I was questioning: why me? Why did I get that [breast cancer]? I could not digest that. [Interview in English]

Women from lower-class and -caste communities, on the other hand, had mixed responses. Some echoed Jayanthi's comments that they had been good about breastfeeding their infants for a long time. Most, however, thought they may have gotten breast cancer because they had not followed the guidelines for breastfeeding but said that was not because they were bad mothers and bad women but because the circumstances of their lives—notably their need to work to support their children—made it impossible for them to breastfeed properly. A Dalit woman on the inpatient ward at the Government Cancer Hospital put it succinctly:

> My husband was a drunkard. He couldn't get work because of that. So, there was no way for me to stay home with my children when they were born. I did all the housework in the morning, then went for *kuli* work all day, then came home and did all the housework in the evening. It is like this now, just like in the Kali Yuga. My husband and I were living alone [i.e., in a nuclear family] so I had to take my children to stay with my mother when I went for work. Could I give my babies mother's milk while working in the fields? I could not. I think I got this thing [breast cancer] because of that.

Oncologists and psycho-oncology counselors told me that breast cancer patients often expressed a deep sense of remorse for not having breastfed properly. They had to reassure women by telling them that lack of breastfeeding is not the only risk factor for breast cancer. When I asked a surgical oncologist who treated breast cancer patients at the Cancer Institute what her patients thought about breast cancer causality, she replied [in English]:

> Oncologist: Amongst the ladies, the perception about why they got breast cancer is that very often they say, "Oh I didn't breastfeed enough." They all say that. They have some sense of guilt. Particularly the urban women. The rural ladies probably breastfed for two years or until they had the next child perhaps. But those urban women, many of them stop at three or four months because they have to get back to work. And a lot of them say, "Oh I didn't breastfeed enough. I stopped at three months, four months. I didn't have milk. So, do you think that's the reason I got this?" That's one thing that these women say to me. They say, "Oh doctor, I didn't breastfeed for long. Oh!"
>
> Cecilia: How do you respond to a patient who has that kind of concern?
>
> Oncologist: We tell them "Lactation is a protective thing, but that may not have been the only cause for you to develop breast cancer. Even women who did breastfeed can get breast cancer so don't worry too much about that. That's not the only possibility." But they will straight away come and say, "I didn't breastfeed. My mother was giving milk for one year, two years. I did just three months and maybe that's why I got this." They feel guilty.
>
> Cecilia: Like they are not good mothers?
>
> Oncologist: Correct, correct. And that as a result, they landed up with breast cancer.

I have written about the high sociocultural value placed on breastfeeding in Tamil Nadu in my earlier work on the fraught decisions that HIV-positive mothers must make about infant feeding when HIV can be transmitted via breastmilk.[13] Breastfeeding for at least one year (and up to five years) is a cultural value associated with being a good traditional Tamil mother, and breastfeeding has been heavily promoted by governmental, transnational, and local NGO public health campaigns. In the Tamil cultural context, mother's milk is thought to be a conduit for mother's love and mother's love is considered to be the highest form of human love possible.[14] Mother's milk is also considered by some to be a medium through which the capacity for Tamil language flows, and its powers are extolled in Tamil nationalist literature.[15] Since Tamil language has been the emotional and political core of Dravidian ethnic and ethno-nationalist identity, we can further appreciate the high esteem bestowed on Tamil mothers who breastfeed.

Whereas doctors report that women express feelings of guilt about not breastfeeding properly, in my interviews with breast cancer patients they either insisted that they *had* been very good about breastfeeding and were therefore perplexed about why they got breast cancer, or they acknowledged that they had not breastfed properly but also made it clear that it was because of circumstances in their lives that were beyond their control. In most instances, the reason breast cancer patients gave for why they had not breastfed according to public health recommendations was the imperative to work in order to earn money to support the family and the difficulty of breastfeeding while at work. There was widespread consensus that this problem had become more acute for the new generation of young mothers, who were having to earn income to make ends meet for the family and who sometimes were the primary or sole breadwinners for their families. They reported that just one or two generations ago, even women from lower-income families were able to stay home with their newborn children for longer periods of time. Changed socioeconomic circumstances had made breastfeeding more difficult for mothers in the late twentieth and early twenty-first centuries.

As the oncologist above noted, this change was particularly problematic in the city because the types of jobs that urban women do preclude them from bringing their infants to work or going home to feed their children during the day. Many lower-class and -caste urban women in Chennai work as domestic servants for middle-class families, or they work in factories. Middle-class working women typically have white-collar jobs as teachers, call-center work-ers, or other office jobs. Lower- and middle-class women alike were aware that it was medically recommended to breastfeed for at least one year, and some middle-class women were able to do so. But most women in my study felt that that "these days" it was increasingly difficult for women to stay home without working for more than two or three months. Contrary to the oncologist's speculation that this was only an issue for urban women, rural Dalit women whom I met said it was increasingly difficult for them to breastfeed their babies because they were required to do more work for pay than had been the case for women one generation earlier and because they were too exhausted from taking on more responsibility for both paid work and unpaid work as they were now living in nuclear households and, in some cases, their husbands were not earning money for the family. Rural and urban women also lamented that overwork can weaken women's bodies to such an extent that they are unable to produce breastmilk. They felt that women today are facing what Arlie

Hochschild[16] first dubbed "the second shift," burning the candle at both ends and leaving women's bodies too exhausted to produce breastmilk.

Kasamma, a breast cancer inpatient at the Cancer Institute, suggested that she got breast cancer because she had too much "tension," akin to comments made by cervical cancer patients. Furthermore, she said the medication she was taking for her "tension" precluded her from breastfeeding because it would be harmful if transmitted to her baby. She also thought her tension itself may have prevented her from producing milk. The following excerpt reveals her varied causal explanations and makes clear that although she knows that lack of breastfeeding could have been a factor, she does not consider it to be her fault that she did not breastfeed.

> *Cecilia:*  Did you have any thoughts about why you got this [breast cancer]?
>
> *Kasamma:*  I think it is because of my "tension."
>
> *Shweta:*  Who told you that?
>
> *Kasamma:*  My husband. Who else? [She laughs]. He thinks I shouldn't have so much "tension." Too much "tension" from too much work might have caused this. I did not breastfeed. I took tablets for the "tension" so I could not breastfeed her because that might affect the baby. Anyway, there was no milk because of the tension. This [breast cancer] could be because I didn't breastfeed. I discovered the lump [*katti*] while I was taking a shower. I touched my breast and saw this. That is how I found out. That month I worked a lot and had too much "tension." I thought that is why I got it.

By stating that her heavy workload exacerbated her tension and made her unable to produce milk, thus putting her at risk for cancer, she framed the problem as out of her hands.

In group discussions, mixed generations of rural and urban Dalit women expressed both sorrow and derision about the decline in breastfeeding that was leading to sicker, weaker children and putting women at risk of breast cancer. Those in their forties and older were both boastful and nostalgic as they recounted that they had breastfed their children for up to five years and that this had made their children strong in body and soft-natured compared to children today. Some older women blamed younger women for not breastfeeding due to concerns about beauty and body image. The following exchange among women who were all older than forty from a poor, government-subsidized housing complex in Chennai illustrates disputes about where to place the blame for changes in breastfeeding practices:

*Woman 1:* I breastfed one child until it was four, another until it was three. My children are healthy even today. But the children of today, they don't get enough of their mother's milk, they look like scrawny rats. Even rats seem healthier in this neighborhood!

*Woman 2:* Yes, in those days we used to breastfeed for five years.

*Woman 3:* Nowadays women work and they are busy so that is not possible now.

*Woman 2:* Well they are worried about their beauty nowadays. Apparently, it fades if you breastfeed.

*Woman 4:* That is not true [she says laughing].

*Woman 3:* My daughter-in-law works very hard! She does not have the time to breastfeed. She is exhausted by the end of the day after cleaning in other people's houses all day and then taking care of her children here. It is the Kali Yuga these days. Everything is harder for women these days than it was in those days.

*Woman 2:* Younger women today are afraid of what it will do to their body and then they say, "Oh, I have too much work! Oh, there is no breast milk!" as an excuse but really they are afraid that their beauty will fade.

Lower-class and -caste women in Tamil Nadu also worried that lack of breastmilk due to anemia (*ratta sogai*) could put women at risk for breast cancer. Anemia is a deficiency of red blood cells or of hemoglobin in the blood, usually due to iron deficiency, that can result in low breastmilk production. My interlocutors told me that women are prone to anemia both because their poverty leaves them malnourished and unable to produce enough blood and because they lose a lot of blood during childbirth and menstruation. When they have less/little blood (*rattam kami*), they cannot produce breastmilk. This idea is supported by the Ayurvedic theory that food is converted into blood and blood is converted into breastmilk. Anemia can be caused by extreme blood loss during birth, but many women in India are already severely anemic even before giving birth. Anemia is a major public health crisis among women in India and is particularly acute among women in poverty who have severe nutritional deficiencies. Over 50 percent of all Indian women between fifteen and forty-nine suffer from iron-deficient anemia, contributing to India's exceptionally high rates of maternal mortality. In several states, including Tamil Nadu, the problem of anemia is getting worse despite the Ministry of Health and Family Welfare National Iron+ Initiative.[17] In light of this, it is not surprising that some people would make causal connections between blood loss, anemia, low milk production, cessation of breastfeeding, and breast cancer.

In addition to concerns that not breastfeeding properly could cause breast cancer, many young women in rural villages in Tamil Nadu asserted that if left untreated, a *paal katti* (milk lump) in the breast would harden and develop into a *puttrunoi katti* (cancer lump) in the breast later in life. They said their doctors had told them this. They described *paal kattis* as lumps that form and become sore from blocked milk ducts, referring to mastitis, a problem that might arise when a woman is breastfeeding or weaning her child. The American Cancer Society states, "Having mastitis does not raise your risk of developing breast cancer."[18] It would be helpful to investigate whether doctors in Tamil Nadu were indeed telling women that *paal kattis* could cause breast cancer and if so, why.

## CANCER GERMS, OPEN BODIES, CONTAGION, AND HEREDITY

Some young women worried about breast cancer occurring as a result of blocked milk in their breasts hardening and becoming cancer; however, there was a much graver and more pervasive concern about the *flow* of substances and the possibility that cancer itself could seep into bodies. In addition to their concerns that stress and excessive work could put them at risk of cervical and breast cancer, women felt that the open nature of their bodies rendered them prone to cancer entering into their bodies. Many thought that "cancer germs" and "cancer bugs" could enter their bodies, giving them cervical or breast cancer. Apprehensions about cancer germs and bugs were linked to fears that both types of cancer were contagious. More importantly, cervical and breast cancer patients worried that *others* believed that cancer was contagious and would, therefore, stigmatize them and their family members. The possibility that these cancers could be hereditary also weighed on the minds of cancer patients. Women thought that if others perceived their cancer as contagious and/or hereditary, they would be held responsible for the downfall of the social standing of their children and of their extended family more broadly.

Public health messages debunk the idea that cancer is contagious. They view that idea as a "cultural misunderstanding" about the biology of cancer that needs to be corrected through education. Amy Moran-Thomas found that people in Belize worried that diabetes—which was on the rise among them—must be contagious, despite public health educators' insistence that it is not. This perception prevailed in Belize because of people's lived experience with a disease that was devastating families and communities like a transmissible epidemic. Moran-Thomas suggests that instead of insisting on the binary of communicable versus noncommunicable disease, we should learn from her interlocutors' assessment and view increasingly chronic diseases such as diabetes and cancer as "para-communicable." She defines para-communicable diseases as "chronic conditions that may be materially transmitted as bodies and ecologies intimately shape each other over time, with unequal and compounding effects for historically situated groups of people."[19] As noted earlier, lower-class women in Tamil Nadu certainly believed that transformed bodies resulting from transformed economic and environmental ecologies were causing cancer to manifest itself in their communities. But they also worried that cancer itself had agency to move across body boundaries, and public health and medical practitioners sometimes inadvertently perpetuated this idea. Furthermore, cervical and breast cancer patients in my study had a clear sense of the negative social ramifications when other people in their communities perceived cancer as contagious, and they struggled to mitigate the resulting social harms.

I knew that *noi* is a common word in Tamil for any disease and is added onto other words to denote the specific disease. But I had not considered the derivation of the word *"puttrunoi"* and what this word might connote until one day when I was sitting on the floor with a group of rural Dalit women at an educational program for a RUWSEC cancer screening camp. We were listening to the organizer explain what cancer was and why cancer screening was so important. She said we all have cells in our bodies that multiply normally and that *puttrunoi* is caused by the abnormally rapid multiplication of cells, which can affect many different parts of the body. She asked the women present, "Do you know why it is called *puttrunoi?*" When we all shrugged our shoulders, she explained:

> This disease is called *puttrunoi* because it is similar to a *pambu puttru* [a snake hole]. Just as a snake's hole grows rapidly in size—is small one day and very large the next day—and it throws up dirt as it grows, in that same way, cancer also grows rapidly which is why it is called *puttrunoi.*

That night I searched for the word *"puttru"* in my Tamil–English dictionaries. In the more recently published Cre-A dictionary, the word *"puttru"* is defined simply as "anthill."[20] The older Winslow dictionary provides three definitions for *puttru*: "(1) anthill, any hillock thrown up by animals; (2) anything scurvy, scrofulous, or cancerous, considered as resembling anthills; (3) holes of snakes, ants, rats, etc."[21]

There are remarkable similarities between the meaning of the Tamil word *"puttrunoi"* and that of the English word "cancer," which is derived from the Greek word for crab (*karkinos*). In *The Emperor of All Maladies: A Biography of Cancer*, Siddhartha Mukherjee notes that the first time the word *"karkinos"* appeared in medical literature to refer to cancer was around 400 BC in the writings of Hippocrates. Hippocrates referred to cancer as *karkinos* because "the tumor, with its clutch of swollen blood vessels around it, reminded Hippocrates of a crab dug in the sand with its legs spread in a circle."[22] Others have since embellished on this association: "Others felt a crab moving under the flesh as the disease spread stealthily through the body. For yet others, the sudden stab of pain produced by the disease was like being caught in the grip of the crab's pincer."[23] It is interesting to consider similarities in meanings for the words cancer and *puttrunoi*. Both conjure up biting and pinching animals that move furtively and silently, digging holes and burrowing into the ground, leaving behind messy clumps of sand or dirt in their wake.

People in Tamil Nadu often told me that cancer slips stealthily into the body through apertures in the body and burrows into and through the body, wreaking havoc as it moves. I heard many comments from women—particularly lower-class women with low levels of formal education—about cancer traveling into the body through various orifices. The greatest anxiety was about cancer entering through the mouth. People speculated that it might also enter the body through tooth cavities, the nose, the ears, the vagina, the openings in the nipples, and even the pores of their skin. Recall the comments by Parimala and Vallamma in the previous chapter, who described how cancer germs (*puttrunoi kirumi*) enter mouths and dental cavities via chewing tobacco and *paan*.

One woman in a group discussion in a village in Kanchipuram district told me she knew a young man who had brain cancer and died from it at the age of eighteen. She said he had a lump on the top of his head and that it looked like he had termites (*karayaan*) crawling under his skin on top of his head. She believed that "cancer bugs" (*puttrunoi poochi*) had come in through his ear and then traveled through his brain to the top of his head. He had complained of an earache so she thought the cancer came in through his ear.

Some people think of cancer as germs/worms (*kirumi*) or as bugs/insects (*poochi*) that can enter directly into the body and move on their own. Others say the cancer germs or bugs are transported into the body via other substances such as tobacco or *paan*. While many worried that cancer could be caused by the potentially carcinogenic effects of food grown with agricultural chemicals, they also wondered if food itself could be a conduit for cancer entering into the body through the mouth. Kumutha, a cervical cancer patient whom we met while she was undergoing treatment at the Cancer Institute, said she got this idea from her conversation with the medical staff:

> *Cecilia:* Do you have any thoughts about what causes cervical cancer?
>
> *Kumutha:* In the hospital they told me that I must have gotten "cancer" bugs ["cancer" *poochi*] in my body because I ate stale food. The bugs [*poochi*] that were in the stale food died, and in their place, I got this lump [*katti*].
>
> *Shweta:* They told you so in the hospital?
>
> *Kumutha:* Yes. The people who had the meeting told me.
>
> *Shweta:* Are they doctors?
>
> *Kumutha:* Yes, they are. They said that bugs gather in old stale food. I shouldn't eat stale food. They asked me to eat freshly cooked warm food, not old food. I said, okay I will do that.

In addition to fears about cancer entering into the mouth, many speculated that it could enter a woman's body through her vagina via semen. People said that any cancer may be sexually transmitted, including breast cancer. But this mode of transmission was particularly associated with cervical cancer. The term for cervix in Tamil is *garbha pai vai*, which literally translates as "womb/uterus bag mouth." Cervical cancer is referred to as *garbha pai vai puttrunoi*. Given that oral cancer is the leading cause of cancer among men in India and that cervical cancer is the second leading form of cancer among women, it is perhaps not surprising that people might conclude that the open nature of these two "mouths" renders the body vulnerable to cancer. According to this logic, the fact that women have two "mouths" puts them at added risk for cancer. Recall from the previous chapter that women expressed concerns that "inhaling" agricultural chemicals through their vaginas when working in the paddy fields put them at risk for cervical cancer.

Just as women's bodies are thought to be hotter than men's bodies in Tamil Nadu, they are also considered to be more "open" than men's bodies, particularly during their reproductive years between puberty and menopause. This concept of open versus closed bodies and the gendering of that distinction is prevalent throughout much of South Asia from Sri Lanka[24] to Bengal.[25] Sarah Lamb's research in Bengal suggests that because women's bodies are deemed more "open," women are thought to be particularly vulnerable to impurity (*asuddhata*), and that this notion of impurity structures inter-caste transactions.[26] Because women's bodies are considered to be more open than men's bodies, they are also viewed as being particularly vulnerable to impurities and to diseases that enter the body through its openings. People say that cancer can enter into the mouths, noses, and ears of men and women alike, and for women, there was the added fear that it could enter through the vagina or even through the nipples, which are "open" while women are breastfeeding into the open mouths of infants. These anxieties about cancer parallel fears of HIV/AIDS as a sexually transmitted disease and as a disease that can be passed from mother to child via breastmilk.

Governmental and NGO cancer prevention and care programs in Tamil Nadu have put enormous energy into dispelling people's fears that cancer is contagious. Since the late 1980s, public health educators have tried to draw clear distinctions between HIV/AIDS as an infectious disease and cancer as a noncommunicable disease. They want to provide accurate information about what is and is not known about the etiology of cancer so that individuals can make lifestyle choices to prevent cancer. They also want to ensure that people are not dissuaded from cancer screening because of the stigma they could face if they are found to have cancer in a context where cancer is viewed as contagious and sexually transmitted. Cancer patients whom I met also sought to dispel such stigma by insisting: "This disease is not like AIDS!"

Cancer is stigmatized in India, but that stigma pales in comparison to the stigma faced by people living with HIV/AIDS. In India HIV/AIDS is widely thought to be highly contagious and people who are HIV-positive are assumed to be immoral and sexually promiscuous. This was shown emphatically in the 2010 Bollywood film *Aashayein* (*Hopes*), in which a sex worker with AIDS is stigmatized by cancer patients, who refuse to sit next to her in a hospice facility. I encountered a similar dynamic in my earlier research with women living with HIV/AIDS who were trying to keep their HIV status secret from others because of the stigma. To avoid revealing their status, when people asked why they were not breastfeeding, HIV-positive mothers who were bottle-feeding their infants to prevent the risk of HIV transmission via breastmilk would sometimes say it was because they had breast cancer and did not want to pass it on to their infants. They reported that their doctors had recommended this subterfuge even though it reproduced inaccurate ideas that cancer can be transmitted through breastfeeding.[27] This subversive strategy restigmatizes

people living with HIV/AIDS. Furthermore, it does not succeed in dispelling suspicions that people may have also gotten cancer as a result of sexual
impropriety. Women with cancer, of the breast or the cervix, said they had to
deal with the stigma of these suspicions that cancer was contagious, sexually
transmissible, and caused by sexual promiscuity. This stigma was particularly
acute for women with cervical cancer.

Those who provide educational programs about cervical cancer find it
a challenge to distinguish between HIV/AIDS as infectious and cancer as
noninfectious. Although cervical cancer itself is not communicable, in most
cases it develops as a result of the sexually transmitted HPV. Despite efforts by
public health and medical professionals to explain that sexually transmitted,
infectious HPV may lead to noncommunicable cervical cancer, several women
I met merged these things in their minds and viewed cervical cancer itself as
contagious. This was due in part to the use of terms such as germs (*kirumi*) and
bugs (*poochi*) by both laypeople and public health and medical professionals.
Karpagam, a forty-four-year-old woman who had been treated for cervical
cancer at the Cancer Institute eight years prior to our meeting in her home in
Chennai, explained how she had to counter other people's assumptions that
her cancer was like AIDS:

> *Karpagam:*  My brother's wife is from a village near Thuthukuddi and she was
> worried that this [cancer] is like AIDS. My husband was dead and I was
> sick. So, she began to think this is like AIDS. I would sometimes not know
> how to counter that. Then I told her that the doctors and other people in
> the hospital told me that it won't spread. They told us that all of us have *the
> germs that cause cancer [puttrunoi erpaduttham kirumigal]*. But some people
> have *more cancer germs [adiga puttrunoi kirumigal]* than others, and when it is
> more in number, you get cancer. I had cancer because it was very active in me,
> but at the same time, this germ is alive inside everyone. So, anyone can get it.
> My brother's wife nodded in a way that made me think she understood, but
> I was afraid of what other relatives thought. I was staying with my maternal
> uncle for a while, and they gave me a separate room. I was afraid they believed
> I was infectious. [Emphasis added].
>
> *Shweta:*  Did you worry about what they thought, or did you think it was actually
> contagious?
>
> *Karpagam:*  I thought they would think I am contagious. In times like this, even
> if people take care of you, they are afraid to be near you. My aunt would
> go by herself to the vegetable market every morning and pick out healthy
> vegetables and fruit and she would make soup for me. I was so tired during the
> treatment, but she would come to me every day, and bring so much good food

and juices, and make sure I ate something. So, I knew she cared. But I would worry that she would start to worry that I might infect people in her home.

It is significant that Karpagam begins by saying that the doctors have told her that "all of us have *the germs that cause cancer.*" As I discuss in the next chapter, public health educators in Tamil Nadu tell women that although HPV is found in the bodies of approximately 80 percent of married women, it does not harm most women due to natural immunities, though it can lead to cervical cancer when the body's natural immunity is weakened. Yet Karpagam follows up by saying that "some people have *more cancer germs* than others, and when it is more in number, you get cancer." Here she seems to conflate HPV and cancer and to understand both to be germs. Furthermore, we can see that although Karpagam herself seems convinced that her cancer is not contagious "like AIDS," she worries that others might think it is.

That women understood cancer itself to be *kirumi/poochi* was also apparent in women's explanations of how some cancer treatments work. Many reported that surgery removed *kirumi/poochi* from the body through excision and that radiation and chemotherapy killed the germs/bugs internally. Karpagam stated:

> The doctors said I would get twenty-eight external radiation treatments, two internal radiation treatments and four chemotherapy treatments. But in the end, they said I needed five more external radiation sessions and two more internal radiation sessions to kill the cancer germs [*puttrunoi kirumi*].

Similarly, Shantamani reported that the nurses who took care of her on the cancer ward spoke about cancer germs. When she was first diagnosed with cervical cancer, her doctors said she had three months to live. We met her ten years later and asked how she felt about beating those odds. She replied:

> *Shantamani:* It is all because of Jesus, that is all I can say. Secondly, I would thank the medicines, they cleared the cancer from my body. The "current" [radiation] got rid of the germs [*kirumi*]; that is what I think.
> *Cecilia:* What is the connection between cancer and germs?
> *Shantamani:* The nurses and others who care for us in the hospital say "cancer" means "*kirumi*" [germs]. They said that because it is a germ, they cannot touch what I touch because it is a contagious disease [*totrunoi*]. They said they cannot touch the clothes I wear or wash them.

I do not know how common it is for public health educators, medical professionals, and other hospital staff to actually present things these ways or if these were just the ways that the patients interpreted the information. There is certainly some misinterpretation by patients and by women attending the educational cancer screening camps, as I discuss later. Nevertheless, I heard a public health worker describe radiation treatment (colloquially known as "current") for cancer as a process that kills bugs (*poochi*). In trying to reassure a group of women that radiation treatments are nothing to be afraid of, she said: "They kill the *poochi* with the 'current.' If the cancer is in the cervix, then they put the 'current' straight into the cervix and the cancer *poochi* die because of the heat."

Women's concerns that cancer could enter through openings in the body was often linked to fears that cancer could spread through sexual transmission, through direct touch, or through indirect touch such as preparing someone's food or washing someone's clothes. Cancer was, thus, sometimes considered to be a *totrunoi* (a "touching disease," i.e., contagious). People who had cancer were stigmatized for a variety of reasons; paramount among them was this dread of contagion. I do not want to leave the impression that everyone in Tamil Nadu thinks that cancer is contagious. That is not the case. Many people—particularly more highly educated, middle-class women in my study—were convinced that cancer was not contagious. They viewed such beliefs as backward and ignorant beliefs of lower-class and -caste people.

Despite the efforts of governmental and NGO organizations to dispel beliefs about cancer contagion, many patients agonized over this. Poongodai continued to worry about the possibility of contagion even though her doctors and the health workers at RUWSEC were trying to disabuse her of this notion:

> *Poongodai:* I am scared because some people say it is a contagious disease [*totrunoi*]. In the RUWSEC "support meeting," they said it is not contagious. But...
>
> *Cecilia:* Do you worry that it is contagious even after they tell you it is not?
>
> *Poongodai:* Yes, I do.
>
> *Shweta:* But they told you...
>
> *Poongodai:* Yes, in the "meeting" they told us it is not contagious.
>
> *Cecilia:* And yet you feel scared?
>
> *Poongodai:* They told us it is not contagious and that we can be around everyone. I asked if we can feed our grandchildren and they said we can do that. They said it is not contagious. In fact, my daughter-in-law also told me that she knows it is not contagious. She said there are signs there at the "Adyar hospital" [Cancer Institute] that say it is not contagious. She says that she will wash my clothes.

*Shweta:* But you still worry?

*Poongodai:* Yes. I worry that it might spread through my clothes or the food. While I eat, my grandchildren come to take food from my plate. Then sometimes I feed the children. But I worry, thinking, "Will they get this thing [cancer]?" See, for example, I drink water and put the glass down. The child comes and drinks from it. My husband sometimes gives it to the child, and I scold him. I tell him not to share the water. I ask him to get rid of the remaining water in the glass. I don't want the children to drink it.

Frequently such stories centered on emotional pain women suffered, thinking that they might endanger their grandchildren or children and that as a precaution, they should not hold these loved ones.

Many people said that although *they* did not think cancer was contagious, they worried that *other* people would think so and then the other people in their families and communities would not want to come into contact with them. This is one of the main reasons why patients felt the need to assiduously manage the information about their cancer. Vijaya said she knew cancer was not contagious but that people in her village would think it was. She was keeping her cervical cancer secret from her own husband because he was too old and not educated enough to understand and he was not a tactful person who could keep this secret; he would tell the whole village and then no one would come near her. She had only told a few of her female relatives and her sons-in-law who came to visit her at the hospital. She told her husband she had a digestive problem and was having an operation for her stomach when in fact she was getting a hysterectomy as part of her cancer treatment. It is remarkable that Vijaya was able to keep her cancer secret from her husband given that she was being treated at the Government Cancer Hospital. Administrators and medical practitioners at that hospital and at the Cancer Institute told me that some people prefer to seek treatment from government general hospitals, which provide oncology care in addition to healthcare for other medical problems, in order to keep their cancer diagnosis secret from others. The fact that Vijaya kept her cancer secret from her husband was an anomaly in my study. In fact, this was the reverse of the more common occurrence—that is, doctors usually inform the husband and other relatives—particularly male relatives—about a woman's cancer diagnosis and prognosis while keeping the cancer patient herself ostensibly in the dark, as I discuss in Chapter 5.

Women were not always able to keep their cancer secret, and when word got out, they sometimes faced intense social ostracism due to fears of contagion.

When we met Parimala, she had been in the Cancer Institute hospital for three months and had not been able to travel home to see her family except on one occasion: to vote in the elections. The hospital staff had made special concessions to let patients return home for the elections and then get readmitted to the hospital without losing their place in the queue for their treatments. This is a testament to the strength of India's democracy, where the turnout for elections is routinely high. Yet Parimala was not warmly welcomed during her four-day stay back home, where others in the village had learned about her cancer. She explained:

> No one spoke to me when I went back to my village. People who used to speak very comfortably with me avoided me completely out of fear that it [cancer] would spread to them. Ordinarily the children nearby would come to my house and play with me, but now they were getting beaten and dragged away by their parents if they came to see me and they were warned to never come to my house. My neighbors thought it was a contagious disease so they would stand behind the walls and then ask me how I was doing from behind the walls.

Although she had been told by people in the hospital that this was not a contagious disease, when she saw how others in her community were staying away, she thought it would be best not to take risks, and she used her own plates in her home and did not touch her husband or her children.

Fears of contagion were compounded by apprehensions that cancer could run in the family. Although some breast cancers are sometimes linked to genetic markers, that is not the case with cervical cancer. Nonetheless, both breast and cervical cancer patients said their anxieties that their disease could run in the family were exacerbated when doctors treating them for cancer would always ask them whether there was a history of cancer in their family. Well-educated, middle-class breast cancer patients I met understood this through the framework of genetics and said that if a woman has breast cancer, her daughter may be at increased risk for breast cancer due to genetics. Some of the less-educated, lower-income women understood the concept of cancer heredity within the framework of contagion, or a combination of genetics and contagion. For example, some said cancer could pass from a mother to a son and then from that son to his wife (through sexual transmission) and then from that wife to the wife's own child. The concept of cancer passing from mother to child in these instances could have been understood as genetic, or as contagion akin to HIV transmission during pregnancy and birth or through breastmilk.

Doctors and laypeople use the term *"parampariyamma varum noi"* to refer to hereditary diseases. This phrase literally translates as a disease that could come through the family lineage (*paramparam*). The concept of lineage carries the connotation of ancestry in a cultural context in which one's identity is tightly wrapped up with one's ancestry and individuals are expected to respect their ancestors and their family elders in order to protect the prestige of the whole lineage. When people view cancer as a *parampariyamma varum noi* it can have serious social consequences not only for the individual patient but potentially for the social standing of the entire extended family lineage. This is another reason why cancer patients and family members who know about the diagnosis may go to great lengths to try to keep this information secret. Among the women in my study, the greatest concern about the association of cancer as a *parampariyamma varum noi* was that it could endanger the marriage prospects for other members of the family, particularly for daughters and sisters, but also for nieces and other extended members of the family. Karpagam's comment exemplifies this concern:

> I thought it [her cervical cancer] would affect my children. See, in the hospital, they ask for family history. I had no one in my family with this thing [cancer] and still they asked me. But tomorrow when it is time for my daughter to get married, won't the fact that her mother had cancer, affect her too? Won't it affect the way she is perceived? Won't they think she is at risk if it is a *parampariyamma varum noi*? So, I do not want to tell anyone that I have this thing [cancer].

Puniamma, a sixty-year-old widow and breast cancer patient from a small town near the Andhra Pradesh border, described the complex logic behind how she managed information about her disease and how marriage and kinship alliances mattered in her decisions about whom she could and could not tell. Although her own married children (a son and a daughter) knew she had cancer, she did not want her sister and her sister's family to find out. She worried this could cause troubles for her sister's daughters. She was not worried about telling her own children because they were safely married through arranged marriages. Her son was married to her own brother's daughter—a form of Dravidian cross-cousin marriage that is not uncommon in Tamil Nadu and is not considered incestuous in a patrilineal kinship context where lineage descends through the male line. Her daughter was married to a relative of her sister-in-law from her sister-in-law's mother's side of the family (also an acceptable marriage arrangement in Dravidian kinship). Because of the nature of these marriage alliances, she did not think this information about her cancer would threaten her son's or daughter's standing among their respective in-laws. She trusted these relatives to keep the information about her cancer secret because they were *sondam* (belonging to one's own family). On the other hand, her sister had daughters who were married but their husbands were not *sondam*; they were *asal* (outside of one's own family). She did not want to put her sister's daughters at risk; their in-laws might treat them poorly because of Puniamma's cancer diagnosis and fears that it could be a *parampariyamma varum noi*, which could jeopardize the marriage prospects of the children of her sisters' daughters.

Puniamma became philosophical as she explained that although she was ready to die because her children were married and well settled, she worried that her children would be stigmatized after her death if others outside of the family lineage discovered she had died from cancer. As she put it:

> If I had an unmarried daughter, it would have been a problem. Now that problem is gone. And since my children were already married, at first, I thought I was ready to die and I did not want treatment. Anyway, you have to die someday. He [god] made me, and one day he will take me. That is true for me, for you, for all of us. The creator will one day take us back, and all of us will go. If there is birth, there will be death. But you cannot die in peace if people say, "Your mother has this thing [cancer]." If there are mouths, there will be talk. The prestige [*kauravam*] of my children will become less. I cannot die in peace thinking that.

The Tamil word "*kauravam*" can be translated as prestige, honor, or respect and means all of these things combined. I translate this as "prestige" because Tamil speakers themselves typically use the English word "prestige" to denote these related concepts. Puniamma was trying to accept the possibility that the cancer could take her life. But she wanted assurance that if she were to die, she could die in peace. She was haunted by the thought that her death to cancer could endanger the social standing of her own children.

Cancer imperils more than the reputation of the patient; the prestige of the family as a whole is also at stake. Women cancer patients felt the weight of responsibility for managing the physical, social, and emotional impact of this disease as best as they could for the sake of their children and their extended families. They understood that as women, the prestige of the family as whole was tied to public perceptions of their respectability, and that public fears of contagion (particularly suspicions of contagion through sexuality), and of a disease that comes through the lineage via them as bearers of children, could be socially disastrous for their family. Instead of dismissing these women's concerns as irrational, unscientific, false beliefs about cancer etiology that need to be corrected, my research demonstrates that my interlocutors in fact have a clear grasp of the complex social realities of living with cervical and breast cancer and that they take reasonable measures to mitigate the potentially negative social impact this disease may have on themselves and their families.

## CONCLUSION

Views presented in this chapter and the previous chapter shed light on key frameworks through which lower-class and -caste women in Tamil Nadu understand cancer causality in general and the etiology of cervical and breast cancer in particular. In the previous chapter, we saw that they attribute cancer to changing economic and environmental conditions that negatively affect their health. This chapter reveals that they understand the nexus of their class, caste, and gender to render them vulnerable to cervical and breast cancer in a changing socioeconomic context. Their explanations for cancer causality contrast significantly with the discourses of cancer causality that are the mainstay of public health interventions for the prevention and early detection of breast and cervical cancer, to which I turn in the next chapter. Whereas the public health messages about cancer causality for women emphasize sexual and reproductive practices as well as diet and exercise and urge women to make healthy choices to avoid cancer, the women in my study highlighted the unhealthy social and economic context of their lives, over which they felt they had little or no control. And whereas public health campaigns aim to dispel misunderstandings about cancer and contagion, in this chapter we see that ideas about cancer contagion seem to be inadvertently conveyed by public health and medical practitioners themselves. Women's comments that they need to be vigilant to avoid the social harm that can ensue when other people raise the specter of contagion and heredity reveal the precarity of the social positions they occupy within their families and communities. These women's narratives about cancer causality and their evocation of the Kali Yuga serve as a social critique through which they assert that for lower-class Dalit and MBC women, life has become more difficult and less healthy in the present than it was in the past.

# CHAPTER 4

# Screening and Morality

One early morning in July 2015, I was sitting in an open-air waiting area of the outpatient clinic at the Government Cancer Hospital.[1] I looked up to see a series of posters on the wall. Most were straightforward public health announcements about the dangers of smoking and the importance of breast self-exams and regular cervical cancer screening. But there was one that caught my eye. The top of the poster stated the name of the hospital. At the center was a large picture of a Hindu couple during their marriage ceremony, dressed in traditional wedding garb, with bountiful jasmine garlands around their necks. Below this couple, in red font, the poster said (in Tamil): "There is no protection like moral sex [*ozhukkamana udaluravu oppatra padukappu*]." The only indication on this poster that it was even about cancer was the name of the hospital at the top and the small international cancer symbol of the crab in the bottom right corner. There was no mention of what kind of cancer this referred to. What was clear was that cancer was being associated with immoral sexuality. Since this poster hung directly across from the gynecological oncologist's office of this public government hospital that caters primarily to low-income patients, it was also clear that this message was intended for lower-class women like those sitting next to me who were waiting to see the doctor. The idealized Tamil bride depicted in the poster stood in for cancer prevention for women. As I was to discover, such moralizing messages were a mainstay of public health programs to prevent cancer and to promote screening for reproductive cancers in Tamil Nadu.

This chapter analyzes messages conveyed through visual and oral presentations at public health camps that are designed to educate primarily lower-class and -caste women about cervical and breast cancer and to encourage women to undergo screening for these cancers. I argue that in the process of conveying information about the importance of regular cancer screening, these messages also convey normative, middle-class ideas about gender, morality, and modernity and about neoliberal assumptions regarding individual responsibility. In doing so, these programs may inadvertently further the stigma of these two forms of cancer among women in South India. These educational messages also seem to serve as conduits for simultaneously promoting several other public health and social development campaigns without clearly demonstrating how proscriptions for or against various practices are specifically associated with cancer risk. While these educational campaigns recommend individual behavior changes to prevent cancer, they do not address broader sociocultural transformations needed for individual women to be able to change their practices to follow the recommended guidelines.

At the end of this chapter, after analyzing the educational portions of the reproductive cancer screening camps, I briefly describe the clinical portions of these camps. I conclude with insights gleaned from short interviews with women immediately after their participation in these camps. These interviews demonstrate that some women attending these camps misinterpret the information presented. They also reveal that attendees absorb the moralizing messages of the educational sessions to some extent. Nonetheless, the discrepancy between the moralistic messages conveyed through the public health prevention programs discussed in this chapter, and the social, political, and economic critiques articulated by lower-income, lower-caste rural and urban women discussed in the previous two chapters, is striking.

## A CRITICAL FEMINIST MEDICAL ANTHROPOLOGY LENS

Inspired by Michel Foucault's concept of biopower,[2] feminist medical anthropologists have shown that biomedical and public health science and practice can serve to reify patriarchal values and hierarchies even when such power is resisted. They have also demonstrated that gender inequalities are interwoven with other social relations of power such as class, race, ethnicity, nationality, and colonial and neocolonial relationships within biomedical and public health projects.[3]

Similarly, historians of medicine in India have documented ways that public health measures were used to serve biopolitical projects in colonial India, in part by disseminating middle-class Victorian values about gender roles, marriage, reproduction, and sexuality.[4] Scholars of post-independence India have shown how this tendency has continued through state and NGO public health programs that have been part and parcel of developmentalist and nationalist projects to craft modern Indian citizens. Programs to improve women's health have promoted idealized, homogenizing middle-class norms for culturally appropriate modern reproductive and sexual behavior.[5]

Sontag's seminal work[6] revealed how metaphors of cancer in American and European literature and public culture blamed victims of breast cancer for being overly repressed while shoring up historically specific configurations of capitalism that encourage conspicuous consumption. Mary Douglas[7] further argued that the discourse of risk in the science of epidemiology supplanted a discourse of sin while masking a persistent assumption of moral blame and individual responsibility. The work of these two authors set the stage for an emerging field of critical ethnographic research that interrogates discourses of cancer causality and risk. Anthropologists have drawn similar conclusions that moralizing discourses often blame victims for their own cancer and deflect attention from other political-economic and environmental factors contributing to cancer and cancer mortality.[8] Some anthropologists have shown that discourses of cancer causality blame cancer victims for not following appropriate gender scripts.[9] This chapter examines the discourses of cancer causality, gender, and individual responsibility that circulate within public health educational programs in Tamil Nadu.

I draw inspiration from these above-mentioned studies in critical feminist medical anthropology, critical studies of public health in colonial and post-independence India, and discourses of cancer causality and risk. I show that while these educational campaigns at cancer screening camps provide an important public health service to low-income communities, they simultaneously act as a conduit for promoting modern middle-class, upper-caste norms for Tamil women. These programs frame cervical and breast cancer as resulting from individual lifestyle "choices" related to marriage, sexuality, and reproductive behaviors and practices associated with sanitation, diet, and exercise that echo long-standing colonial and postcolonial international and national development agendas in India. They do so in ways that condemn these practices and equate them with either uneducated, backward traditionalism (attributed to the lower class) or overly westernized modernity (attributed to the upper class). Embedded in the messages is the promotion of parallel social and public health campaigns that discourage child marriage and chewing *paan* and promote family planning, latrine use, menstrual hygiene, and breastfeeding. Yet there is a lack of clear information about how these issues are directly related to cervical and breast cancer risk.

Public health planners in India conceptualize cervical cancer as overwhelmingly affecting rural, lower-class, undereducated women. Cervical cancer is constructed as a disease arising from practices of "backward," uneducated women who get married too young, have too many children, have multiple sexual partners, have too many abortions, and do not eat nutritious, fresh foods. In contrast, public health planners conceive of breast cancer as primarily affecting affluent, educated, urban, upper-class women. Breast cancer is viewed as a disease resulting from an overly modern westernized lifestyle, one that strikes women who marry too late, have too few children, do not breastfeed, eat too many fatty foods, and do not get enough exercise. In both instances, there are underlying messages about inappropriate behaviors among women from different class backgrounds that may put them at risk for cancer. The juxtaposition of these two opposing critiques brings to light how idealized middle-class normative behavior is promoted for Indian Tamil women.

## REPRODUCTIVE CANCER SCREENING CAMPS

Shweta, Shibani, and I observed six cervical and breast cancer awareness camps run by three organizations. The term "camp" is used in India to refer to temporary health services that are brought directly into communities on a given day to promote public health education and to provide medical services. Typically, these camps are held in underserved rural and urban sites and are facilitated by the government or NGOs. Although the forcible sterilization camps of Indira Gandhi's Emergency period in the 1970s were widely condemned, generally members of lower-income communities have a favorable impression of public health camps in India and view them as convenient alternatives to visits to government hospitals for preventative health screening and minor ailments. Four of the cancer camps we observed had been organized by the Cancer Institute—two in a village near the Andhra Pradesh border and two in a suburb of Chennai. One was organized by RUWSEC at their clinic. Another, run by an NGO called the Noble Foundation[10] and working in tandem with the Government Cancer Hospital, was held in a village near Kanchipuram.

RUWSEC used its community health workers to recruit women from villages where they worked to attend their camps. These RUWSEC health workers lived in the villages from which they recruited women, and they had been involved in these screening and testing programs for several years before my research. Over time, they had managed to convince women in their communities of the value of these programs, and women and men generally agreed it was beneficial for the whole family for women to undergo cancer screening. The other two organizations used a combination of recruitment methods. These included door-to-door recruitment in the vicinity of the camp, with the organizers going to individual homes in nearby villages to inform women that they were holding a free health camp and encourage them to attend. The Cancer Institute also approached groups at MGNREGA sites, where women gathered in the hope of getting work. Those who had not been chosen for MGNREGA work on a given day were encouraged to attend the free health camp instead. Several women who were recruited through door-to-door methods or at MGNREGA work sites were under the impression that they were coming to a general health camp. They only learned that these were screening camps for cancer once the meetings were under way. Two of the Cancer Institute camps were organized at the request of women who belonged to women's microfinance self-help organizations, which are prevalent among lower-income, lower-caste communities in India.

The Noble camp and the two rural Cancer Institute camps were held in government elementary school buildings; the other two Cancer Institute camps were held on the flat rooftop of the home of a self-help group member, under the shade of a huge, colorfully embroidered canopy. Women attending these camps received light snacks and drinks; the self-help group that organized the rooftop camp also provided a full vegetarian South India *thali* meal served on banana leaves.

At each camp, groups of around twenty women between the ages of twenty and seventy, but mostly middle-aged, sat on the floor listening to presentations by primarily female public health social workers and general practitioner doctors.[11] The aim of the presenters was to assuage women's fears about cancer by telling them that notwithstanding the depictions of cancer they see in movies, they should not assume they will die immediately if they have cancer. Rather, with early detection through screening, cervical and breast cancers can be stopped in their tracks. They encouraged women to undergo clinical screening immediately after the educational program, to spread this information in their communities, and to get checked regularly free of cost at the PHC in their localities, at the Cancer Institute, or at the RUWSEC clinic.

Presenters at these camps began by asking women if they knew what cancer was, if they had heard of cervical and breast cancer, and if they knew what caused these cancers and what the symptoms were. These initial inquiries were met with silence, or with a few murmurs by some women indicating that they had heard of these cancers, or had not; that they had recently heard on television that they should begin screening at age twenty-five or thirty; that they did not know what the symptoms were; and that smoking and chewing tobacco or *paan* caused cancer. Many of the younger women in these groups displayed their embarrassment and discomfort over talking about women's reproductive and sexual practices with shy smiles, giggles, and downcast eyes. In some cases, this may have reflected their genuine discomfort, but it was also a way of publicly performing gendered norms of modesty. When it was clear that most of the women in attendance were not inclined to say anything publicly, the leaders would move on to give a presentation on all of these issues, with very little interaction between the presenters and the women in attendance for the remainder of the session, apart from one exceptional anecdote described below. This does not, however, mean that women accepted wholesale the moralizing messages about cancer causality that are the focus of this chapter. As the previous chapters have revealed, lower-class and -caste Tamil women held substantially different views about the causes of what they perceived as an increase in cancer incidence in their communities.

*Listening to Sundari*

Each NGO running these camps had its own presentation style and materials, using oral, video, and paper-based media. Yet the content of the messages was strikingly consistent, and so was the degree to which they promoted highly normative ideas about appropriate behavior for women in Tamil Nadu. The social workers and doctors who facilitated the Cancer Institute awareness programs handed out two pamphlets—a green one for cervical cancer and a pink one for breast cancer—and used these to guide their presentations. These pamphlets contained cartoon pictures along with some words in Tamil. A fictional character named Sundari (literally "the beautiful one") was on the cover of each pamphlet and appeared on each page.

By Tamil standards, Sundari has a fair complexion, indicating probable upper-caste identity. She is wearing a clean and neatly tied sari that covers her ankles, indicating respectable middle-class status. The *pottu* (*bindi*) on her forehead indicates her Hindu identity. Her long hair, braided with jasmine flowers, indicates her femininity but also her controlled sexuality. Her *tali* (marriage necklace) indicates her status as a married woman. Like the picture of the bride on the poster in the Government Cancer Hospital described earlier, Sundari embodies an idealized Tamil woman. And she is here to educate. The cover of each pamphlet says: "Let's listen to what Sundari has to say!" I will let Sundari be our guide and will bring in similar points made in the RUWSEC and Noble camps to show how these cancer screening camps reproduce normative gendered values while providing an important public health service. Echoing the format of these camps, I begin with an analysis of the longer set of educational messages about cervical cancer; this is followed by a shorter discussion of messages about breast cancer; I then discuss the cervical and breast cancer messages combined.

*Cervical Cancer: Causes and Prevention*

The public health workers tell the women gathered that in India two hundred women die every day of cervical cancer but that it need not be so thanks to cervical cancer screening and early detection and treatment. They open the green cervical cancer pamphlet and begin by giving lessons about behaviors that could lead to cervical cancer and that must be avoided in order to reduce risk. There are six pictures to teach us about practices that should be shunned.

First, we see that you should avoid marrying at a young age. There is a picture of an older husband and a child bride. It is a Hindu marriage, as noted by the Vedic worship of Lord Agni (the fire deity) and by the clothing and accessories. It represents what is considered a "backward" form of marriage, one that is not acceptable to a modern, educated Hindu woman like Sundari, our teacher. Marriages between child brides and older husbands were historically considered acceptable in upper-caste Tamil Brahmin communities. Such marriages were condemned by colonial administrators, Indian nationalist social reformers (such as Muthulakshmi Reddy), and women's rights advocates. As a result, as Fuller and Narasimhan report, marriages with child brides have become "an anachronism inconsistent with a modern, middle-class way of life" in Tamil Nadu and throughout India.[12] In Tamil Nadu today, marriages with brides who are not legal adults occur primarily among lower-class and -caste communities, and recent campaigns against these practices have targeted that demographic. From the picture in the pamphlet, we know that the marriage ceremony depicted is bad by the darker complexion of the husband's skin and his exaggerated handlebar mustache, both of which are common tropes used to represent villains in Tamil cinema.

Early marriage was also the first thing mentioned as a causal factor for cervical cancer by the woman leading the RUWSEC screening educational program. She told her listeners that early marriage exposes women to sex at an earlier age and that this is a risk factor for cancer. She explained that the ideal age for marriage is twenty-one for women and twenty-five for men, although legally they can get married at eighteen and twenty-one respectively. According to her, twenty-one was the optimal age for a woman to marry because by that age her body and mind are better adapted to the requirements of a marriage. Her body will be able to withstand the stress of pregnancy and childbirth, and she will be more mature to handle the new relationships that come with marriage. She will be able to "adjust" better in the house of her husband and in-laws because when she is twenty-one, she will know she has to "live by making sacrifices" (*vittukkoduththu vaazhanum*). The *average* age of marriage for women in Tamil Nadu in 2014 was 21.2,[13] indicating that many in fact married before that age; others married later.

Ever since the colonial era, transnational and Indian women's rights groups have been waging campaigns against child marriage—particularly against child brides. These campaigns have been stepped up in the twenty-first century. In 2016, UNICEF and the UN Population Fund launched their Global Program to End Child Marriage in twelve "of the most high-prevalence or high-burden countries" in the world, including India.[14] It seems that these campaigns are reflected in cervical cancer prevention campaigns. The problem is that there was virtually no discussion about why early marriage per se could put women at risk for cervical cancer. Here we see that because talking about sex is taboo, marriage comes to stand in for Tamil women's initiation into sexual activity. The implication is that Tamil women do not engage in premarital sex. This assumption is not always borne out in reality, particularly as the trend for several decades has been toward women marrying later.[15] The fact that unmarried people were contracting HIV from sexual transmission at the turn of the twenty-first century had forced people in India to acknowledge that premarital sex was more commonly practiced than had previously been acknowledged.[16] Furthermore, the suggestion that delayed sexual activity resulting from delayed marriage will reduce the risk of cervical cancer does not help women understand the links between cervical cancer and the risk of contracting HPV through unprotected sex with multiple partners, or through unprotected sex with their spouses who have multiple partners. This point is raised as a separate issue in these awareness camps.

According to the American Cancer Society, there is an increased risk of cervical cancer if a woman's first full-term pregnancy is before the age of seventeen. There is no conclusive understanding of why this is so.[17] To the extent that marriage is a stand-in for the beginning of a woman's sexual and reproductive life and first full-term birth, these messages may help prevent cervical cancer. However, unspoken assumptions about the relationship between cervical cancer, marriage, reproduction, and sex obscure more than they clarify about the biology of cervical cancer. These messages reinforce modern social movements against child marriage, establish an appropriate age for women to marry, and reassert the cultural value of self-sacrifice for Tamil women as wives and daughters-in-law.

In the next picture of the Cancer Institute cervical cancer flyer we see that we should avoid having too many children; this was also the next thing mentioned by the woman leading the RUWSEC screening camp. The picture in the pamphlet to convey this message shows a mother with three children; the mother here looks very sad. For more than half a century the governments of India and Tamil Nadu and countless transnational NGOs and international governments have been telling Indian women that the "small family norm" is a happy family with one or two children and no more, and that they should undergo sterilization after having their second child. These family planning programs have targeted lower-class communities and represented lower-class people as incapable of controlling their sexual and reproductive practices without the help of such interventions. As if to underscore the assumption that marriage and female sterilization after two children is the norm, the woman leading the RUWSEC program explained that "women could begin cancer screening at the age of twenty-five, after they have married and had two children and have done the *kudumba kattupadu* [family planning] 'operation' [i.e., tubal ligation]."

The American Cancer Society website cited earlier says there is evidence that having three or more children is linked to increased risk of cervical cancer but that the reasons for this are unclear. In the screening camps, messages about having too many children followed well-worn paths of preexisting population control programs without providing any insights into possible causal connections between multiparous births and cervical cancer. The long-standing official policy in Tamil Nadu that set targets to incentivize public health workers and medical practitioners to encourage lower-class women to use various birth control methods ended in 1995, following widespread condemnation of the abusive nature of such targets. Yet healthcare providers and public health workers continued to pressure women to undergo sterilization, believing this to be in the best interests of women and of the nation.[18] It seems that this impulse within the public health sector to urge lower-class women to have fewer children continues to circulate through these cervical cancer prevention campaigns.

The next picture in the pamphlet says that women must avoid unhygienic practices and unclean genitals; they must use a latrine with running water and keep the latrine and their bodies clean. The woman in the picture is frowning as she steps in what might be human feces or might be menstrual blood. In this picture, the woman is in a separate bathroom with a pit toilet and a running faucet. Poor urban people living in subsidized public housing in Tamil Nadu have access to latrines but live with chronic water shortages. Most people from poor, rural communities in Tamil Nadu (and throughout India) do not have their own latrines; rural women use the fields to defecate, and running water is scarce, as discussed in Chapter 2. This is likely the situation for many of the lower-class rural women attending these camps, who come from villages similar to the ones I visited. The woman leading the RUWSEC camp also stated that poor hygiene could lead to cancer. She said that the female organs (*penn kuri*) have openings, so if women are not hygienic during urination, defecation, or menstruation, this could lead to repeated infections of the female reproductive tract, which could cause cancer. She said that this is why women should wash after urination as well as defecation, as well as use sanitary methods and maintain good hygiene during their menstrual period.

These cancer prevention campaigns seem to find common cause with state, national, and transnational organizations' campaigns for sanitation in India. India has a long history of public health sanitation programs, dating back to the colonial era, that represent lower-class and -caste Indian women as dirty and in need of social and moral reform through good hygiene.[19] As discussed earlier, Muthulakshmi Reddy was involved in charity programs to provide latrines to lower-class women in the early twentieth century. Such sanitation programs have been reinvigorated through Prime Minister Modi's Swachh Bharat Abhiyan (Clean India Mission) to encourage communities to build and use communal free-standing latrines to achieve an "Open Defecation

Free India."[20] Menstrual hygiene campaigns in India to prevent reproductive tract infections are also proliferating.[21] The fact that the documentary film titled *Period. End of Sentence*, about Indian women's lack of access to menstrual hygiene products received an Oscar in 2019 is testament to the growing international attention to this issue. Although both these public health campaigns have merits, neither can succeed through education about lifestyle changes alone, without addressing fundamental social, political, and economic problems of lack of access to latrines and water for washing.[22] Unless there is active engagement in such structural transformations, these cervical cancer educational camps may inadvertently blame poor women for getting cervical cancer because they have neglected to keep themselves clean. This may reinforce stereotypes about lower-class and -caste women as dirty and backward and reassert the superiority of middle-class, upper-caste women as represented by Sundari. It also misrepresents the cause of cervical cancer.

The fourth picture in the Cancer Institute cervical cancer pamphlet is of women at an abortion clinic. It states that recurrent induced abortions may cause cervical cancer, a point that was also raised in the RUWSEC screening camp. In this picture, the woman who has just had an abortion and the doctor who has performed it both look glum, and a woman who is in line to get an abortion is giving a suspicious sideways glance. Medically induced abortions have been legal in India since 1971 and have been supported and subsidized by international organizations, the government, and NGOs involved in India's family planning program. Although abortion is considered a *mahapataka* (great sin) in the *dharmasastras* (ancient Sanskrit Hindu texts), morally charged political debates about abortion found elsewhere have been relatively absent in India due to the acceptance that abortion has a role to play in India's population control campaigns. Despite its legality, some researchers in India have found that abortion is a taboo subject that women cannot always openly discuss with their families. Therefore, women sometimes resort to unsafe abortions to maintain secrecy over an unintended pregnancy, resulting in serious health problems.[23] Yet research in Tamil Nadu demonstrated that among the younger generation, women felt that having a large family or being pregnant at an advanced age in life was more shameful than having an abortion, and abortion rates in Tamil Nadu are among the highest in the country.[24]

In this context, it is surprising that the cervical cancer prevention messages present abortion as a risk factor for cervical cancer when epidemiological studies to determine the causal link between induced abortions and cervical cancer are inconclusive. When I inquired about this with the Cancer Institute doctor in charge of these educational programs, she said they were using a 1990 study by Remennick for their preventative messages about abortion. In that study, Remennick lays out a strong case that such a link is "biologically highly plausible"[25] and calls for more robust epidemiological research, while also conceding that "an initial attitude of researchers towards abortion usually determines the way they interpret results, since outcome risk measures are often of moderate value and/or borderline statistical significance."[26] There is some evidence that transnational Christian discourses that view abortion as a sin are on the rise in Tamil Nadu with the growing popularity of the Pentecostal church.[27] This trend may be seeping into public health messages about cervical cancer.

At the top of the next page of the pamphlet there is an abstract representation of the international symbols for men ($\male$) and women ($\female$) in two clusters of interlocking groups. The first is of one woman interlocked with two men and the second of one man interlocked with two women. Beneath this is an explanation that having more than one sexual partner is another cause of cervical cancer. This supports a powerful cultural norm in India that sexual relations should be monogamous and between a husband and wife. The woman leading the RUWSEC screening camp also warned that multiple sexual partners was a risk factor for cancer. As she put it: "For every man, one woman [*oruvannukku oruththi*] is the best way to live. That is in accordance with our Indian culture [*kalacharam*]." But she also recommended that women get their husbands to wear condoms in order for women to be safe from cancer. The organizers of these camps make a point of saying that cancer *itself* is not contagious, and they distinguish cancer from the (usually) sexually transmitted and intensely stigmatized HIV/AIDS disease. Nevertheless, such presentations run the risk of leaving women with the impression that cancer itself is a sexually transmitted disease (without full understanding of the role of the sexually transmitted HPV in cancer), that the best prevention is monogamy (without a clear explanation about protected versus unprotected sex), and that if a woman gets cervical cancer, she and/or her husband must not be upholding Indian cultural standards of morality.

The last picture about causal factors in this pamphlet is of an old, white-haired woman chewing *paan*. Instead of sitting cross-legged like a good woman, the woman in this picture is uncouth, sitting with her legs stretched out, her ankles inappropriately exposed, and spitting out the red juice that is secreted from chewing *paan*, leaving a red puddle on the ground. Since the British colonial era, the government has tried to prevent people from spitting *paan* juice. There is renewed attention to this under Modi's Swachh Bharat campaign, which has resorted to the legal system to punish those found spitting in public places. The campaign against spitting *paan* juice in public has been couched in a middle-class discourse of civility aimed against members of lower-class communities, who are more likely to use *paan* today. Chewing tobacco and *paan* both increase the risk of oral and throat cancers and are now a focus of public health messaging. However, whereas smoking tobacco has been linked to increased risk of cervical cancer, research on the link between smokeless tobacco and *paan* and cervical cancer has been inconclusive. The visual contrast in the pamphlets between the proper middle-class comportment of Sundari and the improper demeanor of the woman spitting *paan* juice may further stigmatize cervical cancer as an affliction associated with the uncivilized lifestyle choices of members of lower-class, lower-caste communities, without sufficiently addressing the social context that compels people to engage in these practices, such as the lack of access to dental care for pain relief discussed earlier.

Below this picture, the pamphlet's text explains that cervical cancer is often caused by HPV. It states that although HPV can be found in the bodies of around 80 percent of married women, it does not harm most women due to natural immunities. But it also warns that for all the reasons illustrated in the above-mentioned pictures, the body's natural immunity may be weakened, rendering women with HPV vulnerable to cervical cancer.

On the last page of this pamphlet is a statement recommending the HPV vaccine for girls between nine and thirteen to prevent cervical cancer. The Government of India considered including the HPV vaccine in the national immunization program but faced stiff resistance from some activist groups due to concerns about the vaccine's potential harmful effects and to negligence in informed consent procedures by multinational pharmaceutical companies conducting research projects for these vaccines among tribal communities.[28] Others questioned the validity of the epidemiological data used to recommend universal HPV vaccination in India.[29] The vaccine is available at private Indian clinics, but the cost, as well as assumptions about sexual promiscuity associated with HPV, have deterred most lower-income parents from getting their daughters vaccinated.

Neither the Cancer Institute nor RUWSEC emphasized the vaccine at their educational camps. Administrators for both organizations said this was due to concerns that once vaccinated, women might not undergo screening, even though the HPV vaccine does not prevent all cervical cancers. The Noble Foundation, however, showed two videos promoting both the HPV vaccine and Pap smears. The first video declares that girls between nine and nineteen should get the HPV vaccine and that all women should get regular Pap smears. It appeals to men's sense of duty to protect the women in their lives. The film states that while women give birth and take care of the family, it is men's duty to take care of women. If men want to be good husbands, brothers, and fathers, they should protect girls and women by taking them for HPV vaccines and Pap smears. This cancer prevention campaign clearly reinforces the patriarchal norm that women are expected to take care of the family while men should be the protectors of women. Although no men were recruited for this camp, the program was broadcast to the whole village through booming loudspeakers installed outside for all to hear.

*Breast Cancer: Causes and Prevention*

In the pink pamphlet the Cancer Institute presenters handed out at the camps, Sundari recommends regular breast self-exams and annual clinical breast exams. It also provides a series of "do's and don'ts" for preventing breast cancer. The first of these is the directive to breastfeed. The public health educators recommend that women breastfeed for at least one full year and suggest that those who do not breastfeed face an elevated risk for breast cancer. In doing so, they tap into another public health campaign to promote breastfeeding for infant health. This other campaign represents modern, upper-class, urban lifestyles and multinational milk-formula companies as posing a danger to infants and to what are purported to be traditional and highly valued cultural ideals of Tamil womanhood. Public health workers present these messages as if individual women have the power to simply change this lifestyle behavior, without addressing the broader socioeconomic constraints that may make it virtually impossible for some working women to breastfeed even if they wanted to—a point underscored in the previous chapter.

The public health educators at these camps also say that delaying the birth of one's first child too long can increase the risk of breast cancer. Therefore, they stress that it is important not to get married at too advanced an age in order to avoid breast cancer. A doctor at one camp stated explicitly, "People who haven't married and haven't had children are more likely to have breast cancer." Once again, we can see an emphasis placed on *marriage* in relation to cancer risk that serves to promote normative gender practices for women. As noted earlier, women are encouraged to get married and have children in their twenties.

Women in Tamil Nadu are increasingly getting married at later ages than was the case one or two generations ago. Those who can afford it are pursuing higher education and career opportunities before marriage and have a greater say in the marriage agreement because their consent is now expected.[30] This can create intergenerational conflicts, with parents castigating their daughters for defying traditional cultural norms and accusing them of being corrupted by Western values if they want to defer marriage, while daughters criticize their parents for being old-fashioned. When educational programs about cancer prevention present "late marriage" as a risk factor for breast cancer without providing more nuanced information about scientific studies linking age at first childbirth with breast cancer risk, they may end up reproducing normative cultural ideas about women and marriage held by older generations. This could contribute to stigmatizing women who get breast cancer if they are then blamed for bringing the disease upon themselves by "selfishly" choosing to delay marriage to pursue their education or career.

As mentioned earlier, the connection between marriage and cancer implied in the cervical cancer prevention messages differs from that implied in the breast cancer prevention messages due to differing demographic assumptions about the relationship between socioeconomic class and these two cancers. Cervical cancer is presented by public health planners as a problem of uneducated, rural, poor women who marry too young and have had too many children. Breast cancer is presented as a problem of overly modern, wealthier, educated, urban, upper-class women who marry too late, have too few children, and who may have difficulty conceiving children when they do marry at a later age. Yet these messages are combined in NGO awareness camps that provide both cervical and breast cancer screening simultaneously to primarily lower-class women.

The breast cancer pamphlet also tells women to avoid eating fatty foods. From the picture of a cut of red meat, it seems that we should particularly avoid eating meat and that a vegetarian diet is best. This echoes early colonial-era claims in British medical journals that cancer did not affect Indians because of their vegetarian practices—an argument that is specious not only because Indians did suffer from cancer during the colonial era but also because the vast majority of Indians are *not* vegetarian.[31] In South India, where vegetarianism is more prevalent than in many other parts of India, it is associated with higher-caste groups, particularly with Brahmins.

This pamphlet further instructs women to get regular exercise to prevent breast cancer. The exercise of choice depicted in the pamphlet is yoga. Although many people around the world have the impression that yoga has been widely practiced throughout India for centuries, and continues to be practiced, in fact it has only recently become trendy in India and is generally a middle- to upper-class and upper-caste phenomenon. Prime Minister Modi, whose main political base is middle-class, upper-caste Hindus, has promoted yoga as a national symbol of pride in Indian "traditions."

The public health messages about breast cancer causality and prevention tap into anxieties about the negative impact of westernized, modern, urban, gluttonous, sedentary lifestyles. The recommended antidote seems to be to engage in what are viewed as good "traditional" middle-class, upper-caste Indian cultural practices such as vegetarianism and yoga. Women who get breast cancer may thus be blamed for not being good traditional Indian citizens because they are not taking care of themselves through such practices.

The only time I saw a woman openly challenge the recommendations of the presenters at these educational camps was in response to the suggestion that women should be getting more exercise by practicing yoga or going to the gym. Upon hearing this, a wiry woman in her fifties abruptly stood up from the floor. Her anger was evident by the intensity with which she looked the public health worker in the eye. "How can you say that we need to exercise more when we have spent our whole lives working all day long in the fields?" she demanded. The doctor who was present replied that women should at least spend time walking fast each day so that they sweat and that it only counts as exercise if it produces sweat. In response, the woman said that all they ever do is work hard and sweat all day long and that *that* is what was killing people in her village. She walked out of the room, bristling. The public health educator continued to explain the health benefits of regular yoga practice. No one else uttered a word.

*Cancer Prevention Messages Combined*

Although different messages about prevention for cervical cancer and breast cancer reflect discreet class-specific moral assumptions, these awareness programs address both cancers together (and the clinical screenings for cervical and breast cancer take place at the same time). The result is that women attending these camps, who are typically from lower socioeconomic groups, are presented with the totality of all of these messages. Combined, the key information provided about cancer causality and prevention at each of these camps can be summarized by nine messages conveyed over thirty minutes to the groups of women gathered:

1. Get married at the right age: not too young and not too old. The ideal age for a woman to marry is twenty-one.
2. Have monogamous sex within marriage only.
3. Have children, but not "too many"—no more than two. Get sterilized after two.
4. Breastfeed for at least one year.
5. Do not have "too many" abortions, and use condoms.
6. Wash your body with clean running water in a latrine when menstruating, defecating, and urinating.
7. Eat a healthy diet (avoid fatty foods, such as meat).
8. Avoid *paan* (and tobacco).
9. Exercise regularly (especially yoga).

When we consider this list of the combined messages regarding reproductive cancer prevention for women in South India, it is clear that the educational programs at these camps facilitate multiple kinds of interventions simultaneously. The stated goal of these programs is to encourage behavior change as a public health measure to prevent cancer. Such educational interventions are an important component of any public health agenda. However, when we review the list of these combined messages, it is apparent that these educational programs also facilitate sociocultural interventions by prescribing behaviors deemed essential for an idealized middle-class Tamil woman. They thus intervene to reproduce gender norms in the society and seek to mold women according to a narrow set of feminine ideals. Furthermore, these public health programs for reproductive cancer prevention are implicitly aligned with and promote several other social and public health interventions. This is so even when the link between cervical and breast cancer causality and these other interventions is not always clearly articulated, not well understood within the scientific community, and, in some cases, not agreed upon within the scientific community.

The public health messages about cervical and breast cancer causality conveyed in these educational camps focus on getting women to engage in particular practices and to avoid other practices. These programs seem to presume that lower-class and -caste women can be empowered to live healthier lives through education about healthy lifestyle choices, while doing little to address political, economic, and sociocultural structural inequalities contributing to their ill health. Educational outreach about healthy practices has an important role to play in health promotion, yet when educational messages attribute cancer risk to individual behavior choices without challenging broader social and economic factors contributing to cancer etiology and morbidity, their public health impact will be limited.

None of this would be a surprise for feminist critical medical anthropologists, critical scholars of public health in India, or critical social scientists interested in discourses of cancer causality and risk. Such scholars contend that biomedical and public health knowledge and practice is inherently and inevitably embedded in sociocultural contexts. We cannot escape this. Nevertheless, we can use this analytical lens to shine a light on how public health interventions intervene and to consider the effects of these multiple simultaneous interventions. This is an important exercise not only for feminists and others concerned with issues of social equity. It is also crucial for public health policymakers since at times the implicit interventions may negatively impact the uptake of the explicit public health interventions. These policymakers also risk further stigmatizing cancer patients despite public health goals to destigmatize cancer.

My ethnographic interviews with reproductive cancer patients and survivors demonstrate that they all grapple with the stigma associated with assumptions that they have brought these cancers upon themselves. Women frequently told me that family members, neighbors, and medical care practitioners would make comments suggesting that they had gotten cancer because they had transgressed social norms. Even if no one said this to them directly, women worried that people thought this. Sometimes they were overwhelmed by feelings of guilt and blamed themselves, but usually they resisted such accusations. They tried to keep their cancers secret to avoid ostracism and to mitigate the impact that moral accusations might have on the prestige of their families.

I did not carefully examine the extent to which the moralizing discourses of these educational programs might inadvertently discourage women from undergoing cancer screening due to fears of social stigma that might result from a cancer diagnosis. This is an important question for future researchers. A counselor at RUWSEC who had gone door-to-door in villages when they were beginning their screening project said that Dalit women initially resisted. This was because these cancers were presented as if they were associated with sexual impropriety and with unhygienic practices. Dalit women were quick to reject the idea that *they* were morally suspect and unclean, having long faced such accusations due to caste-based discrimination. Furthermore, these Dalit women were wary of public health interventions on their reproductive bodies since they have historically been the targets of family planning interventions carried out without consent. The RUWSEC health educators engaged in those early interventions claimed they were able to overcome this resistance in the villages where they worked because they were Dalit women from these same communities.

The moralizing discourses conveyed through these educational programs might inadvertently deter women from undergoing cancer screening if they fear that a cancer diagnosis will threaten their moral and social standing in their communities. For example, stating that cervical cancer can result from sex with multiple partners without thoroughly explaining the prevalence of HPV throughout the population, as well as the relationship between HPV, cervical cancer, and factors that compromise the immune system, could deter women from getting screened for fear that they would be accused of promiscuity. Women who have not been able to follow recommendations for long-term breastfeeding may hesitate to get screened for breast cancer if they think that healthcare workers and their family and friends will accuse them of being bad mothers. My ethnographic research with cervical and breast cancer patients reveals that these forms of moralizing are not hypothetical. Women reported being accused of such things following their cancer diagnosis and suffered psychologically from the stigma of such blame. It is, therefore, not a stretch to suggest that moralizing discourses surrounding cervical and breast cancer have harmful consequences for women's health and well-being.

## CLINICAL SCREENING FOR REPRODUCTIVE CANCERS

While these educational sessions were under way, the organizers of the Cancer Institute and RUWSEC programs were busy preparing for the clinical screenings for women who would agree to undergo screening following the educational programs. Those attending the Noble camp were encouraged to go to the Government Cancer Hospital or the local PHC for clinical screening. At RUWSEC the nurses and doctors prepped the clinic room to see patients for screening by making sure they had the VIA and VILI kits at the ready and sterilizing the specula in the autoclave. They used inexpensive locally produced thin sticks—like those used to make broomsticks—to create the swabs for VIA and VILI testing.

Those preparing for the Cancer Institute clinical screening hastily created a clinic out of thin air where no clinic had existed. It was a remarkable sight to see. All the medical personnel had traveled together in a van to reach the sites for these mobile camps. It took more than two hours to reach the village near the Andhra Pradesh border, where a camp was set up in a government primary school. Medical staff unloaded all the equipment from the van and carried it into the schoolroom. They used half that room to set up the education program and the other half for the clinic. They went to work propping up dark green curtains around the clinic space for privacy. Within just thirty minutes, they had created a clinic and were ready to see patients for cervical and breast cancer screening. Primary school classes were in session in the adjacent schoolbuilding; young children were learning through call and response. The exuberant, high-pitched voices of the children filled the air of the school compound and were clearly audible from within the makeshift clinic. The children's book bags—including many with pictures of Jayalalithaa's face on them, which they had received as subsidies for lower-income families—were lined up outside the newly created clinic.

At the other, suburban site, some of the Cancer Institute medical staff set up their mobile clinic in the main living-room space of someone's home; while others led the educational sessions on the rooftop. I was impressed that the owners of this house felt comfortable using their living space for reproductive cancer screening camps. This was striking in a cultural context in which concerns about ritual purity and pollution prevail and in which reproductive parts of women's bodies are deemed impure and ritually polluting. The entranceway to the house was transformed into a makeshift registration and waiting area for women who wanted to be screened. Following the rooftop education program and a *thali* lunch, women walked down the steep outdoor staircase to get in line for the clinic.

The free clinical screenings I observed at the Cancer Institute's mobile camps and at RUWSEC's rural clinic were similar. The female physician in charge would give the clinical exam, assisted by a female nurse. Women entered the clinical space one at a time, but it was common for the next woman in queue to be standing in the threshold of the clinic room, and this was not felt to be a breach of privacy. Women coming for these screenings were not wearing underpants, and most did not have bras, so there was no need to remove undergarments before the exam. They would simply loosen their sari blouses and petticoats and climb onto the metal examining table still wearing their saris. Many women told me they appreciated that the doctors were women and that they did not have to remove their clothes for the exams. Both these things helped them feel more at ease and less shy (*kooccham*) or embarrassed (*vetkam*). The doctor first conducted a clinical breast exam and showed each woman how to do a breast self-exam, and then conducted a routine manual gynecological exam to palpitate the uterus. This was followed by the VIA and VILI tests. Most women seemed calm throughout the clinical exam. When women occasionally winced or cringed and muttered "Aiyo! Amma!" under their breath, the doctors gently reassured them and asked them to relax. Women remarked to me that they appreciated the kindness of the medical care they received during these clinical screenings, for they did not always receive such respect from doctors they encountered in government hospitals.

The RUWSEC clinic only did the VIA/VILI tests, whereas the Cancer Institute physicians also took Pap smears. The results of the VIA and VILI tests and the manual breast exams were communicated immediately. Women receiving Pap smears were advised to call after twenty days to receive the results. When the doctors felt a breast lump or had concerns about the coloration from the VIA and VILI exams, they impressed upon the patient that it was crucial to get further diagnostic testing, while simultaneously trying to reassure them by saying that these were only first-line screening methods and were not necessarily indicative of a problem.

## POST-SCREENING REFLECTIONS

My research assistants and I conducted a series of brief interviews with women immediately after they had completed the educational programs and finished the clinical screening portion of these camps. Doctors had given these women a clean bill of health, so they were relieved, as well as glad they had done the screening. For most, this was their first time undergoing cancer screening, and they said they would do it again and that they would inform others in their families and neighborhoods that it was an easy procedure and nothing to feel shy or embarrassed about because the doctors were all women. When the health workers had first encouraged them to come for the screening camp, they were hesitant because they did not have any symptoms and feared the unknown. But the health workers had been persuasive, and in the end they had come, in large part because of a sense of obligation to remain healthy so that they could take care of their children, their husbands, and their parents-in-law. In some cases, their husbands or mothers-in-law had urged them to go. This quote from one such interview echoes the sentiment of many others:

> There is a fear in the village about this because of the unknown—what will happen to me? What will happen to my body? At first, I felt a sense of trepidation [nadukkamma irundadu] about coming. But now, I feel it is better to get checked. I overcame my fear and came because I decided it would be better to find out and deal with the reality than to live in fear. Even my husband encouraged me to go find out. I did this for him and for my children.

During these post-screening interviews, women said that although they had heard about cancer in recent years through television programs and over the radio, they had not received any direct and clear information about cancer until they had participated in these awareness programs. Their main takeaway from the educational session was that cancer is caused by certain "bad habits" (ketta pazhakkam). As Kanakavalli remarked following one of the Cancer Institute screening camps:

> I was aware that this disease [cancer] exists but I had no idea what caused it. After "madam" discussed it, I learned that it was because of certain bad habits [ketta pazhakkam], like not keeping your body clean, and not eating properly, that we could get such a disease. A woman may get such a disease in the cervix after marriage when the couple has sex.

When asked whether they had any recommendations for changes to improve these screening camps, most women said that their only recommendation would be to hold these camps more frequently and to include information and screening for men as well. Some women said that since men were more likely to engage in "bad habits," these cancer-screening programs would be even more useful for them. Kanakavalli conveyed this point:

> Kanakavalli: They have done this screening camp for women for female-related cancers. Besides this, if they also did a screening for male cancer and make the men go through a similar thing, that would also be good; for a family to be well, both father and mother need to be in good health. A program for

men to explain that these bad habits [*ketta pazhakkam*] like smoking, chewing tobacco, and drinking can cause cancer would be very useful.

*Cecilia:* Do you think that the men and women should have separate camps? Or should they be combined together?

*Kanakavalli:* Either way is fine. *I* don't have any bad habits. So, I am healthy. My husband, on the other hand, has *many* bad habits and because of his habits, I could get "infected." Right? In that case, not only would his health deteriorate, mine would too. If we are both healthy, then that is beneficial to everyone all around.

*Cecilia:* If the husband has bad habits like smoking, chewing tobacco and drinking, how can the wife get cancer?

*Kanakavalli:* First the husband can get this thing [cancer] from chewing tobacco; it [cancer] comes in through the teeth when they chew those things. Then, when husband and wife have sex, this disease can come through that [sex] to the wife as well. That is what the doctors have said today. In that case, the type of "infection" the husband has will definitely spread to us. They said that when husband and wife have sex, a lump [*katti*] can form in the cervix. In that type of case, "cancer" germs [cancer *kirumi*] or "infection" can come to the cervix.

Clearly, women attending the educational programs at these screening camps sometimes misinterpret the information about cancer causality that is presented. It is also apparent that women who attend these camps are left with the impression that cancer is caused mainly by engaging in certain behaviors that are construed as bad habits. Given the moralizing messages presented at these educational camps, it is predictable that women come away from them with the impression that cancer can be caused by engaging in practices that are deemed socially inappropriate. So it is not surprising that women who are diagnosed with cancer have grave concerns that other members of society will question their morality and they will take great pains to counter such assumptions and keep their cervical and breast cancer secret.

During post-screening interviews, we asked women why they and others did not speak up during the educational programs, even when the presenters tried to draw them into a discussion. They explained that it was because they felt shy to talk about these reproductive cancers in a public group in front of others. They worried about rumors that might spread if they said anything. One woman explained:

We don't participate in the discussion because we will feel shy [*koocham*] to discuss such matters and we are afraid that we will be mocked if we answer the questions. If I speak up, the other women there will remember my answers and then they will make fun of me in front of other people while I am working in the fields. Since the questions are sensitive, it would make me uncomfortable if my answers were repeated in my workplace.

Furthermore, they said that the people giving the presentations at these programs were "big people" (*periyavanga*)—that is, educated people in positions of power—who expect respect (*mariyaatai*) and that being silent and listening is a sign of respect. Many felt that this respect was deserved and said they valued the information provided by the public health workers and doctors, given that they were so well-educated. They also questioned what good could come from questioning or challenging such "big people" when they wanted to avail themselves of these free medical services. This concern resonated with the discussions presented earlier (see Chapter 2) about rural Dalit women's fears of jeopardizing their access to life-saving public services if they publicly questioned and criticized the authorities who were providing these services.

Such silent responses at the screening camps should in no way be taken as an indication that lower-class and -caste women in Tamil Nadu had nothing to say about cancer and its causes or that they passively accepted everything presented at these public health initiatives. They had a great deal to say. As revealed earlier, women from these communities tended to situate cervical and breast cancer causality within the broad social, economic, and cultural contexts of their lives, over which they had little control.

In the next chapter, we turn from screening to the diagnosis and treatment of cervical and breast cancers. As we will see, many cervical and breast cancer patients from socioeconomically marginalized communities appreciated the subsidized medical care they received but felt that their subaltern position prevented them receiving information from medical practitioners about their cancer diagnosis, prognosis, and treatments and rendered them powerless to demand such information.

# CHAPTER 5

# Disclosure and Care

As I sat down on the floor of Chellamma's thatched house to begin an interview about her experiences with breast cancer, she switched on a small white fan in the corner of the room to provide some breeze on that hot August day.[1] In the center of the fan was a round sticker with the face of Chief Minister Jayalalithaa. I had seen the same fan in the homes of other women I met in Tamil Nadu that summer. I asked Chellamma if this was a sign of her support for Jayalalithaa and the AIADMK party, and she replied with an emphatic "No!" explaining that these fans and other small appliances are handed out to women living below the poverty line when they collect their ration cards for subsidized rice and other essential provisions. She gestured to the wall above the whirring fan to a large poster of Ambedkar. She explained that her family was Dalit and that they were supporting Viduthalai Chiruthaigal Katchi (VCK), a Tamil Dalit political party. Not all Dalits were politically aligned the same way. In fact, many of her Dalit neighbors were staunch supporters of Jayalalithaa, and some Dalit women were moving away from the VCK as a rejection of its hypermasculine political culture.[2]

Chellamma sat down, and we began to talk about her cancer. She told me how she had discovered the lump in her breast (which she said was about four centimeters in diameter and felt "like a stone"); how the cancer affected her body and her social relationships; how she struggled with the mastectomy, chemotherapy, and radiation treatments; and how the disease exacerbated her financial troubles and shook her faith in religion. We had been talking for more than an hour about all of these issues when Chellamma got up to fetch her medical record booklet given to her by the hospital staff. She gave it to me so that we could figure out when she was due for her next check-up. As I opened the booklet, Chellamma leaned toward me, peering at the pages, which she was unable to read, not only because she had only completed second standard and was barely literate but also because much of what was written in the booklet were medical terms in English, not in Tamil. She looked intently at me as I turned the pages and asked, "Does it say I have cancer?"

Her diagnosis—"Stage III Cancer: Left breast"—was written boldly in English on the first page. But I was taken aback by this question and felt suddenly trapped in an ethical quandary. She had told me that when she first went to the hospital for tests, the doctors told her son-in-law she had cancer but had not disclosed the diagnosis to her. Yet we had been discussing the course of her cancer in detail. If she still had some lingering doubt about what disease she in fact had, would it be ethically wrong for me, a foreign anthropologist, to be the one telling her the diagnosis? But wouldn't it also be wrong for me to lie and tell her I did not know when the diagnosis was plain as day and when she clearly had been working under the assumption that she had cancer based on everything she had told me? I paused for a moment, turning the pages, pretending to look for the information she was seeking to buy myself time to decide how to respond. Finally, I pointed to the diagnosis and said, "Yes, it says that you have breast cancer." "Aha!," she exclaimed, grinning. "I knew it!"

Chellamma was clearly pleased with herself as she made the proclamation. I sensed that she felt clever for having correctly pieced together the facts of a mystery about something she knew had been intentionally kept secret from her. She was not simply proud that she had solved the puzzle; she also took pleasure in knowing that her son-in-law and doctors had taken pains to not disclose her diagnosis to her; she interpreted this as an act of compassion. Yet some Dalit cancer patients I had met interpreted such acts of nondisclosure as a failure of the public health system and its healthcare practitioners to care about them. On the one hand, the politics of knowledge in the form of nondisclosure served to shore up normative gendered values of familial and medical care obligations working in tandem in the South Indian context. On the other hand, the politics of knowledge in the form of nondisclosure resulted in a critique of the abnegation of care on the part of medical practitioners and the government. It is difficult to say definitively for all of the cases I encountered what accounts for these divergent responses. It seems that when women had a sense that members of their family were aligned with medical staff in keeping information from them, they tended to view this in a more positive light than was the case if they felt that medical staff were keeping both patients and their families in the dark.

Medical practitioners, bioethicists, psychologists, and anthropologists have long worried over the vexing issue about whether it is ethical to disclose information to patients—or withhold it from them—about medical diagnoses, prognoses, and consequences of treatment options for life-threatening diseases. This has been a particularly lively debate in the context of cancer because cancer has historically been a highly stigmatized disease and because it is not a communicable disease for which disclosure would be essential to prevent further transmission. In this chapter, I discuss how lower-class and -caste patients and their families felt about having such information withheld from them.

As mentioned earlier, some of the women interviewed regarded the practice of withholding information from them about their cancer diagnosis, prognosis, and treatments in a positive light, while others were highly critical. I contend that arguments on both sides of the healthcare debate about the ethics of cancer disclosure overemphasize the importance of the *content* of the information that may be disclosed or withheld and underestimate the central ways in which the act of disclosing or withholding information is itself evaluated as a signifier of care. Context matters in this evaluation of care in terms of cultural factors and socioeconomic status.

My use of the concept of care as a key analytic here is ethnographic. It is a concept that rose to the surface when I listened to the Tamil words and phrases that cancer patients and their family members used to evaluate their experiences (both positive and negative) of nondisclosure in their cancer care. As such, I use the term "care" to refer to a concept that was highly valued by the participants in my study. Three sets of Tamil concepts arose in many of these conversations: to look after well, and to attend/watch out for, in a nurturing, protective way like a parent (*nalla paathukuvanga; kavanikaranga*); to give emotional comfort (*aarudhal*); and to include by keeping someone socially and emotionally close (*kooda; nerunga*). Together, these three ideas represent the broader concept of care used in this chapter.

This concept of care aligns closely with the idea of "an ethic of care" as defined by the philosopher, Virginia Held, who views care as both value and practice and argues that an ethic of care values emotion and "focuses on attentiveness, trust, responsiveness to need, [and] narrative nuance."[3] Held contrasts this ethics of care, which presumes "a conception of persons as relational," with the dominant European and American notion of ethics that views persons primarily as "self-sufficient independent individuals."[4] Held considers this ethics of care to be "a feminist ethic" because it "offers suggestions for the radical transformation of society. It demands not just equality for women in existing structures of society but equal considerations for the experience that reveals the values, importance, and moral significance of caring."[5]

Medical anthropologists have recently taken up care as an ethnographic object of inquiry.[6] In these studies, care is broadly conceptualized as it is enacted through state public health interventions, humanitarian projects, and clinical interventions, and also as it is experienced by patients and communities receiving healthcare. For example, in Lisa Stevenson's ethnography of care in the Canadian Arctic, she defines care as "the way someone comes to matter and the corresponding ethics of attending to the other who matters."[7] She describes a biopolitical form of "anonymous care" enacted by the colonial and postcolonial state, which is focused more on populations than on individual people and communities, for whom the state's care is often experienced as uncaring and even violent. She then juxtaposes that biopolitical care with what she characterizes as an Inuit conception of care, which is not focused singularly on saving life but is more attuned to interpersonal relationships and "allows us to listen differently to the lives and imaginations of the people who matter to us."[8] In her conclusion, she calls for an "ethics of care" that is in line with Inuit sensibilities by pushing us to care for ourselves and others as "imaginative beings"[9] rather than as members of a population.

Both Held and Stevenson are calling for a future that embraces a new ethics of care that closely resembles the ethics of care articulated by the South Indian women cancer patients and their families whom I met as they reflected on their experiences with the absence of disclosure about their cancer diagnosis, prognosis, and treatment options. For the patients who participated in my study, a concern with this ethic of care was paramount.

## THE CANCER DISCLOSURE DEBATE

Prior to the 1960s, in North America it was standard medical practice to not disclose a cancer diagnosis directly to a patient and to bend the truth about the prognosis in order to assuage patients' fears and allow them to avoid the stigma associated with what was considered an unmentionable, fatal disease.[10] The 1960s and 1970s, however, witnessed a dramatic shift in North America toward full disclosure. Kathryn Taylor attributes this change to patients' demands for the right to information in a health consumerist movement, as well as to the emergence of laws mandating informed consent for patients participating in clinical trials for experimental cancer therapies.[11] Although it may not be possible to pinpoint a causal relationship between these two impulses—the facilitation of medical research for profit on the one hand, and the protection of patients' rights on the other—they continue to be deeply entangled in the field of bioethics and in global health science.[12]

The field of professional bioethics began to flourish in the US in the 1960s. Kaja Finkler argues that with the rise of bioethics from this point on, the principle of individual patient autonomy supplanted the principle of beneficence as the "overarching bioethical principle." She explains that "the principle of autonomy has various ramifications, calling for truthfulness, full disclosure, confidentiality, privacy, and informed consent."[13] In the United States, the 1971 National Cancer Act led to new ethical and legal guidelines calling for obligatory confidential disclosure of cancer diagnosis to patients.[14] These changes were part of a broader biopolitical shift in Western societies toward emphasizing individual responsibility for one's own health and the responsibility to work on oneself as a project.[15] In 2015 the US National Institutes of Health (NIH) put out a report on measures to be taken to improve the cancer disclosure communication skills of healthcare providers. NIH recognized that there may be variation in terms of the amount of information patients may want to receive and suggested that to provide "patient-centered" or "patient-focused" care, clinicians need to consider such variations in decision-making styles of patients when choosing how to disclose information to cancer patients. Nevertheless, the assumption in this NIH report[16] remains that:

> imparting information to the patient can serve the following key functions:
>
> · Grant patients a sense of control.
> · Reduce anxiety.
> · Improve compliance.
> · Create realistic expectations.
> · Promote self-care and participation.
> · Generate feelings of safety and security.

I draw attention to the NIH here because these assumptions about the inherent benefits of imparting information to cancer patients have been asserted by bioethicists in the US and have been adopted by the global health apparatus and by health policy experts around the globe as bioethics has become part of globalization processes. As I will suggest below, based on my findings, the NIH and global health policymakers should recognize that in some sociocultural contexts the ordering of the "key factors" in the above list might be changed, since patients' desires for "feelings of safety and security" may outweigh their desire for "a sense of control."

Despite guidelines recommending that doctors disclose cancer diagnoses directly and confidentially to patients, in many parts of the world—including India—disclosure of a cancer diagnosis is often neither direct nor confidential.[17] It is not unusual for doctors to withhold information from patients altogether or to disclose information only to family members and let them decide whether to disclose the information to the patient, and how. Physicians in many parts of the world may employ what Finkler has called "a context-dependent bioethics." She shows how physicians in Mexico frequently evaluate the specific medical, social, and economic context of each patient before deciding whether, to whom, and to what extent to disclose medical information.

This ethical debate around disclosure is often framed as pitting universal individual human rights against cultural pluralism. The rights-based argument asserts that adults have a right to information about their own health so that they can use that knowledge to make the best decisions for themselves about the course of treatment they choose to undertake. Not disclosing such information to individual patients in a confidential manner is viewed as a violation of individual rights and as an act of exploitation made possible by unequal power relations between doctors and patients. From this perspective, decisions not to disclose reflect a form of paternalism that infantilizes patients[18] or a mode of avoidance that marginalizes patients.[19] Either way, it is deemed detrimental to the health and well-being of patients. The notion of paternalism is frequently invoked in this debate as an obstacle to the "free will" of the patient and, critically, implies a dynamic between masculine adult doctor and infantile, feminized patient. As Crigger, Holcomb, and Weiss write, "paternalism is said to occur if an institution or individual makes choices for people who should be able to make decisions for themselves."[20] The use of the word "should" here brings to light the hegemonic value of autonomous individuality that is central to the human rights discourse. The decision to withhold information from cancer patients for their own sake is criticized for fostering dependency rather than rational autonomy. This critique is evident in the NIH's use of a study that lays out four patterns to describe how patients' emotional styles affected treatment decision-making—passive, avoidant, panicked, and rational[21]—the implication being that is it not rational to be passive (or avoidant, or panicked).

By contrast, the cultural variation stance posits that the rights framework is premised on a Western cultural conception of the autonomous self, whereby individuals independently assert their free will. Proponents of this cultural diversity view argue that this notion of the self is not universal. Furthermore, the rights-based argument that withholding diagnostic information is a form of exploitation may be ethnocentric and inapplicable in societies that have more sociocentric conceptions of the self.[22] Medical anthropologist Arthur Kleinman points out that the profession of bioethics, which supports the individual rights framework and advocates in favor of full disclosure, is embedded in a particular Western cultural context. So it does not make sense to distinguish between rights and culture since the rights-based agenda is a product of cultural context and is not as universal as it purports to be.[23] Kleinman and Veena Das[24] have argued that it is more appropriate to consider perceptions and practices of morality that are constructed and negotiated in both global and local cultural and political-economic contexts of everyday life, than to evaluate the goodness of medical practices through a narrow, homogenizing, inflexible lens of bioethics. Those who emphasize this side of the debate point out that in many communities the question of whether and how to disclose a medical diagnosis is viewed as more of a collective decision (particularly within the family)[25] and that it may in fact be in the best interests of the patient (psychologically and physically) not to disclose cancer diagnoses, prognoses, and treatment options to them.

Good and colleagues contend that the move toward full disclosure of diagnosis and prognosis of cancer in the American context was also influenced by the discourse of hope in American oncology. They argue that hope is the "dominant symbol" in American oncology and that it is tied to "fundamental American notions about personhood, individual autonomy, and the power of thought (good and bad) to shape life course and bodily functioning."[26] This discourse on hope within American oncology is premised on the belief in the power of individual will. The rhetoric of hope was a necessary ingredient in the shift from nondisclosure to disclosure in American oncology, and it has been the premise behind campaigns promoting positive thinking as the key to survivorship in the "war on cancer." While this has helped destigmatize cancer and raise awareness of its prevalence, critics argue that it also places the burden of survival on individuals, thereby indirectly blaming those who do not survive for not fighting hard enough. Individualizing success in the "battle against cancer" through the discourse of hope can depoliticize causal factors contributing to cancer, such as the proliferation of human-made carcinogens.[27] It can also draw attention away from the social structural inequalities that impact mortality rates for cancer.

The arguments in the debate on cancer disclosure all hinge on the question of the impact that information has on the patient's mental and physical health. The rights-based approach is premised on the assumption that patients have the right to information that will enable them to make the best healthcare decisions for themselves and seek out the practitioners and treatments they deem beneficial. The counterargument is that in some cultural contexts, having access to information about one's cancer diagnosis and prognosis and the consequences of treatment may cause more harm than good due to the psychological trauma this information may cause.

I argue that the significance of the effects of the *content of the information* itself is overemphasized in this debate. My research suggests that whether cancer patients or their family members looked favorably or critically on the practice of nondisclosure, their primary concern was about the *quality of care* that nondisclosure symbolized rather than the content of the information and its usefulness for health-seeking decisions and the trauma it might produce.

Some women valued the *absence* of direct disclosure about their cancer, be it by medical practitioners or family members, as sign of care and love. These women had come to understand that they had cancer; given the circumstances of their care in specialty cancer hospitals, it would have been almost impossible for them not to figure this out. These women and their caregivers were engaged in a kind of performance of ignorance that helped the patients feel cared for and helped others feel that they were good caregivers. This could indeed be characterized as paternalistic, with all the gendered dimensions that term connotes, but it may be experienced as beneficence rather than an abuse of power.

On the other hand, other cancer patients and their family members from whom information had been withheld were highly critical of medical practitioners mainly because that act of withholding information made them feel disrespected and dehumanized. It was not because with more information they could have made different healthcare choices. These women had received cancer treatment from the Government Cancer Hospital. They had gone to that hospital because they could not afford high-end private hospitals but also because they were confident they would receive high-quality technical medical care in this hospital, which they felt they would not receive in many private hospitals. They had confidence in the medical expertise of the doctors treating them. They did not want the doctors to provide them with more information about their illness and treatment plans so that they could make alternative decisions about their treatment options. But they wanted the doctors to show they had compassion for them as fellow human beings. They perceived withholding information as a sign of a lack of such caring.

## "THEY DID NOT TELL ME FOR MY OWN GOOD"

When Chellamma exclaimed "Aha! I knew it!" as I read her diagnosis from her medical record, I asked her at what point she had been informed about her diagnosis. She said that neither the doctors nor her son-in-law ever told her directly. When I asked if she wished they had, she replied:

> No, I don't think like that.... They did not tell me for my own good, so that I would not be upset. It is good they did not tell me. The doctors think I will get scared and so they tell me it is just an ordinary [i.e., benign] lump [*katti*]. They give me courage like that.... They will only tell my son-in-law. When I ask, they will say, "It is nothing; don't worry" [*onnum illai; kavalai padaadinga*]. They would give my son-in-law the details, not me, because they don't want me to feel scared [*payam*]. They asked me to sit away and they called him into the room and told him, "This is the kind of lump this is [i.e., malignant] but she is going to get scared." So then when I ask him, he will say, "It's nothing."

Chellamma interprets this physical distance created when she is asked to sit outside of the doctor's office as a form of emotional compassion.

Even when undergoing treatment for the cancer, the doctors and son-in-law withheld information, and she interpreted this too as a form of caring. Caring here entails the idea of providing ease of mind and comfort and relieving Chellamma of any worries by looking after her needs. When she was about to undergo radiation therapy, she asked her son-in-law what the doctors had said, and he told her simply that the doctors wanted her to have the radiation; he would not give her any more information. Reflecting on this, she said, "I guess they wanted to make me feel courageous [*thairiyam*] by not sharing the details.... They must have thought it will worry [*kavalai*] me. So, they did not give me the details."

However, while Chellamma was receiving treatment at the Cancer Institute, she was surrounded by many other women who were also undergoing cancer treatments, and they all discussed their condition among themselves, comparing stories about their treatments. Furthermore, while in the hospital she had participated in the Cancer Institute's psychological support programs, during which the fact that patients had cancer was openly discussed. Later, when she was discharged from the hospital, Chellamma took her medical record booklet around to women in her village who could read and asked them if they could confirm that she had cancer, just as she later did with me. They told her the diagnosis that was written but said there was no need for her to worry since her son-in-law was taking good care of her.

Chellamma interpreted the withholding of her cancer diagnosis as a form of care in the context of her life story as a widow who had struggled to raise her three children on her own after her husband died when her son was only three months old. Without a husband or a son old enough to support her at the time of her diagnosis, she was enormously grateful to her son-in-law, who took on the role of her primary caregiver. She beamed as she showed me a new gas stove that her son-in-law had purchased after she returned from the hospital so that she no longer had to cook stooped over a hot, smoky wood-burning mud stove (*adduppu*) in a separate cooking hut. For Chellamma the gas stove and the silence about her cancer diagnosis were both symbolic of the magnitude of the care her son-in-law provided. "He looks after me well [*nalla paathukuvan*]," she said softly, as I admired the gas stove.

Chellamma, her son-in-law, and her doctors were all participating in an intricate performance in which all players knew that she knew she had cancer, yet all benefited from pretending she did not know. She knew. They knew she knew. She knew they knew she knew. Yet no one could acknowledge this because to do so would be to violate a contract of care. So she felt well cared for and loved. And the doctor and son-in-law could feel that they were being good caregivers by doing what they were expected to do to relieve her of the anxiety of knowing her cancer diagnosis. As Kristen Bright has shown in her study of caregiving and love in the context of breast cancer in the adjacent state of Kerala, "women use cultural relations of love to make sense of illness and the struggle through treatment."[28] Here the lack of direct disclosure is an expression of such "cultural relations of love." Interpreting the nondisclosure of their cancer diagnosis as an act of care is one way in which women both reflect on and publicly pronounce the goodness of their families; it enables them to maintain their social status in a cultural context in which belonging to a "good family" carries enormous prestige (*kauravam*) and provides a sense of emotional security. As discussed earlier, a cancer diagnosis could threaten the prestige of a family, and women cancer patients felt responsible for mitigating this hazard for the sake of their families and particularly their children.

One dimension of the cultural relations of love that I encountered was that for women cancer patients in my study the preference and expectation was that their grown sons be the primary intermediaries between themselves and the doctors. Chellamma underscored that her son was not old enough to take on the responsibility of caring for her before she went on to praise her son-in-law for taking on this role. This needs to be understood in a patrilocal cultural context in which sons often continue to live with their parents after marriage, whereas daughters move into the homes of their husbands. Even when sons are not living in the same home as their parents, they often live nearby and continue to bear responsibilities for their parents' household. While female relatives (especially daughters-in-law and daughters) may be responsible for most of the bodily care of women cancer patients at home or on hospital wards, a male relative was expected to take the lead in navigating the medical institutions, relations with medical staff, and insurance arrangements when seeking diagnosis and treatment. Grown sons were thought to have a better understanding of how to navigate such institutions than elderly husbands.

Maliga, who lived in a village across the dried Palar River from Chellamma's village, had turned to her son for help to go to the doctor when she had a persistent bad odor coming from her vagina. Maliga was a cervical cancer survivor who, when I met her, thought she was around seventy years old. She was married to the brother of Selvi's husband. When Maliga first began to have excessive white discharge, she thought it was a normal part of menopause. As it continued for a long time and she began to emit a bad smell, her female relatives and neighbors urged her to go to the hospital. When I asked if she had considered asking her husband to help, she laughed: "My husband has no understanding about these things!" She added that she felt too shy to tell her husband:

> I couldn't talk to my husband about the white discharge [*vellaipadudal*], because that is not something we should discuss with our husbands. And my husband wouldn't know that you should go to the hospital for things like this. I wouldn't want to go to the hospital with my husband for *this* kind of thing.

The implication was that she could not simply go to the hospital on her own or with her female relatives or neighbors. Since she did not feel comfortable asking her husband to take her for this condition, she was not going to go at all. After a couple of months, the neighbor women told her grown son (who lived in a nearby village) about the problem. Her son took her to see several doctors at private clinics and also at the Government Cancer Hospital, where she was eventually diagnosed with Stage III cervical cancer.

As with Chellamma, the doctors never told Maliga directly that she had cancer; they only informed her son. And although the diagnosis was written in her medical record—Ca Cervix III B—she had never been to school and so could not read. She praised her son for going out of his way to help her navigate appointments and tests with doctors in five different hospitals before she was finally admitted to the Government Cancer Hospital. This was time-consuming and expensive for her son; she acknowledged the hardship this posed for him since he had a wife and young baby of his own to provide for at the time. She was grateful to him for never discussing the diagnosis with her directly so as not to worry her. But she knew full well what she had, since she had been admitted into a cancer specialty hospital and stayed there for four months, surrounded by many other women with cervical cancer in the same ward.

Maliga was eager to show me the gas stove her son had purchased and hooked up for her when he brought her home from the hospital. Maliga and Chellamma both told me their doctors had recommended that they use a gas stove when they were discharged from the hospital. According to them, the doctors advised this because the gas stove would be less "heating" than a smoky wood stove. Their doctors also said it was important for them to avoid too many "heating" foods and activities during their recovery.

When Maliga returned home from the hospital, she was finally able to discuss her cancer with her husband. As she said, "It was only after I came home that I could talk to my husband about it. I couldn't talk to him about white discharge but I could talk to him about cancer." I wondered why this was so and asked for clarification. At this point in our discussion, her husband was in the house but in a separate small room. Maliga looked in the direction of the room where her husband was and then looked back at us and began whispering so quietly that Shweta had to press her ear up against Maliga's mouth to hear what she was saying. Maliga explained that the doctors had instructed her to abstain from sex for at least a year following her radiation treatments. They told her there were other women who had recently been discharged who had not followed those instructions because they had not wanted to discuss sex with their husbands and they had died as a result. So Maliga felt compelled to tell her husband that she could not have sex and to explain that it was because she had cancer. She feared that if she simply refused to have sex without telling her husband why, he would go out to seek sex from sex workers. As she put it, "I had to tell him, no? Otherwise, he would go out and find sex for money. So, I had to tell him why."

Linda Hunt and Jessica Gregg have both written about how cervical cancer patients in Mexico and Brazil fashion new identities when doctors recommend that they refrain from sexual relationships after their treatments. Mexican women in Hunt's study used this as a moment to refuse sexual demands from their husbands to which they previously felt obligated to acquiesce.[29] Gregg[30] shows that women from poor communities in northeastern Brazil who had accepted the stigmatizing assumption that their cancer was caused by their promiscuous sexual behavior used their post-treatment abstinence to claim new identities as pure and virginal once again. The women in these studies were able to take advantage of their changed identities as cancer survivors to construct narratives that served their interests. Both Hunt and Gregg point out that these women did not fundamentally challenge gender norms that presume women have a marital duty to submit to their husbands' sexual desires or that assume that because women are prone to promiscuity, they must control their sexual desire to be virtuous. The former dynamic was at play with Maliga and her husband as she explained that it was only because the doctors had insisted that abstinence was medically necessary that she felt she could legitimately refrain from sex with her husband. Yet in this case, the presumption was that if she did not explain this to her husband, he would have a natural and justified need for extramarital sex.

I was struck by how prevalent the assumption was that a *son* should take on these responsibilities to take their mothers to hospitals when I met Panjalai, whose mother died of cervical cancer. Panjalai was a thirty-six-year-old Dalit from a village on the Palar River who worked as a community health worker for RUWSEC. She was the one who had pointed out that we had driven across the dried-out Palar River the first time I visited her village. She had a big, warm, buck-toothed smile and always slightly disheveled frizzy hair. Panjalai had no brothers and complained that when their mother fell sick, her sister claimed that she was too busy with her own family to help out. Panjalai described her father as a drunkard, incapable of taking his wife to hospitals; he only did so on rare occasions and only when Panjalai was also present. The responsibility of navigating the medical care system thus fell to Panjalai. It was a monumental task for her to manage while she was raising two young children of her own. The journey through multiple hospitals in search of care for her mother was so complicated that I had trouble following the series of events as she described them. Here is a brief sketch of the long and winding story that Panjalai recounted about her search for healthcare for her mother:

After a prolonged period during which Panjalai's mother experienced symptoms of cervical cancer (heavy, foul-smelling vaginal discharge), Panjalai took her mother to a small private hospital near their village. The doctors there said they could not treat her and they referred her to Chengalpattu Government Hospital. But the family wanted to avoid government hospitals because of their reputation for mistreating people from rural Dalit families. Instead, Panjalai took her to another private hospital in Thirukazhukundram. There, Panjalai's mother was diagnosed with cervical cancer and was referred to either the Government Cancer Hospital or the Cancer Institute. In this case, the doctor had disclosed the diagnosis both to Panjalai's mother and to Panjalai. Panjalai recalled feeling devastated by the news and overwhelmed by the responsibility of having to decide what to do for her mother's treatment. Once again, the family wanted to avoid the public hospital, and they thought the Cancer Institute was too far away. Panjalai decided to take her mother to the Sri Ramachandran Medical Centre hospital in Porur, one of the largest private tertiary care hospitals in South Asia. By the time her mother was admitted there, she was bleeding excessively and was in extreme pain. Panjalai's mother would stay at that hospital for three days for her chemotherapy and then return home for a month before returning for another round of chemotherapy. Panjalai traveled with her each time and slept outside on the hospital grounds while her mother was in the hospital. Her mother received five rounds of chemotherapy over a period of five months. The fees for the treatments were exorbitant—for some visits they were as much as 13,000 rupees. Fortunately, they were able to use the state government's health insurance program to cover most of the costs.

The cost of transportation between their village and the hospital was, however, a burden on the family. The journey was also physically taxing, particularly so for her ailing mother. Panjalai and her mother would leave their village at 5:00 a.m. in order to reach the hospital in time for the chemotherapy in the morning, traveling first by auto-rickshaw to the bus stand and then for hours on a commuter bus that stopped at every small town and suburb along the way. It cost 400 rupees round-trip for Panjalai and her mother—600 if another family member came along. The trips home from the hospital were particularly challenging because her mother was overcome by nausea after her chemotherapy sessions. When her mother vomited out of the window of the bus, the other passengers complained. On one occasion when Panjalai's father was traveling with them, another man on the bus tried to force the family off the bus in the middle of nowhere when her mother was vomiting. When the man shamed Panjalai's father by asking him why he had not rented a car to take his wife home from the hospital, Panjalai's father punched the man in the face.

When the side effects from the chemotherapy became unbearable for Panjalai's mother, her doctors recommended she begin radiation treatments instead, and they referred her to yet another private hospital in Chennai. There she received twenty-eight sessions of external radiation therapy over the course of many more months. The family had to pay 42,000 rupees out of pocket for the radiation treatments, taking out a loan to cover the cost.

As her mother's health continued to deteriorate and she became weaker and weaker, Panjalai wondered if the Cancer Institute would be able to help at subsidized rates. The extended family pooled their money together to rent a car with a driver, and Panjalai and her father took the mother to the Cancer Institute, whereupon the doctors told Panjalai and her father that her mother's cancer was too advanced to cure and that they could, therefore, not admit her to the hospital. They scolded Panjalai for not bringing her mother sooner. They all returned to the village, and Panjalai's mother died at home five days later.

Beth Kangas and others have described journeys in search of healthcare as "therapeutic itineraries."[31] This term may more aptly describe the Yemenis in her study, who were traveling transnationally in search of healthcare. The term "itinerary" conjures up a journey purposely planned for work or pleasure. Yet the circuitous pursuits of healthcare for women I met were anything but planned. Instead, they represented a desperate series of trials and errors riddled with obstacles. The term "therapeutic *ordeal*" better captures this experience.

Throughout this therapeutic ordeal, Panjalai's mother felt badly about burdening her daughter in this way. Her mother was particularly remorseful about this because she felt that daughters should not be expected to take on such responsibilities for their parents once they are married into another family with new responsibilities and obligations to their husbands, their children, and their in-laws. As Panjalai recounted:

> My mother cried a lot about what I had to do for her. She was sad that I had to act like a man and take her everywhere. She felt it was because she did not have a son, and so her daughter had to do it. She would say it again and again, "my daughter is trying as frantically as a son should."

This poignant example of the heavy burden of care that is assumed to be carried by sons is an important reminder that within patriarchy, men too are expected to abide by gendered norms and to perform gendered social roles, which may be onerous.

The practice of nondisclosure of diagnosis and prognosis of cancer is not exclusive to women in India. Banerjee considers this phenomenon as it is practiced for both male and female low-income patients in Delhi. According to him, nondisclosure should be understood as a strategy for testing the relative strength or vulnerability of preexisting relationships among kin and neighbors, as well as other important personal relationships. He shows that for one male cancer patient, the act of nondisclosure within the family served to strengthen positive family bonds so as to allow husband and wife to cope with the present in the face of a looming death. For another male cancer patient who was caught in a web of highly contentious family relationships, nondisclosure was a means to help him avoid social danger in an effort to survive.[32] Banerjee shows that for male cancer patients in India, just as for the women in this study, nondisclosure can be interpreted and practiced in different ways depending on the particular context of the individual's life.

It would be interesting to explore the gendered differences more closely. In the narratives about nondisclosure for male cancer patients in Banerjee's study, there is an emphasis on protecting men from the guilt they might harbor from being unable to provide financially for their families in the face of a poor prognosis. Women in my study also expressed these feelings, particularly those who were raising children on their own after their husband died or had abandoned them. For lower-income women this form of guilt is exacerbated because in addition to the paid work they are required to perform for the sake of their families in the twenty-first-century economy, they are responsible for the lion's share of unpaid domestic labor in their extended families.

In an earlier study on cancer patients in North India, Khanna and Singh[33] also reported that patients were able to figure out they had cancer even though the doctors had only informed the family members. Similar to my study, Khanna and Singh found that although there was no direct disclosure, patients realized they had cancer when their symptoms persisted despite treatment and when they were transferred to the radiotherapy unit of the hospital. Their study, however, suggested that these patients did not appreciate the fact that they were not directly informed of this, and they interpreted this silence as a form of emotional withdrawal on the part of their relatives. Chellamma's and Maliga's narratives resonate more with accounts of American doctors in Taylor's study who were nostalgic for the earlier days in American oncology before full disclosure was mandated. One doctor whom Taylor interviewed said he would never forget one patient who was dying of breast cancer. The doctor, who had never mentioned cancer in his interactions with the patient and had told her instead that he was treating her for fibroplasia, said, "I will never forget, on her death bed…she looked up at me and said, 'Thank you for not telling me.'"[34]

## "WE PAY FOR THE TRUTH"

Although Chellamma, Maliga, and some other women I met considered the lack of disclosure of their cancer diagnosis as a sign of caring and protection, many other people I met were sharply critical of doctors in government hospitals who did not disclose the cancer diagnosis, prognosis, or effects of treatments with them. They viewed this as symptomatic of a broader problem of the impersonal, dismissive, and disrespectful attitudes of doctors in public hospitals toward patients who come from predominantly poor, lower-caste communities. Over and over again I heard people say that the quality of technical medical care that cancer patients received in the Government Cancer Hospital was top notch, as was the general condition of that hospital's facilities. But they also felt that the interpersonal interactions between medical practitioners and patients in the hospital were wanting. During group meetings, women said they received good medical services in the public hospitals in terms of the skills and technologies available but felt they were often dismissed and overlooked by aloof and overburdened public hospital doctors, who did not give them the basic respect due any human being. During a discussion with a group of Dalit women in a village, one woman described to me the extent to which one must dramatize one's ailment in order to get the attention of a doctor in a public hospital. She stood up, grabbed one hip with two hands, bent over, twisted up her face and started hobbling around, screaming out in pain: "Aiyai-yo! Aiyai-yo!" This performance was met with howls of laughter and acknowledgment from members of the group, all of whom agreed that they had to literally stoop to this kind of performance to get the personal attention of a government doctor.

Many people viewed the lack of disclosure about their cancer diagnosis by medical professionals as one dimension of this lack of personal care, and their family members concurred. One man told me about the loss of his wife to breast cancer twenty years earlier. His wife had a lump in her breast and had kept this to herself until the lump began to extrude from her skin, at which point she showed it to her husband. He said it was the size of a pea coming through the skin when he took her to see the doctor. After diagnostic tests, she was sent to the Government Cancer Hospital and admitted for surgery. But, her husband said,

> they did not explain what it was. . . . They never told us it was cancer related. They did the surgery. And then they said she needed radiation and she grew very weak with the treatment. They discharged her from the hospital after the radiation therapy and she died within a week after she came home. . . . They did not give us the opportunity to talk. They just wanted to chase us out. They don't want to share an opinion.

The daughter-in-law of the woman who died chimed in: "In *private* hospitals we pay for the truth. But in *government* hospitals, they will never tell you the truth." The implication was that only if you are a paying patient will you or your relatives be in a position of strength to ask questions and receive information about your diagnosis.

Vijaya, who was trying to keep her cancer diagnosis secret from her husband, made the same point. By the time I met her at the Government Cancer Hospital, she had received the sixth round of radiation therapy for her cervical cancer and had received chemotherapy for the first time. She too was critical of the way patients are treated in government hospitals compared to how they are treated if they are paying patients in a private hospital. When I asked if she knew why they gave her the chemotherapy, she replied,

> I don't know. If we ask, they won't give us a proper answer. I want to find out, but there is no way to find out. The "doctor *amma*" will tell me I don't need to know. I want to ask. You know, how you and I are talking now? In the same way, I want to talk to her. But I am not sure if she will talk to me like that.

The combined English and Tamil term "doctor *amma*" literally translates as "doctor mother." In Indian English, people usually use the term "lady doctor" to refer to a woman doctor; this term has British colonial roots and is polite and affect-neutral. The phrase "doctor *amma*," however, suggests a kinship-like affectionate relationship between mother and child that one hopes will be nurturing but that can also be emotionally punishing.

Shweta and I asked for further explanation about this point:

*Shweta:*  So, why do you feel you cannot ask the nurse or the doctor a question?

*Vijaya:*  See if they ask me what sort of questions I am asking, then I will have "feeling" [i.e., a negative feeling; in this case a feeling of embarrassment for asking]. Whatever we ask, they talk sternly [*eri-pori*].[35] They talk stiffly. They are "government" people [government *aalunga*] and we are just individual people [*thaniarunga*]; that is why we have such fear. It is nothing else.

*Shweta:*  Are they like this everywhere? What about in private hospitals?

*Vijaya:*  *There* you can be bold [*thairiyam*]. It's all money there so you can be bold.

*Shweta:*  You mean when we pay, we can be bold?

*Vijaya:*  Exactly! There we can be bold. We can say, "'Sir,' do I have this?" You can be bold there, but here you cannot be bold. That is the problem.

The politics and political economy of knowledge are on full display here and demonstrate how deferential low-income, lower-caste patients sometimes feel they must be when receiving free medical care. This anxiety has become more pronounced with the neoliberal turn in the Indian economy in which there has been a shift from a government policy of "healthcare for all" toward healthcare insurance coverage for the poor and in which there has been a retrenchment in public health spending and a proliferation of private hospitals, including those catering to foreign medical tourists. The lower-income women whom I met during this research felt as though they could no longer take government-provided programs for granted as they had in the past. They worried that if they were to make too many demands for information and for respectful treatment in government hospitals, they might risk jeopardizing their access to these essential goods and services. This echoes a perception presented in earlier chapters: lower-class and -caste women may calculate that it is best not to complain or question the authority of "big people" (*periyavanga*) publicly for fear of losing their rice ration, their right to MGNREGA work, or their access to free cancer screenings.

## GOOD MEDICAL TREATMENT, DISRESPECTFUL CARE

Everyone I met who received cancer treatment through the Government Cancer Hospital felt confident that they were getting high-quality medical treatment from qualified medical practitioners. Moreover, the Tamil Nadu government insurance scheme—the Chief Minister's Comprehensive Health Insurance Scheme, known in Tamil as the Mudalamaichar Kapitu Thittam—provided them with access to this high-level care at no cost. People referred to this insurance program as the Amma Thittam. The word "*thittam*" here refers to any kind of government program, usually translated as a "scheme." As discussed earlier, "*amma*" means mother and was a term of affection and respect widely used to refer to Jayalalithaa and to promote her administration's welfare programs. Large posters featuring photographs of Jayalalithaa's round face with the Tamil word அம்மா (*Amma*) in huge font announced this health insurance scheme on the walls of government hospitals. All agreed that in terms of the quality of the cancer treatment and the health insurance scheme provided, the state government—personified by Jayalalithaa—was serving them well. Most did not think they would receive better medical treatment in private hospitals. Their concern was that they felt they were being left in the dark about everything, and they found that to be demeaning. Here nondisclosure was felt as the withholding of emotional care and thus an act of exclusion, which in turn was interpreted as a lack of respect. It was not that they wanted more information so that they could be better consumers; rather, they wanted to be emotionally well looked after and comforted by these "government people" who were their doctors and nurses.

From the point of admission into the hospital, throughout their treatment in the hospital, and even during the process of being discharged from the hospital, these patients felt that they were not being given information and that they were not in a position of power to ask. This would begin when they had to sit through a "tumor board meeting" before being admitted as patients. One day I attended a tumor board meeting as an observer. There were fifteen doctors in white coats sitting around a long rectangular table. One by one, new patients entered the room and sat on a stool that was set back from one end of the table. A doctor read the patient's case sheet in English, and this was followed by a discussion among all the doctors about the appropriate treatment. This conversation was mostly in English, with technical medical terms and some Tamil words mixed in. The patients did not seem to understand what the doctors were saying. At one point, the doctors all laughed loudly at a joke made in English that was not related to a patient's case and the patient looked very alarmed. The doctors did not look at the patients and did not ask the patients any questions except on a few occasions to ask about medical records or to ask one patient to stick out his tongue to check for anemia. After the doctors agreed on a treatment plan, they would write it down on a piece of paper and hand it to a nurse, who would escort the patient out. The doctors said nothing to the patients as they were ushered out, or they simply said, "They will tell you what will happen next." Thirteen patients were seen over a period of one hour.

When I asked Vijaya about her experience in the tumor board meeting, she replied,

> There is nothing to say. They just spoke amongst themselves. I was not asked anything. I was upset because nothing was asked. They were all there talking. But they never asked me how I was, or anything like that. They just make you sit down and then they have a meeting. They talk among themselves. Then they said, "You can go home for a week or a few days, and then come back and get admitted here." So, I came back and got admitted here.

Another patient described the tumor board meeting:

> The doctors do not include you in that conversation [*kooditta pesu maataanga*]. You are asked to sit. Then the doctors see your report and they discuss it and then they decide who gets what treatment. They keep you separate [*taniyaaha*]; they don't talk to you in that meeting. When you come out of that meeting they say, "You will get 'current' so go to the third floor."

When I followed up and asked if she was satisfied with the way the meeting was run, she replied,

> No, I think it is better to talk to the patients. It makes you feel a sense of comfort [*aarudhal irrukkum*]. See, whatever it is, it is you who has to live through it. If they include you in their conversation [*kooditta pesuvanga*] you feel comforted [*aarudhal kidaikkum*]. But they don't do that. They just think, "The patient has this disease, so let me read the report and tell them what to do."

Once admitted to the hospital, these patients typically had to remain for a long time while they were receiving treatment. These treatments were typically handled on an inpatient basis. This meant that most of the women I met had stayed or would be staying in the hospital ward for several months. The longest time reported to me was four months. One woman had to wait in the hospital ward for an entire month before she even began receiving her radiation treatments. She had to simply bide her time there waiting to initiate treatment and was told that she could not leave the hospital ward to visit her family; if she did, she would have to go to the back of the line of patients waiting to receive the treatment and this would prolong her wait. She had seven grandchildren living with her at home and played a crucial role caring for them. Her long absence placed a strain on the family, so the fact that she would have to wait such a long time while simply waiting to begin her treatments infuriated her. Delays like this are an inconvenience to families as well as an inefficient use of government resources. Practices such as this led patients to feel that staff in the government hospitals do not see beyond their patients' cancer to recognize that they are also people with social lives.

One day when I was visiting the breast cancer ward in the Government Cancer Hospital, I was chatting with Amaldevi, sitting on the edge of her bed. Soon Saroja, from the adjacent bed, joined in the conversation. This happened often since all of the patients were staying together with their beds lined up side by side in one large, open room. They got into an animated discussion—in hushed tones to make sure they would not be heard by the nurse in the nurses' station—about the impersonal way in which they were treated at the hospital. Saroja pointed to Amaldevi and said, "Look at what happened to her!" She then explained that the doctors had told Amaldevi that she only needed two more radiation treatments. So Amaldevi called her husband to come get her. He traveled all day by bus to take her home. But when he arrived, the doctors suddenly announced that Amaldevi needed to stay longer for more treatments. Her husband was left waiting indefinitely and was sleeping outside on the hospital grounds because there was nowhere else for him to go as they did not have relatives nearby and could not afford a hotel. Amaldevi explained:

> He has left a job and wages behind and has to just wait until I am discharged. But when I mentioned this to the doctors, they said, "Oh, so we should tell you everything?! Don't you know anything?" When they respond like that, we think, "How can we ask them anything when they speak to us like that?" So, we just don't ask.

Saroja added:

> I don't have concerns about how they give the treatment. They give the treatment. But they do not think of how this affects your family. They don't think about the patient's family circumstances at all. That pains me.

Amaldevi agreed:

> That is the problem. They give you the correct medical treatment. In fact, they are like gods. We think of them like that. But when they talk to us they say, "Lie down! This is your fate [*nerum vandhuruchu*]!"[36] That kind of treatment is what pains you. They should ask us how we are managing to be here in the hospital for so long when we have children at home. They should care about us that way [*apadi kavanikkanum*]. That is the problem. There is no other problem. It is good treatment. The medicines are good. But they don't tell us anything and they don't ask us anything.

Devaki, a Dalit woman and cervical cancer survivor whom I met at one of the RUWSEC cancer support group meetings, recounted her experience as a patient at the Government Cancer Hospital:

> The doctors and nurses there never come close to their patients [*kitta nerunga maataanga*]. They are always so distant. It is as if they think I am garbage. They put a distance between us and them, and if we try to get closer to them in the room, they say, "Stay there and say it to me." They say that. They are good doctors as far as the medical care goes. But their "ego" gets in the way. Also, it may be because some people with this disease have a bad smell from the cancerous ulcers. Or maybe they think it is a contagious disease [*totrunoi*]. There is no real occasion when they sit down and talk to you. But a few doctors take good care of us [*nalla paathukuvanga*][37] and will sit with us and talk with us about everything.

When I asked Devaki what she meant when she used the English word "ego," she explained that the doctors are "big people" (*periyavanga*) and "educated people" (*padiccirukkiravanga*) who treat poor Dalit patients in the government hospital as if they are uneducated, ignorant people who are too gross (*asingam*) to come near. This, she added, was the kind of treatment that people like her had to endure. She said it was like living in the Kali Yuga.

The word "*nerunga*" as Devaki used it in the preceding quote (they never come close) conveys the same double meaning of proximity and emotional intimacy that the word "close" has in English. Whereas Chellamma appreciated it when doctors asked her to sit outside while they spoke to her son-in-law, Devaki was humiliated by the physical distance imposed by doctors, who kept her at a distance as they spoke to her. Other women were critical of the fact that they were kept out of the conversation during the tumor board meetings even though they were seated in the same room; they said they would have felt comforted if they had been included. Critical here is how women interpret the context and how they assess whether people care not just *for* them but *about* them.

Physicians working in government hospitals in India commonly only see patients in public hospitals during the first half of the day; they then see patients in private clinics (sometimes in their own homes) during the afternoon and early evening hours. Patients in public hospitals complained that because of this arrangement, physicians prioritize the paying patients whom they see in their private practice and give less attention to the patients in the public hospitals. Thirty-four-year-old Renukha traveled twelve hours by bus from her hometown near Thoothukudi in southern Tamil Nadu to receive free care for cervical cancer at the Cancer Institute's NGO hospital. She explained,

> They do not give proper care in the government hospitals. But here they do. In government hospitals the nurses will say, "What is it? Get out of here!" But here they call you by your name and remember you. It would be good if they could treat us that way in government hospitals. If that were the case, we would not need to go to a private hospital. After coming here, I saw that if a patient is unable to use the bathroom or if they fall down, the nurses carry them. I am not saying that the government hospitals need to do it at *that* level, but they could at least talk to us nicely. When you go to the government hospital, the doctors do not even *see* you. The very same doctors also run private care clinics in the evening. They are very welcoming and interested in learning what is going on when a patient comes to their private clinic. If they could behave that way in the government hospital, that would be nice.

At their core, these critiques of the medical staff in public hospitals were less about not being provided with specific information and more about not being handled with emotional care and comforted as fellow humans. At public hospitals, lack of disclosure was experienced as an act of social and emotional exclusion that for lower-class and -caste women carried the sting of social stigma and disrespect. Patients' anger about nondisclosure in this context was an assertion of the right to the dignity of receiving emotional comfort more than about the right to information per se.

## PATIENT SOLIDARITY ON THE WARD

When patients did not get enough information from medical practitioners, they turned to one another to better understand their diagnosis and prognosis and the effects of treatments. Because patients in the Government Cancer Hospital shared open wards for a long time, they got to know one another well. I spent many afternoons in the cervical and breast cancer wards—spacious, open rooms with freshly painted light-green and white walls and high ceiling fans circulating the air that came in through open windows. Except for a few patients who were severely ill and hooked up to IVs and oxygen tanks, most patients moved about freely in the ward, frequently going to the bedside of another patient to chat. In the afternoons and evenings, after the doctors had completed their inpatient rounds in the wards, the patients remained largely unsupervised by medical staff except for the on-duty nurse. In this context, most interactions patients had were with other patients, and this fostered a sense of solidarity on the ward that served as an important resource for information about medical treatments.

As seen in the story of Chellamma, patients in India are given booklets with their medical records for them to keep while they are in the hospital and after they are discharged. Women shared and discussed these record books with close family members or friends, as Chellamma did. They also shared them with other women in the ward, comparing information to try to piece together the details the doctors might not be inclined or willing to disclose. While I was talking with Amaldevi and Saroja, Amaldevi said, "No one explains that this is the illness that you have or this is the treatment you will get and these are the side effects that you might have. So, we share these reports and talk to each other to understand." It was not only the sharing of helpful information about their health and treatments among patients that women appreciated. Even more important for them was that the other women would ask about their families and take an interest in them as fellow humans with lives beyond their cancer. My past research has taken me into the wards of Indian government hospitals for maternity care and for HIV/AIDS treatment. I have usually perceived the lack of privacy in these large hospital wards as a negative attribute of medical care in resource-poor settings. During my research in cancer wards, however, I came to understand that patients in fact appreciated the social solidarity they found there.

I was impressed by the intimacy of care that I witnessed. Women on these wards swapped stories and photographs of their children; one woman helped adjust the flaps on the woolen cap her friend wore to cover her balding head; women escorted each other to the bathroom when they needed to vomit after their chemotherapy and helped carry a woman back to her bed when she felt too weak to walk after radiation; women held hands while they sat together on the floor watching Tamil soap operas on the single television on their ward; one woman hung a small poster of Lord Siva on the wall near her bed to protect all of the patients in the ward. When I asked women if they would prefer to have a room of their own in the hospital, they were unanimous that they much preferred being all together in one room. Vijaya explained:

> If we were in separate rooms, there would be too much "feel" [i.e., worry/anxiety]. This is a lot better. I can talk to people. See how we live here? We are talking to each other and are on good terms. If we are alone, we are alone with our thoughts. If I were alone, I would feel troubled in my heart/mind [manasu] but now I am not. We talk about our hopes that we will all recover; we discuss our apprehensions about what could happen. When I get back from seeing the doctor, the others here will call me over and ask me what the doctors said and did. We tell each other stories from our homes too. We lay out everything here to discuss. That is a comfort [aarudhal].

Another woman on the general ward of the Cancer Institute echoed that sentiment:

> We share our fears of leaving our families behind and dying. They share their problems, and cry. We share ours and cry. You tell them your problems; they tell you theirs. You cry a little, they cry a little. I feel comforted.

## CONCLUSION

Whereas this environment of open sharing and support was considered by Vijaya and others to provide patients with a sense of comfort that the medical staff failed to provide, for other patients like Chellamma, the fact that doctors and family members did not give them the details of their illness was felt to be a comfort. In both cases, this sense of comfort was associated with feelings of being handled with care. Earlier, I listed the six reasons the NIH gave in favor of full disclosure of cancer diagnosis, prognosis, and effects of treatment. At the top of the list was the argument that full disclosure "grants patients a sense of control." At the bottom of the list is the suggestion that it helps "generate feelings of safety and security." My research suggests that the factor that matters the most for cancer patients in my study in their evaluation—both positive and negative—of the lack of full disclosure was the degree to which the act of nondisclosure was associated with emotional comfort and caring or lack thereof. This suggests that in some sociocultural contexts the item at the bottom of the NIH list should in fact be placed at the top (while in other contexts the current order may be appropriate).

Deborah Lupton similarly cautioned against overemphasizing patients' desires for control within an increasingly consumerist framework of medical care that privileges patients' preference for autonomous rational decision-making over patients' desires to feel comfortable renouncing control to an authoritative figure whom they trust to take care of them. This is often criticized as a form of paternalism. Finkler noted that the rise of bioethics has been accompanied by a shift in the guiding ethical principle in medical practice from beneficence to autonomy. What might otherwise be viewed as an act of beneficence on the part of a physician or a family member is now negatively interpreted as paternalistic in American and now global bioethical guidelines. Lupton argues that in the highly emotional contexts of "illness, disease, pain, disability and impending death," both impulses—of control and of dependency—need to be seen as equally rational.[38] This idea has clearly not been taken up by the NIH, as is apparent in its use of a study that claims there are four mutually distinct categories of patients' emotional styles: passive, avoidant, panicked, and rational.

My research supports Lupton's suggestion that we need to acknowledge the high value that patients in some cultural contexts place in the emotional experience of being cared for and to insert this point more centrally into debates about disclosure. Some women in my study viewed the lack of disclosure from medical practitioners working in government hospitals as an indication of lack of care. It is important to consider this as part of a broader critique that lower-class and -caste citizens may have that government employees are uncaring and aloof. As Vijaya said, "Whatever we ask, they talk sternly. They talk stiffly like that. They are 'government' people and we are just individual people; that is why we have such fear." She implied that as socioeconomically marginalized individuals they are relatively powerless vis-à-vis the government as an institution and vis-à-vis the government employees of this institution. Thus, they critique the government for denying them basic respect as citizens while simultaneously praising the government for providing them with medical services to which they feel entitled as citizens.

In India, Tamil Nadu stands out as a state where the promise of healthcare as a public good has been a cornerstone of populist political campaigns for decades. As a result, the state's health outcomes are better than those of most other states.[39] As Livingston writes about oncology care in Botswana, "the promise of citizenship is manifest in access to novel technologies increasingly understood as necessary to collective health and well-being."[40] The same is true in Tamil Nadu. However, when lower-class and -caste cancer patients criticize the social and emotional quality of the healthcare while praising the technological medical care they are receiving, they are asserting that as citizens they expect more than modern biomedical technical services. They feel they are entitled to be treated with compassion and that they are being denied this fundamental aspect of citizenship because of their socioeconomic position. In this context, lack of compassion is experienced as lack of respect or the denial of dignity. Like many Dalit and MBC women whom I met, Devaki criticized this lack of respect and saw it as emblematic of the Kali Yuga. In these critiques, Held's ethics of care (focused on attentiveness, trust, responsiveness to need, and narrative nuance) is linked with what she refers to as an "ethics of justice," which she says "focuses on questions of fairness, equality, individual rights, abstract principles and the consistent application of them."[41] Held notes that care and justice are distinct modalities of morality but maintains it is possible for them to be conjoined, that is, to foster "equitable caring" or "humane justice."[42] Lower-class and -caste cancer patients used the opportunity of our ethnographic encounter, and my promise to convey their experiences and opinions through writing a book, to criticize this form of disrespectful care and to express their demand for such equitable caring.

Jayalalithaa's face adorned fans, school backpacks, and other appliances in people's homes as well as the posters that hung on the walls of public hospitals throughout the state to announce various public health schemes. But it is the personnel working in government hospitals who became the real human face of the state for these patients. As Akhil Gupta wrote in his ethnographic work on the Indian state, it is local government institutions, such as the government hospital, that are "the site where the majority of people in a rural and agricultural country such as India come into contact with 'the state,' and this is where many of their images of the state are forged."[43] Throughout Tamil Nadu, Jayalalithaa—and by extension the state under her leadership—was represented as a benevolent and protective goddess and mother (*amma*). The medical staff in the government hospitals, on the other hand, were viewed by patients as highly capable and imbued with positive powers ("like gods") in terms of their medical expertise but were reproached for their lack of compassion for patients.

My point is not to condemn doctors and nurses working in these government hospitals. They are doing remarkable work and providing critical medical services to people in need under difficult circumstances. Gregg's ethnography of cervical cancer in Brazil suggests that in addition to trying to protect patients from bad news, nondisclosure of a cancer diagnosis helps the physicians cope because they are working in overcrowded public hospitals and lack the time needed to give solace to each cancer patient following disclosure of their condition.[44] Doctors working in large public hospitals in India face similar problems of overcrowding, with little time to spend with each patient. Recent ethnographic work points to the constraints faced by Indian doctors and nurses in public institutions.[45] But in addition to that, physicians working in government hospitals in India commonly only see patients in public hospitals during the first half of the day and attend to their private practice for the rest of the day. This diminishes the amount of time doctors have for patients in public hospitals.

The state of Tamil Nadu is to be commended for the medical care it offers through the Government Cancer Hospital and for its widely extolled health insurance program for the poor. However, my research underscores the need for greater attention to providing emotional care for patients as well, recognizing that when it comes to cancer, for some this may mean that less direct disclosure is best while for others more disclosure would be preferred. This is not simply because of the content of the information conveyed but also because the act of such communication itself, or the careful absence of communication, can be felt as forms of care. This requires more attention in medical education and in policies regarding the allocation of medical staffing resources and accountability.

In his work on the anthropology of bioethics, Kleinman wrote:

> The cardinal contribution of the anthropologist of medicine to bioethics…is to deeply humanize the *process* of formulating an ethical problem by allowing variation and pluralism and the constraints of the social positions to emerge and receive their due, so that ethical standards are not imposed in an alien and authoritarian way but, rather, are actualized as the outcome of reciprocal participatory engagement across different worlds of experience.[46]

This chapter "humanize[s] the process of formulating an ethical problem" by describing the multiple ways in which socioeconomically marginalized women in Tamil Nadu evaluated the practice of nondisclosure of cancer diagnoses, prognoses, and treatment. It has shed light on lower-class and -caste women's calls for more empathic care for patients. In the next chapter, I explore women's experiences with the biomedical interventions they had to undergo during their cancer treatments. In particular, I examine women's responses to the loss of their body parts resulting from biomedical treatments for these reproductive cancers. We will see how the nexus of gender, class, and caste informs women's encounters with biomedical cancer treatments and how lower-class and -caste women struggle to find creative ways to negotiate the constraints of their socioeconomic position to survive this disease with dignity.

# CHAPTER 6

# Biomedicine and Bodies

The shock of receiving a cancer diagnosis was profound for women, whether they got the news directly from a doctor or indirectly through a family member, or simply figured it out themselves. In that moment they entered into what Sontag referred to as the "kingdom of the sick," an experience shaped as much by socially constructed metaphors and cultural meanings of an illness as by the physiological effects of the biology of disease.[1] The immediate response was fear of death, since a cancer diagnosis is often thought to be a death sentence in India. A cancer diagnosis also led people to speculate about why *they* had gotten cancer, bringing up feelings of guilt, exasperation, resentment, suspicion, or anger. While they tried to make sense of their diagnosis, more immediately women and their family members had to make quick decisions about how to proceed with treatment. Participants in my study who received free healthcare at the Government Cancer Hospital and the Cancer Institute faced the prospect of the three most common treatment modalities for cancer: radiation, surgery, and chemotherapy. They did not receive new experimental cancer treatments such as immunotherapy or other therapies in clinical trials. They had to contend with fears about how biomedical cancer treatments would transform their bodies while also, hopefully, eradicating the cancer and saving their lives. They worried that they might experience severe nausea, weakness, dizziness, and pain from the treatment. Above all, they were anxious about how cancer treatments could result in loss of body parts—uteri, ovaries, breasts, and hair—that would compromise their womanhood. Despite these apprehensions, they were willing to go through with treatment in the hope of saving their lives and staying alive for the sake of their children, and they developed coping mechanisms to deal with the trauma of losing parts of their bodies.

The most common sequencing of treatments among the breast cancer patients was: four doses of chemotherapy, followed by a mastectomy (surgical removal of the affected breast), followed by four more doses of chemotherapy, followed by twenty external radiation therapy sessions on the area where the affected breast had been removed. These treatments varied depending on the unique circumstances of each woman. Some had double mastectomies. One had a lumpectomy and no mastectomy. They reported a range of chemotherapy treatments from three to eight and a range of radiation sessions from ten to twenty-seven. Four breast cancer patients also had hysterectomies (surgical removal of the uterus), and two had oophorectomies (surgical removal of the ovaries); these additional surgeries were performed to prevent the recurrence of cancer.

The primary mode of treatment among the cervical cancer patients was radiation therapy. They underwent multiple sessions of external beam radiation on their abdominal area, followed by a few internal brachytherapy radiation sessions via vaginal insertion. Most had twenty-five to thirty external radiation sessions and two or three internal radiation sessions. Women reported having up to sixty external radiation and four internal radiation sessions. Eight of these cervical cancer patients also received between one to six chemotherapy treatments. Several said that medical staff had informed them they could not receive chemotherapy because they were over sixty years old and their bodies would not be able to tolerate it at that age. Two cervical cancer patients had hysterectomies: one to treat the cancer itself and the other to prevent a relapse.

Although there are commonalities in women's experiences with these treatments globally, this chapter demonstrates how the sociocultural context of the lives of the reproductive cancer patients in my study in South India had a direct bearing on their perceptions of and experiences with cancer treatments and their modes of coping with the effects of these treatments. The idea of getting radiation therapy terrified them initially, whereas they were nonchalant about the prospect of having a hysterectomy. And while they were apprehensive about having a mastectomy, it was their fears of chemotherapy-induced hair loss that traumatized them the most. Such disparate things as linguistic translations of medical terms; local conceptions of food and the body; the legacies of international, national, and state birth control programs; cultural constructions of gender, kinship, and marriage; and South Indian religious practices, informed women's experiences with these treatments. These ethnographic accounts of their engagements with cancer treatments illuminates how the nexus of their class, caste, and gender identities combined with distinctive Tamil cultural and religious practices to create unique experiences of cancer for these women. Comparisons for what I found in the South Indian context come from social science literature on women's experiences with cancer treatments in the US and around the world.

Anxiety about chemotherapy-induced hair loss loomed larger than concerns about the effects of all other treatments, including the loss of breasts, uteri, and ovaries. This surprised me, because the losses of these other body parts involve invasive surgery and are permanent, whereas the loss of hair is painless and temporary. Deeper reading on women's experiences with chemotherapy-induced loss of hair elsewhere made me aware of how much women worldwide agonize about hair loss because it is publicly visible.[2] Yet even though chemotherapy-induced hair loss is stressful for women everywhere, I suggest that it poses unique challenges in India, where women's hair and the ritual head shaving of widows carry particular cultural meanings that exacerbate the stigma for women cancer patients. Other uniquely South Indian practices of ritual head shaving provide women with a strategy to deflect the stigma of their baldness.

RADIATION THERAPY

When I first broached the subject of cancer treatments during group discussions with Dalit and MBC women, there was widespread consensus that the thing people feared the most was the possibility of having to undergo "current" or "current shock." Although we were all speaking in Tamil, they used these English words to refer to radiation therapy. People were quite terrified of this because it conjured up visions of electrocution through electroconvulsive therapy. Electroconvulsive therapy is sometimes used for patients in mental health institutions in India, and the idea of it provokes dread.[3] Some medical practitioners tried to avoid using the term "current" because they knew this might frighten patients. Instead, they used the Tamil word "kadiriyakkam" (radiation). But this was a very formal word, and patients did not understand what it was, so they fell back on the more familiar term, "current."

Cancer patients and survivors similarly reported grave fears initially about undergoing radiation therapy because they assumed it involved being zapped with electric current that would burn them severely. Women who were coaxed into having radiation therapy complained about some of the effects of the treatment but felt that it was not as drastic as the term "current shock" had led them to believe. One woman commented, "When they told me that I would have to get 'current,' I was scared. I thought it might burn me to a crisp! I was scared for the first day, and then as I began taking it more regularly, I lost the fear." Similarly, another woman explained:

> I thought they would give me "current" like this.... [She pointed to an electric outlet in the wall and started shaking her hands vigorously in short up-and-down motion as if she were receiving an electric shock]. Even my husband got scared and told me that if they give me "current" I would get burns and wounds over my stomach and die. I might become even sicker. He said, "If they are going to give you 'current,' then you should not get the treatment. Instead, you can live out your last days well at home. If they give you 'current' you will die of burns in your stomach." But after I came here [to the Cancer Institute], they said it won't hurt me like that. They said the "current" will dissolve the lump. And the other patients in the hospital ward told me not to worry because the "current" is just a light beam [oli].

Although women were not "burned to a crisp," many were alarmed when the skin around the area where they received the external radiation became dark. However, they were reassured by doctors and other patients that this would fade.

Cervical cancer patients who also received internal brachytherapy radiation applied through vaginal insertion suffered from the physical discomfort of this treatment as well as from psychosocial discomfort due to feelings of shyness (*kooccham*) and embarrassment or shame (*vetkam*) about having a stranger insert an instrument into their vagina. They referred to the internal radiation treatments as "*ool* current" (inside current). At both the Government Cancer Hospital and the Cancer Institute, patients who received brachytherapy radiation reported that although they were given anesthesia before receiving the internal radiation, they still felt some discomfort and pain from the procedure and from the heat inside their bodies during and after the procedure.

Some reported that their arms and legs had been strapped down during brachytherapy so that they would not move. They would only have one hand loose to ring a bell for help if they were in too much discomfort. Karpagam described her experience:

The "*ool* current" is so hot! All the machines use "current" [electricity], and they all cause heat. The heat was painful. They would strap your hands and legs down for the "*ool* current" so that you can't move at all. Your hands and legs are strapped. Even if they give you a pain injection, you feel so much pain. But I would bite my teeth and think, "This is for my children. God gave me this option, and I will have to take it." If I am alive today, it is probably because I tried so hard for my children. I think that is why my children feel like they should take care of me.

One woman expressed concerns about the potential carcinogenic effects of radioactive radiation treatments when she was diagnosed with cancer of the parotid (salivary) gland two years after her breast cancer radiation treatments. She was a seventy-five-year-old Tamil Brahmin breast cancer survivor from Chennai who had been a paying patient at the Cancer Institute. Her daughter, who lived in New Jersey, had proposed this theory, but her oncologists dismissed it. Lower-class and -caste women had other theories about the iatrogenic effects of radiation.

Selvi, who had toiled on construction sites as a young orphan girl and then under the hot sun in the paddy fields after her marriage, also discussed the potentially lethal iatrogenic effects of radiation. She said that radiation therapy rendered the body "too hot" and that this overheating could be life-threatening. Reflecting back on the time when she had completed her radiation therapy at the Government Cancer Hospital and was preparing to return home, she said the doctors and other patients on the ward stressed the importance of eating "cooling" foods and avoiding work in the heat as well as mental stress. She explained:

> They said, "Don't think about anything; don't let yourself feel 'tension.'" They said I should eat well. I should not eat heating foods and I should not work in the heat or over a hot wood-burning stove. That is very important for your recovery after the "*ool* current" because that is very hot. *What keeps you alive is medicine, what kills you is also medicine.* You should not eat just the medicine, you should also eat good food [emphasis added].

Recall that Selvi and others were convinced that overheating was a causal factor for their cancer. Here we see that some thought radiation treatments for their cancer caused their bodies to overheat. They believed that radiation was necessary for their survival, but they also viewed it as something that would compromise their health by overheating the body and that it could place them at risk for a cancer recurrence or other problems. Whether women had received cancer treatments from the Government Cancer Hospital or the

Cancer Institute, they said they had been given strict dietary guidelines from doctors, nurses, and counselors about what they should and should not eat when they were discharged from the hospital. They interpreted these restrictions as necessary for recovering from the effects of the cancer treatments themselves, particularly from the "heating" effects of radiation.

The array of dietary prescriptions reported was dizzying. Parimala had recently completed all her external and internal radiation treatments for cervical cancer and was getting discharged from the Cancer Institute. When we asked whether she had been advised to follow any particular diet after returning home, she replied:

> They said we could eat whatever we want. But they said we should not eat oily food. So, it is best to avoid food bought from shops. We should instead eat food made at home. They asked us to avoid sour varieties of spinach, and also dried fish [karuvadu]. We should avoid spicy and sour foods. We can eat everything else. Eggs must be eaten boiled. Fish should not be fried. Everything can be eaten. But not poori [a kind of fried bread] made from maida [refined flour], the kind they sell in stores. We can make poori on our own. If we make things at home, everything including the spinach has to be boiled and cooked thoroughly. Fish should not be made with oil, but you can eat it in a curry. The curry should not be too spicy. "Medium" spices are okay. They said it won't harm us. We can also eat meat as long as we don't eat it fried. We need to let it cook thoroughly by boiling it. They asked us to make "soup" and eat that. We shouldn't eat "broiler" chicken. But we can eat country chicken [naattu kozhi]. We can eat mutton [goat] curry, but not the white chicken curry. We should also avoid anchovies [nethili] as well as the dried fish. They told me to avoid lime pickles because those are sour. We can have rasam [tamarind-spiced soup] but not too much because that is made with tamarind, which is sour. We can eat everything but we must avoid sour and spicy foods. They say we should not eat fruits with seeds and we should not eat the skin of fruits. You can eat bananas and peeled apples.

Others mentioned that they should avoid grapes, pomegranates, oranges, mangoes, and watermelons because these too are seeded fruits. Some were advised to not eat white pumpkin or brinjal (eggplant). Several were advised to drink tender coconut water and eat gooseberries.

Most women said they were told to avoid certain foods because they are "heating" foods, especially spicy foods, mangoes, white pumpkins, dried fish, and "broiler" chicken. They explained that they needed to avoid these things because their bodies were overheated from the radiation treatments; they needed to counteract that with a "cooling" diet. Selvi explained:

Since the "current" is hot, it might cause wounds to come inside the body. So, we need cooling things to counteract the heating of the "current." The "current" causes diarrhea. So, we are advised to take water and green vegetables.

Chicken posed its own set of problems. Although all chicken was said to be "heating," it was the white chicken—referred to as "broiler chicken"—that patients were told to avoid. There was a growing public concern about these chickens in South India at the time because of the manner in which they were raised. The heavy doses of antibiotics and hormonal treatments given to these chickens were considered deleterious to the health of people who consumed them. In addition to these concerns, cancer patients said these chickens posed a health risk to them because they were hatched and raised in incubators using very hot electric lights—"current." One cancer patient who had recently been discharged explained: "We should not eat the 'broiler' chicken. It is hatched in 'current' so they told us not to eat that. Even if we eat one piece of that chicken, we will get stomach pain because of the heat from the 'current' used to raise the chickens."

Despite concerns that radiation "current" therapy caused their bodies to overheat, rendering them once again potentially vulnerable to disease, including cancer, all were convinced that radiation (and other biomedical cancer treatments) could rid them of cancer and save their lives. This was a risk worth taking. Following cooling dietary regimens after radiation therapy would mediate the risks of radiation. As Selvi noted (see above), "What keeps you alive is medicine, what kills you is also medicine. You should not eat just the medicine, you should also eat good food."

Were women able to follow these dietary guidelines at home? That would depend on their circumstances, which were challenging for many, especially those living in poverty. Most said their families strove to ensure that they followed these diets, even if it was difficult. Others like Poongodai were not so sanguine. Poongodai was ashamed that she and her husband had become financially dependent on their son because they were both recovering from cancer treatments, which had depleted their strength and left them unable to engage in manual wage labor. When I asked if she was able to follow the doctors' dietary recommendations, she hung her head and replied:

I cannot say to my son, "Bring me milk, bring me country chicken eggs." I am not able to make these demands because we don't have the money. What can I do? This is the Kali Yuga, isn't it? They want us to drink milk and buttermilk. They want us to eat peeled apples. How can we eat like that every month when he earns 10,000 rupees a month and there are six of us to feed? We had to sell our cows to pay for all these medical tests. How can we afford to drink milk now?

A few women confided that it was only while they were in the hospital and receiving food for free that they were able to eat a healthy, balanced diet, even if the food tasted a bit bland. The problem was that they felt too nauseous from the radiation and chemotherapy treatments to eat the hospital food. Then, when they returned home after their treatment, many faced food insecurity once again.

## SURGERY I: THE ROUTINIZATION OF HYSTERECTOMIES

If the idea of receiving radiation—"current"—was initially shocking, the prospect of getting a hysterectomy or oophorectomy did not seem worrisome to the women I met, even though these are invasive surgeries. This was true for women in group discussions as well as for cancer patients who had these surgical procedures as treatments. I suggest this nonchalance about hysterectomies was a result of the routinization of hysterectomies and tubal ligations as part of the long-standing international, state, and NGO push for family planning among lower-class women in India.

I came to this realization about the connection between family planning campaigns and cavalier attitudes toward hysterectomies during my first group discussion meeting in 2015. I was sitting under the shade of a tree on the edge of a field with a group of around fifteen Dalit and MBC women. Two gigantic white terracotta horses belonging to Lord Ayyanar, a guardian deity of Tamil villages, hovered behind us, seemingly listening in on our conversation. Women in this group said they were afraid of the unknown of "current shock" since none of them had had that kind of treatment, whereas they were all familiar with "operations" because of the *kudumpakkadduppadu* (family planning) operation (female sterilization/tubal ligation). They reported that doctors insisted on sterilization after the second birth; if women refused, doctors would scold them. All but four of the women in this group had been sterilized, even though most were between twenty-five and thirty-five years old. When I asked if any of them had had a hysterectomy, five women raised their hand—around one third of the women in this group. They explained that women over thirty who have two children will often have a hysterectomy. Older women whom they knew had undergone hysterectomies as a result of fibroids, severe discharge, heavy bleeding, or a prolapsed uterus. Doctors nowadays were recommending a hysterectomy after two children as a form of family planning and as a preventative measure against other reproductive health problems they might encounter when they were older. The same comments were repeated in other rural and urban communities in Tamil Nadu.

My research on maternal healthcare in Tamil Nadu in the mid- to late 1990s made me aware of the extreme pressures that the family planning programs in Tamil Nadu had exerted on lower-class women to undergo sterilization after two births and to use intrauterine devices (IUDs) for birth spacing between births.[4] These programs were set in motion in the 1960s when the World Bank and the US Agency for International Development (USAID) demanded that the Indian government demonstrate evidence of implementing population control programs as a stipulation for receiving aid, based on neo-Malthusian theories about population size and economic development. National, state, and district-level targets were established to get people to "accept"—sometimes through coercion—various methods of birth control. Over time, lower-class and -caste women became the focus of these efforts; it was they who were pressed and coaxed into having tubal ligations. My research in the 1990s demonstrated that although some women in Tamil Nadu complained that they had been forced to accept these family planning methods, many others embraced them as normal and good for them. Women used the English word "operation" in Tamil conversations to refer to the tubal ligation procedure. If they had undergone another kind of operation, they qualified it with another word, such as "*garbha pai* operation" (uterus operation), to refer to a hysterectomy.

Lawrence Cohen connected my findings to his work on organ donation and sales in India to develop the concept of "operability"[5] as a critique of how marginalized people's bodies are too easily made available to invasive medical interventions that serve the interests of others more than those of the individuals undergoing the operation. Anthropologists have expanded this concept to include other medical interventions, such as surrogacy and clinical trials, using terms such as "bioavailabity" and "bioviolence."[6] Women's blasé attitudes toward hysterectomies and oophorectomies for cancer fit under this analytical rubric of operability or bioavailabilty.

Women cancer patients who had had hysterectomies for their cancer treatment said it was easy to accept the idea of having a hysterectomy because they knew other women who had had one. These surgeries had been so routinized that women and their doctors did not view them as "big" operations. I gleaned from interviews with patients that doctors seemed to leverage the normalcy of hysterectomies when recommending them to cancer patients. Tharani, a thirty-nine-year-old breast cancer patient and wage laborer from a village in Viluppuram district who was receiving treatment at the Cancer Institute said that in addition to getting a mastectomy, she also had a hysterectomy to prevent a recurrence of the cancer. I asked why she was getting her uterus removed:

> I am not sure but the doctor told me to do it so that so that the cancer would not come back. The doctor said I should not worry because it is not a big "operation." It is just a uterus [*garbha pai*] "operation." My periods have stopped because of the chemotherapy. My doctor said since I don't have my periods anymore, it could cause problems later. There are germs [*kirumi*] that could cause problems if you don't remove your uterus. So, I said, "Okay, remove it." My sister-in-law had the same "operation" and I have known many others who had this "operation" too. I think it is better to do it rather than suffer later.

Lalitha, a forty-nine-year-old woman who had been treated for cervical cancer at the Government Cancer Hospital, had a similar attitude toward her hysterectomy. I met her when she was checking back into the hospital for this surgery. Doctors had informed her that her earlier radiation treatment had successfully removed the cancer from the cervix but that she should have a hysterectomy to ensure that the cancer did not return. When I asked why she replied:

> I think it is because if it [the uterus] is there, then it [the cancer] might spread again. Now it is fully "clean." But to prevent it [cancer] from coming back, they advised that I remove it [the uterus]. If I remove it, I can be free of the fear that it [cancer] will return. This [hysterectomy] is because you don't want problems later. I went home and discussed it with my family. They told me that I should remove it because we know of so many people who have had this "operation" and they are fine. Nowadays they do it for many reasons. If you don't want a child, this [hysterectomy] is a kind of family planning [*kudumpakkadduppadu*] "operation." I already had an ordinary family planning "operation" [tubal ligation] after my second child. This is another kind of family planning "operation." Some women have the uterus removed if they don't have enough blood or if they have too much blood. I know so many people who have it removed for so many reasons. If you remove it, you won't have any problems. If you have it, you might have all sorts of problems with heavy periods, or with white discharge, or with "cancer" so it is better to take it out. It is better to have it removed and be without fear of a problem.

Lalitha decided to get a hysterectomy not only to prevent her cancer from relapsing but also to be free of the fear that it might return. She and her doctors rationalized this decision by pointing out how common and prevalent this surgery had become in India.

Women were increasingly getting hysterectomies for heavy periods and white discharge. As discussed earlier, many women thought these things—which are symptoms of cervical cancer—were caused by overheating and actually led to cervical cancer. Some women who were diagnosed with cervical cancer, therefore, regretted not having had a hysterectomy to prevent heavy white discharge and bleeding in the first place. Parimala lamented:

> There are a lot of women in my village with white discharge and with heavy periods. They went and had their uterus removed. They all had the uterus "operation." Now they are fine and they are able to work well. They can work well without having to worry about getting their periods anymore. They are well. I was cheated. I did not know then that I would get this disease [cancer] from that white discharge. I too would have removed my uterus. But I did not know I would get this illness.

Hysterectomies have been on the rise in India as the healthcare system becomes increasingly privatized, creating a profit motive within the medical industrial complex for all sorts of medical interventions, including hysterectomies.[7] This has raised concerns about human rights violations of marginalized women. There are other factors at play as well. Parimala's comment that women who had had hysterectomies "can work well without having to worry about getting their periods anymore" is ominous in light of reports that contractors for laborers in sugar cane fields in Maharashtra, North India, are insisting that women cane cutters undergo hysterectomies to avoid labor time lost due to menstrual periods.[8]

Hysterectomies and other forms of reproductive surgery have become routinized among low-income communities in India. I am not suggesting that women should *not* have hysterectomies or oophorectomies when medically indicated for cancer. Rather, I am suggesting that past and present-day medical interventions on lower-class and -caste women's reproductive bodies in India influence how cancer patients and medical practitioners view these surgical interventions. This analysis serves as a warning about the potential for medical overreach in cancer treatments for low-income women in India. It also underscores the importance of providing patients with a clear understanding of why they may want to consider a hysterectomy for cancer, without suggesting it is not a "big operation," since it is in fact a major surgery.

Hysterectomies and oophorectomies are both invasive surgeries, yet they cannot be detected publicly. It is easy to keep these surgeries private. Furthermore, because hysterectomies are so common, women can tell others they are having this procedure without raising suspicions about cancer. In a social environment where cancer continues to be stigmatized, women cancer patients welcome this scope for discretion. By contrast, the loss of one or both breasts from a mastectomy, and the loss of hair from chemotherapy, *can* be seen by others in public. Both may lead others to speculate that a woman has cancer, and this visibility poses a social risk that needs to be managed. Furthermore, breasts and hair are both powerful cultural symbols of femininity. This is perhaps a universal truth, but these symbols take on distinctive meanings in diverse cultural contexts.

## ANATOMO-POLITICS OF CANCER TREATMENT IN THE UNITED STATES AND BEYOND

Maren Klawiter's 2008 book *The Biopolitics of Breast Cancer: Changing Cultures of Disease and Activism* provides insights into "regimes" of breast cancer—social, cultural, political, and medico-technical attitudes and practices—in the US throughout the twentieth century and at the beginning of the twenty-first century. Of particular relevance here is her discussion of the "biomedicalization and the anatomo-politics of treatment"[9] and the role of Reach to Recovery. This program began in 1952 and was adopted by the American Cancer Society (ACS) as a national program in 1969. Using ex-cancer patients as peer volunteers, Reach to Recovery was designed to provide newly postoperative breast cancer patients with the support, information, and goods they needed to be able to return to normal life after treatment. Key to this was helping women regain a positive body image by re-creating "normal" women's bodies after mastectomies with prostheses—and later reconstructive breast surgery—to conceal the fact of the mastectomy. Klawiter explains that such programs did not exist for other cancer patients as they did for breast cancer patients because "women with breast cancer came to be seen as having a unique set of needs, and those special needs were directly connected to the cultural significance of women's breasts in American society and the importance of women's 'breasted existence'[10] to their individual and social identities."[11]

Klawiter argues that although the techniques of concealment taught through Reach to Recovery helped breast cancer patients avoid the stigmatizing shame of cancer in the mid- to late twentieth century, they also "strengthen[ed] the architecture of the closet that enabled these stigmatizing discourses to continue circulating freely" because they kept the evidence of cancer hidden.[12] In 1974, Reach to Recovery programs were established in other countries, and eventually a broad international umbrella group—Reach to Recovery International—emerged, which remains active around the world, including in India.

During the 1990s, breast cancer awareness campaigns to promote mammography screening and increase funding for biomedical breast cancer research took off in the US, galvanized in part by the success of the Susan G. Komen Foundation, which was founded in 1982 and heralded a new model of fundraising for health causes with its first Race for the Cure, conducted in 1983. The driving force behind the Komen Foundation and campaigns that followed was the corporate sector, particularly the fitness, fashion, and cosmetics industries.[13] Although these breast cancer awareness campaigns—symbolized by the pink ribbon and the positive discourse of the breast cancer "survivor"—succeeded in bringing breast cancer out of the closet and into mainstream American discourse, they also perpetuated gendered body norms for women by advocating and marketing products to conceal the effects of mastectomies and chemotherapy-induced hair loss.

The ACS gave institutional support to these initiatives. In addition to linking up with Reach to Recovery's programs to provide information and resources for prostheses, it helped launch the Look Good Feel Better program in 1989 (in collaboration with the cosmetics industry's Professional Beauty Association), with affiliate programs around the world. This program's website states: "Look Good Feel Better is dedicated to improving the quality of life and self-esteem of people undergoing cancer treatment. The program offers complimentary group, individual, and online sessions that teach beauty techniques to help people with cancer to face their diagnosis with greater confidence."[14] This program provides information about makeup, skin products, wigs, and other head coverings ("chemo headwear").

Not all women in the US have subscribed to body techniques to conceal mastectomies or the balding effects of chemotherapy. Some have pushed back against what they see as gendered aesthetic norms that tie a woman's value to her sexualized body. They view such techniques as problematic because they keep cancer in the closet as a taboo topic. So they reenter the world without breasts (permanently) or without hair (temporarily) to promote greater public awareness and acceptability of living with cancer and to destigmatize cancer by challenging the social code of invisibility.[15]

Others have refused these normalizing body techniques as part of a radical feminist environmental activist movement. These activists publicly display the bodily effects of their cancer treatments in protest marches to draw attention to the physical ravages and deformities caused by cancer treatments. They expose their mastectomy scars as a form of confrontational politics to shock the public into rage against the "cancer industry" (including corporations and government policies that protect them) that has been responsible for creating a carcinogenic world.[16] More recently, some women have used their breastless chests as canvases on which to create artistic tattoos.[17]

Despite all this, normalizing techniques are used today by the majority of breast cancer patients in the US, who prefer to fit in and move on after cancer treatments rather than draw public attention to their condition. It is precisely because the vast majority of women do use breast prostheses or breast reconstruction and do wear wigs while they are undergoing chemotherapy that *not* engaging in these practices is an act of defiance.

This brief discussion of the anatomo-politics of the management of breast and hair loss following cancer treatments in the US and beyond provides a backdrop for understanding similarities and differences in the experiences of women in South India. As elsewhere,[18] most women in Tamil Nadu seek to regulate their bodies to conform to gendered bodily norms in order to cope with the loss of both breasts and hair due to cancer treatments. Some used prostheses and wigs, while others did not. The difference fell primarily along socioeconomic lines. Middle-class women used and advocated for prostheses and wigs, whereas lower-class women did not, because of the costs and also because they interfered with manual labor. Most women in Tamil Nadu who moved about publicly with bald heads and missing breasts following cancer treatments did not do so as a mode of protest; they too found ways regulate their bodies so as to avoid the stigma of being bald and breastless. I am not suggesting that women in India are not engaged in activist resistance against gendered norms imposed following cancer treatments or against carcinogenic-producing industries. Many are. Rather, my attention is on the experiences of women in my study, whose responses to the loss of breasts and hair aligned with normative practices in Tamil Nadu. Although there are commonalities across the experiences of breast cancer patients in the US and India, there are also important differences both in terms of the meanings and social responses associated with the loss of breasts and hair and the techniques used to reconcile these losses. Furthermore, I highlight differences across class *among* women in South India.

## SURGERY II: MASTECTOMIES AND THE CULTURAL
## POLITICS OF BREAST LOSS IN TAMIL NADU

"The day I went in for surgery was the day my femininity came under attack. When I came out of that surgery, the loss of my breast began to haunt me," Padma said, recounting her story (in English) about coming to terms with her mastectomy. She had been forty-three at the time of her cancer diagnosis in 2002. She came from a middle-class family and had completed a bachelor's degree in Commerce. Her only prior knowledge of cancer had been through family experiences and films. She reflected on the moment she received the diagnosis:

> I felt it was the end of the road. To me cancer was the ultimate disease. It was like death. I thought there was no medicine for cancer; if you have cancer, you will die. I thought I was finished and that this cancer was the end of my story. I thought this because I saw my relatives die and we saw this in Hindi movies. They would show the hero is diagnosed with cancer, he coughs blood, and then he is dead. So that was my basic understanding about cancer. Cancer means death. There is no medicine for cancer. You may undergo treatment but ultimately you will die.

Doctors at the Cancer Institute encouraged her to have the mastectomy and gave her hope. Nevertheless, the absence of her breast haunted her. It was a constant hovering presence, like a phantom limb, reminding her of her lost femininity. I met Padma fourteen years after her mastectomy. By then she had not only survived the cancer but also become a strong promoter of breast prostheses and was engaged in Reach to Recovery kinds of networks, providing information about the benefits of breast prostheses to patients in the hospital.

Padma's concern about losing her femininity after a mastectomy is a common one among cancer patients around the globe.[19] In India, as elsewhere, women's bodies are sexualized through aesthetic forms that exaggerate large, rounded breasts. This idealized form of the feminine body is famously exemplified by erotic sculptures at the ancient Hindu temple of Khajuraho and can also be seen in the sculpted forms of goddesses in many temples throughout India, as well as in Bollywood and Tamil Kollywood films.

Ethnographic research on gender and sexuality in India indicates that although the female body is sexualized in aesthetic forms, women's own sexuality is valued only when it is safely contained within the boundaries of conjugality and serves a reproductive purpose. Women's experiences of their breasts enter the ethnographic record in discussions about breastfeeding and descriptions of the embarrassment adolescent girls feel as they develop breasts and go through puberty. Pubescent girls feel ashamed when their parents restrict their movement in public and force them to cover their breasts up with more clothing, and when their breasts draw the unwanted attention of strangers, who give them lewd looks and sexually harass them in public (known as "eve-teasing" in India). Jyoti Puri's ethnographic account of middle- and upper-class urban pubescent girls' embarrassment about their breasts provides this quote:

> Before marriage I used to feel very ashamed of my breasts. People are looking at you, passing comments. I used to get comments. But after the wedding I felt that I have such an asset. Before I was shy about them. In school I was very shy. "What are these people around me thinking?" Later you realize they are an asset for ladies.[20]

"Asset" is a highly utilitarian term that is not evocative of women's own pleasure. This woman seemed to be implying that women's breasts are useful within marriage because of the pleasure they give to their husbands or perhaps because of their use in breastfeeding. Although breasts can bring them pleasure personally, women view their breasts as an asset because they can strengthen bonds of marriage and family.

So it is not surprising that some women who had to undergo a mastectomy feared that their husbands would abandon them because the disfigurement from surgery would make them unattractive and unfeminine. This has long driven American oncologists' recommendations to their patients that they have breast reconstruction following a mastectomy, as revealed by a breast cancer survivor in Klawiter's study, who reported that her oncologist said, "You know, you really need to have reconstructive surgery. . . . I have seen many a marriage founder on the shoals of a mastectomy."[21] Women in my study were not just worried that their husbands would no longer find them attractive; they were also concerned that their parents-in-law would view a mastectomy as grounds to seek another wife for their son. In the Indian context, decisions surrounding marriage are typically diffused throughout extended family networks. A woman's parents-in-law, with whom she may be living, can play a key role in regulating her relationship with her husband.

Oncologists told me they had witnessed situations where husbands and in-laws had made women feel un-human after a mastectomy. One surgical oncologist explained [in English]:

If it is breast cancer and you have a mastectomy *that* is the most difficult thing a lady can have in this part of the country. When you have to lose your breast, people don't accept it. People look at you as though they are looking at some *thing*, not at a human being. People come to look at you for that alone. It puts the lady in an awful position. When I joined this hospital in the late 1980s, there was a lady who committed suicide because she had a mastectomy and she was not accepted in her husband's home. Thirty years back that was the situation. Now that is not so much the case. To some extent nowadays the lady is ready to say, "Ok, get lost. I am not bothered." But not in most situations because they have to live for the sake of their family, for the children. In India, even if the lady does not like the man, she lives with him until the children are married because they are the more important thing.

Another woman had counseled breast cancer survivors for more than three decades and provided prostheses to survivors. She knew women who faced abuse from their husbands after having a mastectomy but endured it for the sake of their children. This problem was so acute that she advised young unmarried women with mastectomies to avoid marriage all together. She explained [in English]:

> I am providing breast prostheses for two unmarried women who both had mastectomies when they were young. I tell them, "Don't get married. Work and enjoy life." If they do get married, they will have to have a "love marriage" because the other family won't accept an arranged marriage because the stigma of cancer is there. But I don't like them to get married at all after they have had breast cancer because I have seen many instances where a husband will taunt his wife about the loss of her breast. He will make her feel ugly and deformed and will threaten to leave her because of that. But a woman won't divorce. She will stay in the marriage for the sake of the children and she sacrifices and puts up with all of these taunts from her husband who makes her feel bad about not having a breast. Sometimes a husband will follow through with his threats to leave his wife if she gets cancer, though it is rare.

Some breast cancer survivors reported that they feared their husbands might shun or desert them because of their mastectomies but then found that their husbands were in fact supportive. In his study of cancer care in Delhi, Banerjee observed that a cancer diagnosis can strengthen family bonds *or* exacerbate preexisting rifts.[22] These competing tendencies operated in tandem for Akila as she navigated the complex social relations of her family after her cancer diagnosis and mastectomy. She was thirty-five years old when she underwent a mastectomy for breast cancer. She had had an inter-caste "love marriage" and said that while her own family was from an MBC community, her husband was from a Forward Caste and an economically and politically powerful community in Tamil Nadu. His family was wealthier and more highly educated than hers. According to Akila, this inter-caste marriage had caused more problems with her own kin than with her in-laws, whom she perceived as less concerned about caste status because they were more educated. Her own family felt that she was marrying above her standing and that she would look down on them now that she was a member of her husband's family. Her kin were always trying to sow seeds of doubt in her mind about her husband, claiming that he would eventually leave her. Akila attributed this to jealousy. It was from this vantage point that she interpreted her family's incessant comments that her husband would surely leave her because of her mastectomy. Yet in fact, her husband and in-laws went out of their way to care for her during her recovery.

Breasts are also useful for breastfeeding. None of the patients and survivors I met had undergone a mastectomy while they were breastfeeding. They already had as many children as they wanted, and most had already had a tubal ligation (or hysterectomy) as a permanent form of birth control. Some commented that having a mastectomy was not so devastating precisely because they did not expect to have more children to breastfeed. One thirty-nine-year-old woman on the general ward of the Cancer Institute who was waiting to have her mastectomy stated:

> I have two children and they are grown up. If I lose my breasts it is okay because I don't need to give them mother's milk. For me it is not so bad compared to other people who have to cut off a leg or who lose some vital organ. I do not need my breast anymore. It is not like an arm or a leg.

Further ethnographic research with women who were breastfeeding children or who still intended to have children when they had to undergo a mastectomy would be important to appreciate this experience and the ways in which women cope with that situation. My previous research with women in South India who were living with HIV/AIDS revealed how emotionally and socially agonizing it was for women to follow doctors' recommendations *not* to breastfeed in a cultural context in which breastfeeding is a central feature of motherhood and in which public health campaigns extol breastfeeding.[23] Furthermore, public health messages that promote breastfeeding to prevent breast cancer could compound fears about the recurrence of cancer among women who cannot breastfeed after a mastectomy.

Concerns about being sexually attractive to husbands and about being able to breastfeed their children touch on intimate experiences that women with mastectomies may have to negotiate. Yet the greatest challenge for women— especially middle-class women—regarding breast loss was how to avoid being seen without breasts in *public*—on the road, at work, or at a social function. Lakshmi summed this up [in English]: "If you don't have a breast, it is so very awkwardly visible, and people will stare at you so there is a lot of fear about that. It is very difficult for women socially." Jayanthi, who was thirty-two when she had her mastectomy, found that being seen in public without a breast at her age was particularly challenging. She said [in English]:

> I wear a prosthesis. Otherwise the abnormality is felt, no? And there is no need that I have to reveal this to each and every person on the road. I have to be confident and lead a normal life so definitely the prosthesis is required. Because it [the breast] is a part of you and it is gone. You have to accept that and then move on. But it's not that easy. Because losing your figure is not easy. I was totally upset. At first, I felt disfigured when I would go out and walk on the road. I thought: "How will I attend social functions like this?!" But with this [prosthesis], I feel confident when I go out. With this, women feel confident about going back to work, especially if they work in an office.

Jayanthi's comments reflect anxieties about the visibility of being "a mastectomee"[24] and the discourse of confidence achieved with a prosthesis that is central to the Reach to Recovery and Look Good Feel Better campaigns. Middle-class women experienced the visible absence of their breasts as an acute problem that required prostheses as a solution. Lower-class women were more likely to say this was not such a big issue, though they adjusted the way they wore their clothing in public.

## Managing Breast Loss across Class

Surgical breast reconstruction and silicone implants are rare in India except among the wealthy. The middle-class women I met used breast prostheses made of latex or cotton after a mastectomy. For years, middle-class breast cancer patients receiving treatment at the Cancer Institute have been advised to go to Naidu Hall, a well-known women's clothing store in Chennai, to get a special bra and cotton prosthesis. Many do so. But some complained that purchasing these items in a store was too awkward and embarrassing because of the public nature of the experience, with other customers overhearing and watching the sales transaction.

There was a network of middle-class cancer survivors who had received treatment at the Cancer Institute and who continued to return to the hospital as volunteers to provide psychological support to patients undergoing treatment. They had located a new mail-order source in Delhi for their prostheses and bras. This was more satisfactory because of the fit and feel of the products and also because of the privacy it allowed when buying them. For Padma, "This was a boon. It was a blessing. I feel much more confident."

I traveled to Delhi to meet Mira, the woman who was supplying these prostheses to women in Chennai. Mira was a warm, wealthy, elderly breast cancer survivor. When she had been diagnosed with cancer and had a mastectomy in 1980, no prostheses were available to her. So she had made it her mission to help other women avoid suffering the same indignities of being visibly breast-less as she had encountered after her surgery. In the mid-1990s she participated in a Reach to Recovery training program to lend support to other breast cancer patients, eventually starting an NGO for this work. She showed me her Certificate of Achievement from Reach to Recovery International, along with numerous other certificates for her work that she kept together in a file. Laughing loudly, she said, "These are all of my achievements thanks to my breast cancer!" Mira explained [in English] why she thought wearing a prosthesis was essential for women:

> For any woman who is going out of the home, the prosthesis is a must. In India most women are working. We are very advanced now. And it is important for women to look normal and respectable. When a woman wears the prosthesis, she feels she is a full woman. You should look like a full woman. Old ladies and poor, uneducated women don't bother. But, to be respectable, a woman must wear a prosthesis when she goes out of the house.

For Mira, having a breasted form was not only important for women's sense of femininity, it was also a crucial ingredient of middle-class respectability for women.

Mira was supplying latex prostheses and cotton bras to middle-class breast cancer survivors throughout India to help them feel more confident moving about in public as well as more comfortable, in that they could buy these goods in a discreet way. She and the network of women in Chennai who were using her products also claimed that there were "health benefits" to wearing a prosthesis. I could appreciate that wearing the prosthesis helped women have a better body image and feel comfortable being seen in public, but I wondered whether there actually were "health benefits" to wearing a prosthesis. Mira and others attributed a range of problems to not doing so: pinched nerves of the remaining breast, neck and shoulder pain, hunchback, and loss of balance. Yet it seemed that health benefits were being touted to encourage women to wear prostheses when the real reason these products were being promoted was for them to meet societal expectations about what "respectable" women's bodies should look like. The values promoted through such programs as Reach to Recovery and Look Good Feel Better prevail among middle-class women in India even if the sociocultural context in which they operate may differ somewhat from that of women in the United States.

The latex prostheses and bras supplied by Mira were more affordable for middle-class women than either imported silicone prostheses and bras or breast implants and reconstructive surgery; for lower-class women, they presented a significant cost. Padma acknowledged that breast cancer patients in the general wards of the Cancer Institute who came from lower-class and -caste communities and were receiving medical care for free through subsidies were not purchasing the prostheses: "Right now the lower-classes still cannot afford it. For them medicine is more important than their image."

When I asked lower-class women who had had mastectomies whether they felt the need to manage the social stigma of not having a breast, they gave short, pat responses that they were not particularly bothered about the loss of their breasts and that they did not worry too much if people noticed it because what mattered was that they had survived for the sake of their children. They added that it was easy to drape their saris in such a way that the missing breast was not visible. Those women who had a mastectomy of the left breast felt especially confident that it was not noticeable under their sari since they could drape the end of the sari fully and loosely over their left shoulder, completely covering the left side of their chest. A mastectomy on the right side posed more of a problem since the sari is usually pulled up tightly along the edge of the right breast. But even that could be finessed by adding extra pleats to the sari on the right side and letting it hang a bit loose. Women demonstrated these sari techniques to me as they explained the simple adjustments they made. Furthermore, the cotton "jacket" (short-cut blouse) that women wear under the sari was convenient for managing the loss of a breast. With a tight-fitting jacket, they did not need to wear a bra at all, and the empty side of the blouse would lie flat and would not show under the sari in the same way that an empty bra-cup would show through a shirt.

They told me that women who wear *salwar kameez*[25] outfits—as I usually do in India—could also easily cover up the missing breast by draping the accompanying *duppata* (loose scarf) low and loose across the chest. They tugged gently down on my *dupatta* to show me how I would need to wear it to do the trick.

Although lower-class women claimed not to be bothered about visibility of their missing breasts, it was clear that they did in fact strategize how to manage this simply and without cost, and they felt that Indian clothing was particularly convenient for such purposes. When girls go through puberty in India and as they become mature adult women, they are usually required to wear clothing that covers up their bodies. A key component of this sartorial change is wearing two layers of loose cloth over their breasts to hide the contours so that their breasts are not visible. This is done to promote modesty and prevent unwanted sexual advances and is an important symbol of women's respectability. Both the sari with accompanying "jacket" and the *salwar kameez* with accompanying *duppata* ensure this double layering of loose cloth over women's breasts. The cultural practice that allows women to be discreet about their emerging sexuality and femininity is the very same one that allows women to be discreet about what they fear will be interpreted as the *loss* of their sexuality and femininity after a mastectomy.

Older, lower-class women seemed blasé about how they looked after losing their breasts, except that it could make people wonder if they had had cancer. A sixty-year-old Dalit woman stated:

> I don't need to do anything with my sari to try to hide this. I am not worried about that. If people ask me why I am missing this thing [her breast], I tell them that I had a lump [*katti*] so I had my breast removed but that it was not that kind of a lump [i.e., not malignant]. I am old and no longer menstruating so it doesn't matter that I don't have a breast.

The implication here is that once women have gone through menopause and are no longer in their reproductive years, their breasts are no longer imbued with the cultural values of fertility and sexuality. It is difficult to determine whether older women were genuinely not concerned about the loss of their breasts or whether the utilitarian argument that they were not bothered because their breasts were no longer of use to them was another way to cope with their feelings of loss, as Waleska De Araújo Aureliano[26] suggests was the case with elderly working-class women in northeastern Brazil.

CHEMOTHERAPY

*Cultural Significance of Hair Loss in Tamil Nadu*

Women felt the loss of their breasts as a social and emotional challenge, but it was the loss of their hair that they worried about the most. They felt it to be the most traumatic aspect of their cancer treatments. Jayanthi explained [in English]:

> I had forty radiations and six chemo treatments, a mastectomy, and an oopho-rectomy. After the first chemotherapy, I lost all my hair. I went through so many physical changes. But of all these deformities, I was completely taken aback by losing my hair. I had very long hair before it fell out. I had to explain to my young children why I had lost my hair. That was the most pathetic part of it; they had to understand [she begins crying quietly].

Others recalled the sense of impending doom about hair loss that they and their family felt when they were first presented with the breast cancer diagnosis. Lakshmi recalled:

> A biopsy showed I had a "Stage II breast cancer. Malignant." It was such a "psy-chological shock." My brother who had taken me to the hospital began to cry. Why did he cry? Because with cancer I would have to take "chemo" and I would lose all of my beautiful hair. I was so scared; I cried too. I had such beautiful hair.

On a few occasions, husbands were present during my interviews. They were usually silent while their wives recounted their journeys with cancer. Yet when the conversation turned to the issue of hair loss, they always chimed in, such as one husband who said: "I felt bad about that more than anything else! She had such long, thick hair!"

Doctors and counselors who treated cancer patients understood women's deep concerns about hair loss in the Indian and Tamil cultural context. One oncologist explained [in English],

> As far as India is concerned, hair is the most important thing for women. They are very, very particular about grooming their hair. You need to have flowers in your hair. Your flower is the most important thing as far as Tamil Hindu culture is concerned. If a lady is married and her husband is alive and she wants him to be with her until the end, she needs to have this thing [she points to her *pottu/ bindi* on her forehead], and the flowers in her hair, and the bangles on her arms. These are the three things that a lady needs. Once she loses those things, people will assume that she has lost her husband. Once she loses her hair, she cannot wear the flowers. Then it will seem as though she has lost her husband. It is because

many years back—sixty, seventy years back—when the husband died, they would tonsure [shave off all the hair] the lady. That was a ritual in a certain community. That is why women don't want to lose their hair. That is what is in their minds when they lose their hair from the chemotherapy. Today it is in the minds of ladies from all communities. Once the husband died, they tonsured the widow and she became inauspicious so whenever they see a lady who is tonsured, they feel she is an inauspicious widow.

When mentioning "a certain community," this doctor was referring to the Brahmin caste. These Hindu rituals of widowhood, including shaving a woman's hair, were associated with Brahmins. Based on his analysis of ancient Tamil literature, George Hart has argued that this practice originated in South Indian Dravidian societies and predates the Indo-Aryan civilization; but Brahmins later adopted and enforced this practice strictly so that it came to be associated with them.[27] Lamb[28] and Patrick Olivelle[29] argue that during the colonial and post-independence eras in India, widows were considered inauspicious and impure because of their association with the death of their husbands and thus with the antithesis of fertility and life. In high-caste communities, widows were sometimes prevented from remarrying, even if they were still young. Over time, these ideas were emulated and practiced by other caste communities as well. Due to their perceived inauspiciousness, widows may be shunned, as well as barred from participating in auspicious life cycle events such as weddings and rituals associated with pregnancy and birth. Widows' experience of stigma and the restrictions on their activities have weakened during the twentieth and twenty-first centuries due to social movements that counter discrimination against widows. Nevertheless, the association between bald-headed women and the taint of widowhood persists.

In all societies, hair communicates social meanings. Anthropologists and others have analyzed symbolic meanings of hair and hair grooming cross-culturally and over time and contend that hair is universally associated with sexuality; in addition, rituals and customs surrounding hair grooming are related to social and religious mores regarding the expression and/or control of sexuality.[30] This has been documented in ethnographic accounts of South Asia.[31] Throughout South Asia, women's hair is associated with powerful sexuality and fertility. Women's sexuality is viewed as a positive force when properly channeled into reproduction within marriage, but it can also be dangerous when it escapes the bounds of conjugality. Similarly, women's hair should be tightly bound in public and should only be loosened in the private domain of the home and intimate relations with husbands. There is a cultural norm in South Asia for women to grow their hair as long as possible and to keep it combed and oiled, parted in the middle, and tightly braided in public. In some *seemantham* rituals for pregnant women that I observed in Tamil Nadu in the mid-1990s, the husband traced a porcupine quill along the part of his wife's hair to symbolize the opening of her vagina to facilitate a smooth birth.

Women's long hair is more than a symbol of sexuality and fertility; it also embodies and enhances sexuality and fertility. Women are thought to have more *sakti* (power associated with fertility and divine heat) than men.[32] Their long hair symbolizes their *sakti*; indeed, it imbues women with more *sakti*. Because a woman's hair represents and embodies her sexuality and fertility, some communities in India have shorn the hair of widows to represent the end of their sexual and reproductive years and to transform women's bodies in order to reduce their sexual heat, rendering them cool and asexual.[33] This is why Hindu ascetics may shave their hair as part of a rite of passage as they move from the status of a householder and member of society to that of a spiritual renouncer (*sanyasi*). Olivelle argues that the ritual shaving of hair among Hindus, be it of widows, or ascetics, or even criminals, publicly marks that individual as "excluded from the two central institutional spheres of society: the sexual and the economic." Thus, "shaving the head amounts to the ritual separation of an individual from society," and the shaven person is "placed outside the social structures and denied a social status and role."[34]

Women's long, braided hair is also a national symbol of traditional Indian culture and of India's superior morality, which is contrasted with Western modernity and immorality. Conflicts between tradition and modernity and the prerogative of Indian women to uphold tradition are represented dramatically and sometimes comically through women's hair and clothing styles in popular Indian films, novels, and other media.[35] Women with short and/or unbraided hair in Indian films are intriguing but ultimately unreliable, overly individualistic, and not suitable for marriage and family life. Although shorter hairstyles for women are becoming more acceptable in major cities in India, they remain rare in most rural areas and in lower-class communities. Also, it is less common to see women with short hairstyles in metropolitan cities in South India than in the North, and the prerogative for women to wear flowers in their braided hair is a distinctly South Indian practice.

The loss of hair for women—particularly a bald head—is also a sign of illness. Today it is increasingly interpreted as a tell-tale sign that someone is undergoing chemotherapy for cancer, a fact that people do not want to publicize. When I asked a patient in the Government Cancer Hospital if she would tell people in her village about her cancer, she replied: "My bald head will speak for itself. They will not have to ask me." Rachana, a seventy-two-year-old woman who had been treated for cervical cancer, expressed the extent to which women worry that their visibly bald heads would lead others to suspect they had cancer. She was immensely relieved that she did not need chemotherapy and would not be losing her hair:

> If you take "chemo," you lose your hair, and that loss of hair makes you look different. People fear that. But I did not need "chemo," so I don't look like a patient. Can you tell I have cancer? When you lose your hair, it is obvious that you are a patient. That you've lost your hair means you have cancer so your disease becomes obvious and then everyone knows. One couldn't tell I was sick. My children made sure that I did not look or feel sick.

Most of the breast cancer patients and survivors I met did experience hair loss and spoke about how emotionally painful this was, particularly when they were in public. Lakshmi explained:

> See, women never go bald. Have you ever heard of women going bald? You have seen men going bald. But not women. Every Friday, women take a bath and wash their hair and put *kum kum* [red powder placed at the center of the forehead and sometimes at the start of the part of the hair]. That is Tamil culture. You need to wear flowers in your hair to go to the temple on Friday. That is all "psychological." You can't go to the temple with no hair! People will comment. It is because of this "social pressure." That is why women like to have hair. If you are the only one without hair, people stare at you and wonder if you have this thing [cancer]. That is very embarrassing. Your prestige [*kauravam*] will be reduced.

There was intense anxiety about the visibility of one's cancer. Women feared that a bald head would make their cancer visible. People worried that their illness or the illness of a family member would become known publicly and negatively impact their prestige. Illness is a sign of weakness that reduces one's prestige in the community. This is particularly so for cancer because it is a dreaded disease that is assumed to be fatal, is sometimes thought to be contagious or hereditary, and is associated with immoral behavior. Cancer affects not just the patient's prestige but that of the entire family and may make it difficult to arrange respectable marriage partners for younger members, especially young women. To manage the stigma they face, cancer patients and their families go to great lengths to render cancer invisible.

*Management of Hair Loss across Class*

There were differing strategies for managing the visibility of hair loss from chemotherapy based on socioeconomic class. Middle-class women relied on wigs and cosmopolitan short hairstyles; lower-class women found creative ways to use South Indian Hindu forms of worship involving head shaving to their advantage.

Medical staff and counselors at the Cancer Institute recommended wigs for women who had hair loss from chemotherapy. They referred patients to a nearby store in Adyar called Hair and Care to purchase wigs. Middle-class women generally followed these recommendations and wore these wigs when they went out in public. Some made a point of wearing them in front of their young children at home to protect them from the shock of seeing their mothers bald and from the fear that such an abnormality might induce in children. Women cancer patients from other parts of the world similarly talk about the need to protect other people's feelings by wearing a wig. A Danish woman in Helle Hansen's research stated, "You care for others by wearing a wig and makeup, and I didn't want to remind people of death."[36]

The middle-class women cancer survivors who participated in the network of volunteer counselors to give courage to cancer patients at the Cancer Institute would console women and tell them not to worry about losing their hair because it would grow back. They advised patients to wear wigs in the interim. One of these women had kept a photo of herself when she was bald from the time when she was a patient undergoing chemotherapy. She would show that photo to patients in the hospital and then she would point to her hair in its current state, which was long and thick and neatly tied in a braid. Using this visual before and after comparison of her own hair, she could demonstrate to patients that she was living proof that hair loss is temporary. Alison MacDonald's[37] research about breast cancer survivors volunteering in public hospitals in Mumbai to provide hope to cancer patients indicated a similar emphasis on the power of visually embodying the potential for being cured of cancer. What was interesting to me was that what mattered most in Tamil Nadu was the visual image of women's hair.

Meenakshi stressed the importance of hiding her hair loss at work. Like other middle-class women I met, she had stopped working for over a year while she was undergoing her cancer treatments. When she finished her treatments and began to look for work again, she was faced with what she considered a double stigma of being too old to join a job—at the age of thirty-seven—combined with her cancer history. She explained [in English]: "Nobody employs a person at that age, especially if they know you had a history of some physical ailment like cancer; it's impossible to get a job then." Larger companies with human resources departments required that she provide her medical history, and they had mandatory medical checkups, so she decided to only look for jobs at smaller companies where this was not required. She chuckled as she told me this, pleased with herself for outsmarting the system, though clearly this system discriminated against cancer survivors like her.

Meenakshi had been bald for almost a year as a result of chemotherapy. She waited until her hair had been growing back for a few months before applying for jobs. At that point, her hair was still short by Tamil women's standards. However, since she was a middle-class woman engineer seeking employment in companies that required international travel, she was able to leverage her hair to her advantage or, at least, to pass without anyone intuiting that cancer was the reason for her short hair. She explained:

> My hair was very short when I started applying for a job. But they were thinking, "Okay, this lady has gone abroad and everything. That's why she's into this kind of haircut." They were thinking, "She looks very modern." They didn't have any thoughts like, "She must have undergone treatment and so her hair is growing in after that." They didn't have any thoughts like that so luckily, my hair was not a big issue.

Although she concludes that "hair was not a big issue," she was extremely conscious of her hair as a potential barrier to getting a job. It was only because of her class status and the nature of the industry in which she was seeking work that she felt she could pass as normal with her short hair, all the while thinking she had fooled them by keeping her status as a recent cancer patient hidden.

Having a short, modern, foreign-looking haircut was not a boon for lower-class and -caste women in Tamil Nadu, who were expected to subscribe to the traditional long hairstyle. Nor were wigs a viable option for the lower-class women I met, both because of the cost and because they were engaged in manual labor, either agricultural labor in rural areas or work carrying rocks on construction sites or cleaning houses in urban areas. Even their unpaid domestic labor was physically demanding—handwashing clothes while bent over an open water spigot or beating clothes on the banks of a river. They often had to carry heavy loads on top of their heads, such as plastic jugs filled with water or metal bowls filled with rocks. A wig would not reliably stay in place as they performed such tasks. Furthermore, women said it would be too hot to wear a wig while engaging in physical labor, particularly if they were out in the sun. They too felt it was demeaning and embarrassing to be seen in public with a bald head. There was, however, a clever solution to their predicament.

In South Indian forms of popular Hinduism, women often make vows to a deity, offering to shave their hair and donate it at the temple of a god or goddess if the deity grants their wish and protects them. This practice is more widespread among lower-class and -caste communities and is a South Indian practice that it not commonly found in North India. Making a vow to shave your hair for a deity is not taken lightly. It is something women do only in dire circumstances, for example, if their lives or those of family members are at stake. Women may make such a vow when their own lives are threatened by cancer.

In everyday forms of Hindu *puja* worship, there is an exchange between the devotee and the deity. This consists of offering respect as well as flowers or money to a deity as if to an honored guest.[38] In turn, the devotee receives *prasad* (grace) from the deity in the form of such things as sacred ash, *kum kum*, sacred water, or sometimes *paan* and sweets given by the god (via a priest, in a temple context). On special occasions, devotees may give larger, more lavish offerings, such as coconuts, flower garlands, or large lotus flower stalks. One of the loftier reasons for *puja* is to "achieve identity" between the deity and the worshipper.[39] Although some dismiss or criticize the notion that *puja* may also be practiced in the interests of pragmatic bargaining with the gods for favors, in fact, this is often a central goal of *puja* in the minds of many devotees.[40] The expectation is that if one is conscientious about performing *puja* regularly, and shows utmost respect, the gods and goddesses will protect you. If one falls short in devotion, the deities may demonstrate their wrath by causing misfortune to fall upon you or your community. Illness, including cancer, may be interpreted this way as a punishing misfortune caused by the lack of protection of a deity who is not satisfied with your level or sincerity of devotion. People may feel compelled to offer a sacrifice to the gods to demonstrate the magnitude of their devotion either for future protection or to fulfill a vow to the gods that have responded to their prayers for healing and health.

The ultimate sacrifice is life itself. In Tamil Nadu members of lower-caste, non-vegetarian communities may offer animals—chickens or goats—as a sacrifice to non-Brahminical, non-vegetarian gods and goddesses, or they may offer to undergo painful, ecstatic public austerities with their own bodies, such as doing the *kavadi attam* (burden dance) or piercing one's body. They may also offer to shave off their hair and donate it to the deities. Women's long hair is considered a sacrifice to the gods because it is associated with life force—it is imbued with *sakti*, a sacred power of sexuality, fertility, and heat. When a woman offers her long hair to the gods, this is experienced as a penance because it deprives the devotee of her *sakti* and of her sexuality, thus temporarily removing her central social role and placing her outside of society.

Based on his analysis of Brahminical texts, Olivelle discusses Hindu head-shaving in the context of "penitential separation," in which a person who is undergoing a vow as penance and is separated from society will shave prior to the penance. He argues that this is done because "sins become lodged in the hair" and a "person who wishes to expiate sins should shave the hair."[41] In South India, however, hair is not simply shaved prior to enacting penance. Women shave their heads and offer their hair to the gods as an act of penance itself. Women who offer their hair to the gods as fulfillment of a vow perceive their hair as something of great value and full of *sakti*, rather than reviling it as an embodiment of sin. When women offer their hair to the gods, it is considered a great sacrifice and is experienced by women as a deprivation of the power of their fertility and a loss of their identity as women. When we consider the religious and cultural significance of the donation of women's hair to the gods as a great sacrifice, it clarifies why the loss of hair women experience from chemotherapy is traumatic.

Lower-class and -caste cancer patients whom I met made such vows to deities, offering to travel to the deity's temple to donate their hair if they were cured. As Parimala explained:

> I have promised to shave my head. I have promised to drop money in the money box [*undiyal*] in the Mariamman temple in my village. I have promised to give one hundred rupees. I have promised to sacrifice a goat and a chicken. If I get well, I will shave my head, sacrifice a goat, sacrifice a chicken, and put one hundred rupees into the money box. And I have promised to wear the garland and walk on the fire at the temple for the goddess in Melmaruvathur for every year that I am alive. I have always believed in such things. If not for this, we would not have survived, suffering so much, without work or food in this Kali Yuga.

Women like Parimala made such vows out of deep conviction that deities possessed healing powers. Typically, people make a vow to offer something to a deity once they (or their loved ones) have been cured, and this was the practice followed by some of the cancer patients I met. Several had donated their hair this way to Mariamman at local shrines and temples in the towns and villages where they lived. One woman from a village in Salem district had returned to the hospital when her cancer recurred after two years of remission. When she was discharged from the hospital after the first round of treatments, her family fulfilled a vow by sacrificing a goat and donating *pongal* rice to Mariamman. This time, she had vowed to shave her hair for Mariamman if she survived her cancer recurrence. She explained, "If you tell Mariamman you are willing to give her your hair if you are cured, then she will help you to get well. If a woman prays and offers to shave her hair and give it to Amman [the goddess], she can get cured."

This practice was also a convenient way for women to manage the stigma of the visibility of their hair loss from chemotherapy. It served as a cover for the shame they felt when they lost their hair in that way. Women discussed this strategy with one another when they were inpatients in the general wards of the hospitals. Medical staff and counselors at the hospitals sometimes recommended this as well. In such instances, women took a more flexible approach to the sequencing of the vow. Often, they would shave their hair for a deity as soon as their hair began to fall out from the chemotherapy treatments rather than wait until they could be considered cancer-free. Tharani, a thirty-nine-year-old Dalit woman from Villupuram district who did daily wage labor making bricks for a living, exemplified this strategy. During my interview with her while she was an inpatient on the general ward of the Cancer Institute, she said,

> I had chemotherapy and I lost all my hair. After three injections, I looked bald. I lost all of my hair everywhere. Not just the hair on my head. First, I just let it fall. But other women on the ward with me told me they got their head shaved before their hair began to fall so I also got my head shaved. I did it at a temple in Chengalpattu because my children are working there. I went and gave my hair to that temple and came back to this hospital. It was a Murugan temple but I was thinking of Venkateswara in Tirupati. In my heart/mind [*manasu*], I dedicated my hair to Venkateswara.

Venkateswara is a form of Visnu and is the god who presides in the large temple in Tirupati in Andhra Pradesh, just over the border from Tamil Nadu. This temple is famous as a place to go to fulfill major vows, and many cancer patients and survivors I met said that they kept Lord Venkateswara in their hearts/minds when they offered their hair, even if most of them could not actually make the pilgrimage to Tirupati. In actuality, they usually reported that they had gone to either a Mariamman or Murugan temple to have their hair shaved. Some women shaved their hair at home while thinking of god and saved their cut hair in a braid for a time when they were healthier and could travel to Tirupati to donate the hair. In a bizarre twist of globalization, women's hair that is donated to fulfill all sorts of vows at Tirupati—including but not limited to these vows of cancer patients—is exported to the United States and elsewhere to make hair weaves and wigs for women—including for women cancer patients experiencing chemotherapy-induced hair loss.

Several women confided that although they had devotion for gods and goddesses and believed in the value of offering their hair, the main reason they had shaved their hair at a temple was so that they would have a legitimate excuse for being bald; this would prevent other people from surmising that they were bald because they had cancer. Puniamma had been able to offer her hair to Venkateswara in Tirupati because she came from a nearby village. She explained that because everyone in her family had gone together and they had all offered their hair to Venkateswara, "people in our village won't ask about why I am bald when everyone in my family will be that way."

A few women said they had completely lost confidence in gods and goddesses when they were diagnosed with cancer: they had always been good and had prayed regularly, yet the deities had betrayed them by not protecting them from this disease. In two such instances, women had shaved their hair at home, without praying to the gods, but then told others they had offered their hair to the deities since this was a valid explanation for their baldness. Middle-class women found it necessary to purchase wigs to hide their balding heads; some lower-class Hindu women in Tamil Nadu used religion as a cover instead.

## CONCLUSION

Cancer wreaks havoc on the bodies and on the social lives of those who suffer from it. Moreover, the three most common forms of biomedical treatment for cancer—radiation, surgery, and chemotherapy—cause excruciating physical and psychosocial pain. For cervical and breast cancer patients, these treatments have been increasingly successful at saving people's lives, particularly if the cancer is detected and treated early. Yet the effects of the treatments for these two cancers pose unique social and psychological challenges to women around the world because of how they transform parts of women's bodies that carry heavy symbolic weight within cultural systems of gender and sexuality.

This chapter has demonstrated that how women think about these different treatment modalities, how they experience them, and how they cope with the physical and psychosocial fallout of treatments for these reproductive cancers is context-specific and far from universal. Being attuned to how women articulate their experiences as reproductive cancer patients can provide insights for medical practitioners, counselors, and policymakers who are tending to the growing numbers of cancer patients in India. Listening to Tamil women describe their encounters with cancer treatments also reveals much about the broader sociocultural context of South India in the early twenty-first century and about how women make sense of and navigate the social worlds they inhabit.

People's decisions about treatment modalities are informed by the conceptual frameworks through which they understand cancer causality. In addition to viewing cancer as a biological disease that should be treated through biomedical interventions, the lower-class and -caste women I met in Tamil Nadu contemplated whether deities and spirits may have played a role in causing their cancer and whether these entities could help heal them. As we will see in the next chapter, women often sought help through the religious realm and from biomedicine simultaneously. They did so for therapeutic reasons and to mitigate the stigma of immorality associated with their cancer.

# CHAPTER 7

# Sorcery and Religion

Panjalai, the RUWSEC community health worker who took her dying mother around to multiple hospitals for treatments, told us she believed her mother died of late-stage cervical cancer due to biological processes.[1] But, she added, many of her relatives and neighbors hinted that it might have been karmic punishment for immoral behavior. Her sister Roja suspected that their mother's illness and death was caused by a ghost sent via sorcery.

In order to be out of earshot from her husband and neighbors in the Dalit section of her village, we followed Panjalai along raised footpaths dividing neon paddy fields to an open area with two cremation pyre platforms side-by-side. Panjalai explained that the fully constructed cremation platform had been there for years and was used by higher-caste people in the village, who consider themselves to be ritually purer than Dalits. Dalit villagers like herself had been strictly prohibited from using the old pyre and were forced to burn their dead in the surrounding scrubland. This was because a central aspect of Hindu death rituals involves carefully managing the impurity associated with death.[2] Those who subscribe to the ideology of caste consider Dalits to be inherently impure; thus, higher-caste villagers viewed their presence in the form of a corpse and of family members involved in death rituals as dangerously polluting. Angered by this caste discrimination, Dalits in the village raised funds to build their own funeral pyre, which was still under construction at the time of our interview. We settled in under the bit of shade afforded by the cement roof over the new platform, and Panjalai shared her experiences as both a community health worker promoting cancer screening camps in nearby villages and as a daughter who had cared for her ailing mother in her final days. She was dismissive of her sister's fears of sorcery and ghosts; nevertheless, it was unsettling that we were having this conversation at the cremation ground, precisely the site where ghosts are thought to linger. Perhaps her choice to sit there was a further assertion of her lack of concern about ghosts and a way to prove she was not superstitious. More importantly, it was a sign of the extreme stigma of cervical cancer for Dalit women and their families, given that Panjalai felt compelled to take me to this most marginalized of all spaces in order to speak privately of her mother's plight.

Panjalai impressed upon us the importance of early detection through cervical cancer screening. She explained that most women in this region, including her mother, do not complain openly about their physical symptoms or seek treatment until the disease reaches an advanced stage, primarily because women put the needs of others—especially their children and husbands—first, and neglect their own needs. But it was also due to concerns about the cost of treatment and lost wages from time spent seeking healthcare, to feelings of embarrassment associated with women's reproductive health, and to assumptions that white discharge is a normal part of menopause. According to Panjalai, all of these factors had dissuaded her mother from seeking help when she first began having white discharge. It was not until the discharge was so heavy that she was changing sanitary pads as frequently as if she were menstruating and the foul odor from the discharge became too strong to hide and the pain became impossible to bear that she informed Panjalai of her problem and Panjalai began taking her to various doctors, from whom they received mixed messages and unsuccessful treatments.

Having witnessed the devastating physical, financial, emotional, and social suffering that cervical cancer can cause while she was supporting her mother during her final days, Panjalai asserted that cancer screening for early detection is of paramount importance. Though she did not know what exactly caused her mother to get cancer, she fully accepted the biomedical explanation that cancer is the result of biochemical processes that lead to uncontrollable proliferation of cells in the human body. She considered cancer to be an *odambu noi*—a "body disease"—caused by physiological factors. She viewed it as a disease that if detected early can be cured by biomedicine.

Others, however, felt that a specific cancer episode may be karmic retribution for an immoral act committed in the past (including in a past life). Or it could be due to a malignant ghost sent by another person through sorcery to cause harm. Or it could be divine punishment for neglecting the gods, or even a result of the negligence of the gods themselves. Many believed it important to determine whether such occult forces had played a role in causing someone to get cancer or whether it was an *odambu noi* caused solely by physiological processes.

The conceptualization of "the body" as it relates to the diagnosis of cancer as an *odambu noi* in Tamil Nadu needs clarification. As discussed earlier, multiple systems of medical knowledge about the body coexist, including biomedicine, Ayurveda, Siddha, homeopathy, and "country medicine" (*nattu marundu*). When people asserted that cancer was an *odambu noi* and not a disease caused by forces beyond the body—referred to in hushed tones as *vera madiri noi* (another kind of disease)—they considered it to be a disease that required biomedical treatment and perhaps also the modulation of the hot/ cold balance associated with Ayurveda and Siddha. Although I interviewed practitioners of other systems of medicine who had treated cancer patients,[3] I did not meet or hear of anyone who used other medical systems as their sole mode of treatment for cancer, and some used biomedicine exclusively.

Determining whether an illness was an *odambu noi* or a *vera madiri noi* was necessary in order to know how best to proceed with therapeutic interventions to heal the afflicted person. Women in my study did not feel they had much agency to change the socioeconomic structures of their lives that they thought had put them at risk for cancer, but most felt there were concrete steps they could take to respond if sorcery, ghosts, or unreliable deities were involved in causing this disease.

Members of Panjalai's family were rattled by the lack of a specific causal explanation for her mother's cervical cancer. In their understanding, illnesses associated with women's reproductive organs—glossed generally as "women's diseases" (*pombalai viyaadhi*)—are attributed to a woman's moral depravity, particularly her sexual promiscuity. Panjalai said they were bewildered:

> How could such a good woman get such a *pombalai viyaadhi*? Even with a handi-capped arm, she had spent her life taking care of her family and selling milk from the family cow for the children of other families in the neighborhood. And despite this, she had suffered such agonizing pain toward the end.

They felt that she was not the kind of woman who could possibly have deceived her husband by having an affair. In fact, they said, she was so honest that she never even added a drop of water to the milk she sold (a tactic used by unscrupulous people to add to the volume of milk and increase profits).

A few months after the death of Panjalai's mother, her family was offered an explanation that, even if distressing, quelled their initial shock and fear that people would assume that their mother had been immoral. A cousin told Panjalai's sister, Roja, that their mother's illness had been his doing and was the result of sorcery (*seyvinai*). The cousin made this claim when Roja moved into their mother's house after the death and helped her father manage their property. During this time, she discovered that this cousin—their father's brother's son—had illegally encroached on their lands and was building his house on what was her father's rightful property. When Roja confronted him, she learned that their mother had challenged him a few months before she was diagnosed with cancer. This cousin told Roja that her mother's cancer had been incurable because it had not been an *odambu noi*. It had been caused by sorcery performed at his behest to remove the mother from his path. Then he threatened Roja, telling her that if she interfered in his business, he would ensure that she would face a similar death. After that, Roja began to believe that cancer could be sent through sorcery. To find out for certain, she consulted with the local village *samiyar*, a medium for local goddesses and gods. When possessed by a deity, a *samiyar* can ascertain whether the family is a victim of sorcery and can provide instructions for escaping the hex. The *samiyar*'s verdict confirmed Roja's suspicion that sorcery was at play. As an NGO community health worker, Panjalai adamantly rejected this:

> After that, my sister has been scared. But I don't believe in it. In the medical report, it said "cancer," and we did everything we could. So, I think, "Let him brag! I don't believe it's true." But my sister thinks he did *seyvinai* on my mother, because my mother never recovered. Now he keeps threatening my sister that he will do something to her. She is afraid.

Unlike Panjalai and Roja, two sisters who were grappling with reasons for their mother's painful death, women who suffer from cancer themselves often do not choose between biomedical and spiritual ways of thinking about causality and treatment as separate frameworks. Even as women came to accept the biomedical explanation for their cervical and breast cancer as an *odambu noi* and took biomedical treatment to heal from the physical suffering caused by the disease, many turned to explore the role of sorcery, malicious ghosts and spirits (*pey pisasu*), and deities to understand the disease's causality. This was part of their attempts to heal physically from the cancer and to heal from the social, spiritual, and emotional suffering caused by it.

In this chapter, I explore how women in Tamil Nadu wove together biomedical understandings of cancer and spiritual and religious ideas as they sought explanations for their cancer as well as cures for it. The biomedical explanation—the overproduction of cells—appealed to Panjalai because it was scientific, but it failed to explain adequately *why* a particular person gets a particular disease. In turning to the possibility of the occult *and* to biomedicine for diagnosis and treatment, women with reproductive cancers were seeking not only to be healed but also to deflect assumptions about the immoral behaviors and individual "bad habits" associated with reproductive cancer. They were hoping to avoid the intense social stigma that such ideas entail. Assumptions that improper behavior could karmically result in illness were bolstered by moralizing public health messages about the etiology of reproductive cancers. In this way, moralizing public health discourses can inadvertently lead people to contemplate whether sorcery played a role in cancer.

Lower-class and -caste women often experience cancer as a biological, social, and spiritual affliction that can be cured only when biomedical treatments are complemented with religious and spiritual modalities of healing. These explanations of cancer causality and engagements with cancer treatments do not negate those discussed in previous chapters; rather, they add to the multidimensional layers of meaning that people attribute to cancer and expand our understanding of the social and cultural dimensions of the experience of cancer in South India.

This chapter also reveals how the intersection of class, caste, and gender affect women's religious practices and modes of worship in myriad ways. Belief in sorcery was deemed backward by middle-class society and public health practitioners. The predominantly lower-class and -caste women at the heart of this ethnography were, therefore, cautious about linking sorcery to their illness. They also had to contend with the absence of shrines to worship local Tamil deities such as Mariamman (either directly or through *samiyars*) within the space of the public and NGO hospitals, where more socially respectable forms of middle-class, upper-caste Hindu worship and yoga practice were available. When women speculated that they had been neglected by Hindu gods despite their lifelong devotion to those gods, they sometimes began praying to Jesus instead. The highly fluid nature of religious worship and tendencies toward conversion from Hinduism to Christianity in the face of calamity follow a long tradition of Christian conversion among Dalits in Tamil Nadu. In the twenty-first century, the Pentecostal church has come to play a particularly important role in lower-caste conversion and faith-healing in Tamil Nadu (and elsewhere). The majority of Pentecostal converts in the state are Dalit women.

Understanding all of these dynamics requires us to conjoin three well-developed approaches in medical anthropology that are typically not integrated in ethnographic analyses. The first is the analytic of "moral reasoning"[4] attributed to cancer diagnoses and the stigma and blame that ensues from such moral reasoning. Many have noted the gendering of such moral reasoning in the context of women's reproductive cancers. Second, following Evans-Pritchard's classic 1937 ethnography of magic and witchcraft in central Africa, medical anthropologists have explored how sorcery is leveraged to help explain why a particular person or family is afflicted with illness and to provide guidance for what can be done socially and spiritually in response.[5] These anthropologists argue that sorcery accusations can both reproduce and challenge the status quo of power relations. Third, medical anthropologists have shown that for many people around the world, religious and medical healing are not separate systems of knowledge and practice.[6] Anthropologists have documented such religio-medical healing practices in South Asia.[7] I suggest it is necessary to combine these three frames of analysis in order to understand the decisions that lower-class and -caste Tamil women make as they seek explanations for their cancer and take measures to be healed.

## CANCER AND SORCERY

People used several Tamil words interchangeably to refer to sorcery, including *seyvinai*, *suniyam*, and *manthirivaatham*.[8] A key component of this sorcery is *kuri*. As a noun, *kuri* can be translated as mark, target, or aim.[9] It can refer to a negative outcome from malicious acts of sorcery. In these cases, the cancer itself was the *kuri*. People also use the term as a verb—as the act of marking or taking aim at the victim, as if at a target, with black magic. Sometimes they use the term as a verb when referring to processes of divination and prognostication carried out by ritual specialists, who are adept at detecting present traces of past acts of malicious sorcery, including malicious spirits sent via sorcery. Finally, *kuri* can refer to the *samiyar*'s role in aiming the afflicted person in a direction that will provide redress for the affliction.[10] These ritual specialists are sometimes referred to as *kurikarihal* (if female) or *kurikarar* (if male).[11] My interlocutors referred to them as *samiyars* ("god persons"), whether they were male or female (even though grammatically the term is masculine) and regardless of whether they become possessed by male or female deities.

Through outreach awareness camps in low-income communities and through mass media campaigns, governmental and nongovernmental organizations work to debunk what they view as irrational, superstitious, and backward beliefs about cancer and to introduce what they assert are more rational, scientific, modern ways of thinking about cancer in order to encourage people to visit hospitals for screening and treatment. These discourses of modernity and development have been a cornerstone of public health programs in India since colonial times. The idea that sorcery could be a cause and counter-sorcery a cure for cancer is one of the "superstitious" beliefs that public health educators attempt to combat.

So it was not surprising that Panjalai and other community health workers and medical practitioners were dismissive of claims of sorcery associated with cancer. In my initial meeting with members of the RUWSEC community outreach team for healthcare, they reported that many people in their communities held such beliefs. They laughed out loud as they accused some *samiyars* of duping unwitting and vulnerable people into shelling out money for their services. They described one *samiyar* in a nearby village who sits in his *kuri meydai* (a consultation platform for *samiyars*), watching out to see if anyone is coming down the road. When he sees someone approaching, he will go into a possession as a show for the passerby. They considered him a charlatan, putting on an act to make himself look like he had become possessed by god. They explained that a *samiyar's kuri meydai* is like a business that works by referral, and they likened this business to the work of lawyers and private doctors, who also profit from people's misfortune. One woman explained:

> This is like a business. If someone has a problem, that person will look for a place they trust already and a place that others have recommended. Just like how a lawyer has a "set-up" where he consults cases, the *samiyar* has a similar place, which can actually be scary! If the problem is big, it costs more, just like when we go to a lawyer or a doctor. If we go to a doctor for tablets, we pay one fee; for a caesarean, we pay something else. If we get a caesarean and if that leads to another caesarean later, then that also costs more money, no? The doctors may recommend a cesarean knowing that they can charge a lot. This is like that. The expenditure can be very high. The *samiyar* will ask you to buy various things that you need in order to fol-

low his instructions and you also have to give a fee to the *samiyar* for his service. It is like giving a doctor his fee. Sometimes all of this can be very expensive. It can cost 15,000 rupees, or 50,000 rupees. It can even cost one lakh [100,000] rupees! People will figure out how much it will cost for the *samiyar* and what they will need to save for that just as they do for a doctor or a lawyer. People are willing to spend that money for the *kuri meydai* just as they are willing to spend money for a doctor because they have the belief [*nambikai*] that it will work.

Although they were critical of exploitative biomedical doctors, they did not question the efficacy of biomedicine itself. Much of their work involved encouraging women to seek biomedical care. On the other hand, they characterized all *samiyars* as quacks and all those who consult them as foolish and unmodern.

When I raised the issue of sorcery and its role in cancer in group discussions among low-income communities, women would look around to see how others would respond first. Following an awkward moment of silence, one or two women would speak up and say that although people in *their* village or neighborhood did not lend credence to such superstitious beliefs, people in *other* nearby communities did believe such things. Middle-class, upper-caste cancer patients said they did not believe in such things and that these were only ideas to which uneducated, rural people subscribe. Several of the lower-class and -caste women with little or no formal education were also unequivocal in their disbelief of such ideas. Renukha was a thirty-four-year-old cervical cancer patient in the general ward of the Cancer Institute. She had dropped out of school while still a child to do daily wage labor as a sweeper and a fruit-picker in her village. She stated succinctly, "I don't believe in anything like that. Diseases happen to humans but they are not caused by other humans."

In other instances, people conceded that sorcery and malignant ghosts did pose a danger but that only some kinds of affliction were caused by sorcery and cancer was not one of them. They distinguished between a bodily disease (*odumbu noi*) caused by physiological causes and "another kind of disease" (*vera madiri noi*); the latter could be caused by black magic used in sorcery or by a haunting ghost. One woman explained,

> If something like this [cancer] happens in our body, then you don't go to the samiyar. If it is something caused by an evil spirit [*pisasu*], then it will happen very suddenly, then you can call upon the samiyar. But for these body illnesses [*odambu noi*], you are the god [*sami*].

It is not clear exactly what she meant by her comment, "you are the god." In this context, it seems to suggest that the cause for cancer lies within the individual's body, not in the spiritual realm. In such instances, the afflicted person should only seek a biomedical diagnosis and treatment. In this vein, several other people said that it is only when something happens very suddenly and dramatically to someone—particularly if they feel a sudden sensation of dizziness and cognitive confusion—that sorcery and spirits may be culprits. Diseases that develop gradually in the body, such as cancer, would not be attributed to sorcery.

Still others were on the fence about the role of sorcery in cancer causality. Those who were uncertain whether sorcery could be a factor did not rule it out, for if sorcery was the source of this affliction, they would need to take measures to address it in order to heal and to prevent further misfortunes. For such people, if a member of their family were to get cancer, they would consult a *samiyar* to determine whether sorcery and malignant ghosts and spirits (*pey pisasu*) were involved and would insist on following the instructions of the *samiyar*; they would not want to later regret that they had not done everything possible to save the person.

Despite the allegations of backwardness associated with the belief in sorcery, many lower-class and -caste cancer patients and survivors said they had considered the possibility that sorcery had played a role in causing their illness, and they tried to ascertain whether it had been a factor in their disease. Where the visit to the *samiyar* fit into the "hierarchy of resort"[12] as they sought out various explanations and treatment modalities in this medically plural context might vary. Most patients who included *samiyars* in the therapeutic repertoire said they first went to the hospital, then consulted a *samiyar* while awaiting the test results, then back to the hospital for treatment, then back to the *samiyar* after they got out of hospital.

Roja was open to considering her cousin's claim that he had used sorcery against her mother, in part because she was certain her mother was not an immoral, promiscuous woman. Similarly, women cancer patients sometimes turned to explanations of sorcery and to assistance from *samiyars* both to deflect accusations of moral impropriety and to be healed by local Tamil goddesses and gods. Speaking through *samiyars*, deities have the power to diagnose the role of sorcery and to prescribe concrete steps to remove its *kuri* and the effects of the *kuri*. In the process, they may also be able to protect the moral integrity and prestige of the afflicted person and her family if the family can make the case that the victim is innocent, as Roja did with her mother. However, engaging in these practices may itself be stigmatizing in wider social circles because they are associated with Dalit communities and are framed as backward and irrational by upper-caste people and within public health discourse. From the perspective of caste hierarchy, such practices are considered to be dangerous and impure; they are also deemed dangerous by public health practitioners, who contend that these beliefs may prevent people from following biomedical treatment protocols. In this way, public health discourses and caste discrimination are conjoined, so that openly engaging in such practices may reproduce the degraded social status of Dalits.

Parimala speculated that her cancer may have been caused by sorcery. In a hushed voice, she recounted how she had had to endure endless village gossip about her husband's sexual relations with other women long before her cervical cancer diagnosis. When she first received her diagnosis in the Dharmapuri Government Hospital, she did not tell anyone she had cancer. She simply told her family and neighbors she had a lump (*katti*) that needed treatment in Chennai. While she was preparing to travel to the Cancer Institute in Chennai, she wondered how her family would be able to make money while she was away. At the age of forty-five, she was supporting her seventeen-year-old son and her husband on her meager income of 150–200 rupees per day through the MGNREGA scheme and as a laborer in the cotton fields. Her husband was unable to get steady work because he was an alcoholic. She had tried to keep her cancer diagnosis secret, but others figured it out. While she was preparing to travel to Chennai, she overheard her neighbors discussing her situation:

> People who live nearby guessed it on their own. They know I have cancer and they are speaking about this. They didn't speak to my face but they stood just a little away, and said, "She has just come back from Dharmapuri and she has this disease [cancer]." I could hear them clearly. Then they said, "He goes all around town [i.e., having sex with other women] and now look at what happened to his wife."

At the Cancer Institute she learned that cervical cancer could be the result of HPV, which is sexually transmitted. This led her to also think that her husband's philandering was to be blamed. When she confronted him, he denied the rumors or any responsibility for her illness. Instead, he told Parimala that she had gotten cancer because she chewed *paan* and tobacco, and he scolded her, telling her to stop these bad habits. Parimala too wondered if she had gotten cervical cancer from *paan* and tobacco.

Ultimately, Parimala was not satisfied by either explanation. She did not accept that it was solely because of her own *paan* habits. The possibility that it could have been caused by her husband's infidelity was too embarrassing, and she was unable to get him to take responsibility. So she turned to another explanation, which gave her some comfort even if it too was disquieting: she claimed that her relatives had used sorcery to destroy her family. She reasoned that their sorcery had turned her husband into an alcoholic who could not find a steady job and who spent whatever little money he earned on alcohol and running around with other women. She said that because of all this, her husband got a disease, which he sexually transmitted to her, the only earning member of their family. This was how she came to have cervical cancer, which led to her ostracism. Lowering her tone even though we were speaking to her behind closed doors in the privacy of a hospital clinical room far from her home and family, she asked: "Who else could have done this?" She attributed such malicious behavior to the Kali Yuga, saying that in the past, people treated one another well, but now, in the Kali Yuga, there was too much competition, it was too difficult for poor people to earn a living "these days," and relatives were increasingly turning against one another.

Roja and her family had tried to deflect rumors and assumptions that her mother must have gotten cervical cancer because she was promiscuous. In Parimala's case, the blame was placed on her philandering husband and the community viewed Parimala as the victim. Nevertheless, what mattered in both these situations was that the prestige of the family was in jeopardy. In both cases the consideration that someone else was to blame for hexing the entire family provided people some sense of dignity, even if contemplating the potential role of sorcery was itself a socially dangerous path because it was deemed unmodern and raised the specter of social conflict.

Some argued that sorcery could only be suspected if someone was suffering from the onset of a sudden mysterious illness that made one dizzy and caused one to faint; whereas others, including Parimala, felt that if someone or someone's family was experiencing an onslaught of *multiple* misfortunes and if cancer was one among several such calamities, then sorcery could be at play. Anjali, a patient in the Government Cancer Hospital, also considered her cancer to be a *kuri*—a sign or mark of sorcery—because it was one among several problems afflicting her family. She believed that her breast cancer was the result of sorcery, explaining that her relatives had first taken down her husband, giving him paralysis, then killed a sister-in-law by giving her breast cancer, and now were targeting her by sending her the same illness. Anjali believed that her relatives wanted to destroy her family's good name and social standing in the village.

Sorcery is often suspected when people become entangled in disputes over private property, particularly land. Roja believed that her virtuous mother developed cervical cancer only because her cousin used sorcery to gain access to her land. Similarly, Poongodai suspected that her father-in-law's sister's son, who coveted their land, to which he had no right, had used sorcery to give her and her husband cancer. After all, he had threatened her maliciously: "Watch out for what I will do to you. Let us see how you live." Although the thought that someone might be using sorcery against them was frightening, Poongodai found this allegation to be more acceptable than the rumors that her cancer was karmic punishment for her promiscuity or for her failure to prevent her goat from destroying her neighbor's sapling.

Some cancer patients and survivors agreed that sorcery could be involved in a misfortune such as cancer, but they felt certain there was no way it could have been implicated in their own cancer affliction because they were so poor they did not have any land or other resources to fight over. Here the logic was that they were too poor to elicit any kind of jealousy or competition for resources that would lead someone to use sorcery against them. Paul Farmer's ethnography of an emerging HIV/AIDS epidemic in rural Haiti presented a similar reasoning.[13] In my study, Chitra categorically dismissed any possibility of sorcery. She was a Dalit woman in her late fifties who said she was always hungry for food because there was no *kuli* work available due to the droughts. Even when work was available, she would get passed over because people thought she was too old to be of any use. Did she consider the possible role of sorcery in her cervical cancer?

> No, I did not. I don't have wealth or property. I don't even have a bowl and I have to eat porridge [*kanji*] out of my own hands. How can I think of that? If I had had a lot of money, and a big home, then maybe I would have thought that someone wants to wish me ill. But I am drying up under the hot sun. I have no wealth, no money, and even my home is given to me by the government. So, I did not think of that.

## AMMANS' DIAGNOSIS AND REFERRAL

Though they speculated that their illness was a result of sorcery, Parimala, Anjali, and Poongodai also thought that once the *kuri* manifests physically inside their bodies as a disease, it needs to be removed by biomedical treatment as well as through the performance of religious rituals. By then, it has become a disease that should be physically cured by biomedical doctors. Even so, the curse on them and on their families—the overarching reason for their predicament—can only be lifted by the deities. They turned to Mariamman for help. Mariamman is a pre-Vedic Dravidian Hindu goddess who is enormously popular in Tamil Nadu, especially among rural Dalit communities. Historically, Mariamman was worshipped as the goddess of smallpox who could both cause and cure this deadly disease, depending on whether she felt appropriately propitiated. Since the eradication of smallpox, she has come to be known for her power to cause and heal disease more broadly, especially diseases associated with "overheating" of the body.

"Amman" means mother goddess. Most local Tamil goddesses are called Amman, and their devotees consider them to be motherly figures who can be fiercely protective of their children but can also punish children who are disrespectful or neglect their responsibilities toward their mother. Some say that the word "mari" in Mariamman is derived from the Tamil word for rain (*maari/maazha*). Mariamman is thus sometimes referred to as a rain goddess who makes the earth fertile. Others say that "mari" in Mariamman is derived from the word "*maaru*," meaning "to become changed/exchanged/altered." This meaning of "the changed one" is evident in a mythological origin story for Mariamman that situates her in a post-Vedic caste-based society. In this story, following a complicated series of events, a Brahmin sage accidentally attached his Brahmin wife's head to the body of a Dalit woman who had saved the wife's life. The wife's life was endangered, and she had become decapitated, because her husband had falsely accused her of sexual promiscuity. Having placed his wife's head on a Dalit woman's body, the Brahmin sage was disgusted with this mixture of substances, and he recoiled from her and banished her from the family. The now enraged wife instantly *changed* into the wrathful goddess Mariamman, who demanded to be propitiated through ritual action. In this story, the ambiguity of Mariamman's caste status threatened caste hierarchy but also enhanced Mariamman's healing powers, particularly for people from Dalit communities.[14] Parimala, Anjali, and Poongodai, and other Dalit worshippers of Mariamman, did not refer to these mythological accounts of Mariamman's origins or mention the caste politics implicit in this interpretation. Nevertheless, it is significant that this origin story links Mariamman and her powers to the politics of caste transgression, given this goddess' popularity among Dalits. Furthermore, the fact that Mariamman's life was threatened by her husband's false accusation of her promiscuity may bolster this goddess's popularity among Dalit women who chronically endure such allegations.

Turning to Mariamman to deal with a dimension of their illness that was beyond the scope of biomedicine, women like Parimala, Anjali, and Poongodai brought biomedical and religious systems together and assigned specific roles to each. People suffering from an illness may consult with a *samiyar* who is a medium for Mariamman so that Mariamman can determine whether sorcery is involved and then cure them with her healing powers. While they consider biomedicine to be an essential means of treatment for cancer that is already inside the body, religious diagnosis and worship of Mariamman through the expertise of *samiyars* is a crucial means for them to rid themselves of the *kuri*, to protect themselves from the moral blame leveled at them, and to heal from the physical and social suffering caused by cancer.

While women turned to sorcery in part to defray moral blame, they also did so to get a second opinion and out of a genuine desire to seek answers for why they got cancer when medical practitioners failed to provide them with adequate explanations. After her sister-in-law's death from breast cancer, Anjali was aware of biomedical explanations for cancer, and she sought biomedical treatment for her own breast cancer. Still, she could find no explanation within the biomedical system for why the disease had specifically affected *her*. So she consulted a *samiyar*, who confirmed her fears that the cancer was a *kuri* that had been caused by envious relatives using sorcery. The *samiyar* told her to seek biomedical treatment for her illness. To be more specific, Mariamman, speaking through the *samiyar*, told her to seek biomedical treatment. Anjali explained, "She said it was caused by sorcery. She said I should go to a doctor. She said if I go to the doctor, she herself will make sure that I will get cured. And I thought, 'How could I know? Only Amman knows what it is' so I chose to come to the hospital."

Sorcery was viewed as the underlying cause of cancer, but biomedicine was considered a key component of the cure for it. Deities speaking through *samiyars* may sometimes refer clients to the biomedical system for cancer treatment while still recommending that they follow ritual prescriptions to get to the root cause of their ailment and thus to be fully cured. Ellamma, a Dalit *samiyar* whom I met in a village in Kanchipuram district, emphatically stated that she always refers cases of cancer to biomedical doctors. I observed her nighttime séances inside her *kuri meydai*, which was a shrine to Muthumariamman. Muthumariamman (Pearl Mariamman) is the goddess whose spirit descends on Ellamma on Tuesdays and Fridays and during new moon and full moon nights, allowing her to diagnose the effects of sorcery and the presence of evil ghosts and spirits causing misfortune. It is in this shrine that Muthumariamman inhabits Ellamma's body and exorcises evil ghosts and spirits from the bodies of men and women who consult her.

Ellamma's story of how she came to be a *samiyar* resembled similar accounts documented by Isabelle Nabokov[15] in her ethnography of mediums and their rituals in Tamil Nadu. Ellamma began by describing the abuse she suffered from her husband for many years until one afternoon she was visited by the goddess in the form of a cobra. As she sat in front of her house, cutting vegetables, the snake fell onto her from the thatched roof above her and licked her right down the center of her face before slithering off to a large tree in the courtyard of the small Muthumariamman temple in her village. Ellamma then lost consciousness. When she regained consciousness under that tree, her whole body was covered with pearl-like boils, evidence that Muthumariamman had taken hold of her. Ever since, Ellamma has had special powers to become possessed by Muthumariamman and to heal those who are suffering. She is much sought after for consultations by people from surrounding villages. Although her husband continued to threaten her—sometimes loudly and publicly in a drunken stupor, as we witnessed one night—she claimed that due to the powers of the goddess she now embodies, he stopped physically violating her out of respect for Muthumariamman and fear of reprimand from Ellamma's clients. Anthropologists studying female mediums elsewhere in South Asia have reported similar gendered scripts of divine justice.[16]

With donations provided by those who seek her help, Ellamma built a shrine to Muthumariamman next to her thatched home. Interestingly, this concrete shrine with a freshly painted light pink exterior and a corrugated tin roof looked, from the outside, like a small replica of the closest government Primary Health Centre. Inside, it was painted yellow—Amman's color—and housed a stone sculpture of the cobra-hooded Muthumariamman and the ritual paraphernalia for Ellamma's nighttime séances. These included limes, used to divine the presence of ghosts and evil spirits (*pey pisasu*); batches of twigs of "cooling" *neem* leaves to heal afflicted clients and calm the goddess down after a possession; and a small metal trident (*alagu*) that Ellamma pierces through her tongue (or the tongue of someone being exorcised) during possession, which she said will fix the goddess inside the body. Toads, lizards, and beetles hopped, crawled, and flew on the floors, around the fluorescent tube lights on the walls, and onto us during her nighttime séances. We had to keep swatting them away as we sat watching the séances, which added to the "scary" atmospherics of the place as described by one of the RUWSEC healthcare workers.

During her séances, Ellamma—while possessed by Muthumariamman—left her long, disheveled hair untied and waved it around wildly as she rolled her head from side to side. Her unbound hair was emblematic of her potentially dangerous power. She handed bundles of limes tied together to clients and their families who came to consult the goddess about their misfortunes and who wondered whether sorcery might be at play. She asked them to hang these lime bundles in the doorway at the threshold of their homes for five or seven days and then return again with these limes. The limes contain the essence of the goddess.[17] If there are *pey pisasu* present in the home, they will sense the presence of the goddess and a trace of these spirits will be absorbed into the limes. We watched too as other families came to see Ellamma after the designated number of days had passed and Ellamma—or rather Muthumariamman inhabiting Ellamma—cut the limes open and sniffed them to decipher whether *pey pisasu* were present. If she detected the presence of *pey pisasu* in the limes, she would recommend that the person return to stay at her *kuri meydai* for several days in order to exorcise the spirit.

During an exorcism, Muthumariamman (inhabiting Ellamma) is able to speak directly to the *pey pisasu* that is possessing the unfortunate person. In this way the goddess is able to determine the nature of the *pey pisasu* and whether it was sent via sorcery or whether it is a lingering, haunting ghost not sent by sorcery. Through her conversations with the malignant spirit, the goddess also gleans what foods that spirit craves. After making the unfortunate client fast for several days so that the person becomes ravenously hungry, the goddess entices the spirit out of the body of the unfortunate person by offering the foods the malignant spirit craves in a pot. The spirit comes out of the body to eat the food in the pot and is then trapped inside the pot. The previously possessed client takes the pot to the cremation ground and there burns the pot with the malignant spirit inside. The newly healed person then pierces her tongue with the small metal *alagu* trident to fix the goddess in her. She will discard the clothes she was wearing, bathe in the river, and don the yellow cloth of Mariamman as protection for a period of time while she convalesces from the ordeal.

According to Ellamma, cancer is most likely caused by something other than *pey pisasu* and sorcery and is therefore considered to be an *odambu noi*.

But, she added, sometimes sorcery and ghosts may indeed also be involved. Regardless of its cause, Ellamma was emphatic that Muthumariamman cannot fully cure cancer through exorcisms. The goddess herself, therefore, advises people afflicted with cancer to see a biomedical doctor. When we asked Ellamma how she can determine whether a person requires biomedical attention, she retorted that she herself cannot determine such things; it is Muthumariamman who divines, diagnoses, and recommends treatment. Ellamma explained that she has no knowledge or recollection of what the goddess says or does while she inhabits Ellamma's body.

Parimala and Anjali both claimed that Mariamman, speaking through a *samiyar*, had directed them to seek biomedical care. Along with the biomedical care, both had also received amulets and charms from Mariamman's shrine to protect them and to keep away further acts of sorcery. Parimala showed us the cylindrical brass amulets she had received from a *samiyar* devotee of Mariamman. She wore them on her wedding *tali* around her neck. During her time in the Cancer Institute hospital, Parimala draped herself in a yellow and red cotton sari with *neem* leaf motifs on it. Women wear these saris when they go to Mariamman temples, especially during the Tamil lunar month of Aadi, for festival processions for Mariamman. Parimala said that she wore this sari in the hospital to please Mariamman in the hope that Mariamman would bestow her blessing on her and help her heal. These same saris were for sale in a small shop inside the compound of the Government Cancer Hospital, and most women patients in the wards there wore them, just as one might find patients wearing hospital-provided gowns in other contexts. Like Parimala and Anjali, several other women who were convinced of Mariamman's powers visited Mariamman temples before they came to the hospital for treatment. They would carry small pictures of the goddess and amulets they had received from her shrines and temples with them to the hospital in the hope that these things would ensure that the blessings of the goddess remained with them throughout their treatment. If Amman had referred them to the hospital, they believed it was her power (*sakti*) that would ensure they left the hospital fully cured of the cancer.

## "IT'S PARTLY IN OUR HANDS; IT'S PARTLY IN THE HANDS OF THE GODDESS"

Cancer patients and survivors often stated that biomedical cancer treatments would only work if they had the protection of Mariamman and other deities.

Faith in both biomedical and spiritual interventions was so deeply intertwined that it was not uncommon for women to say their doctors were "like gods" and the hospital "a kind of temple." Women explained that radiation, surgery, and chemotherapy worked in tandem with prayers and rituals, with the latter being done to appease gods and goddesses, who would then provide them with help to heal from both the physical pain of cancer and the emotional and social suffering caused by the moral blame and stigma associated with a reproductive cancer diagnosis. I met seventy-two-year-old Rachana seven years after her cancer diagnosis. In her family, they did *puja* to the Tamil god Ayappan and to the goddess Perunkootu Bhagavathi from their ancestral village in Kerala. Rachana explained, "It's partly in our hands; it's partly in the hands of the goddess. The treatment will work only if god wants us to survive."

Kalaa's face lit up when we asked her whether gods and goddesses played any role in her healing from cancer. Kalaa hailed from a village in Salem district. As mentioned in Chapter 3, her husband had abandoned her for another woman when their second son was two years old. She had struggled to raise her two sons by collecting firewood in the forest and doing sporadic *kuli* farm work and MGNREGA labor. She explained that her diagnosis of cervical cancer would raise questions about her sexual activity, particularly because people would speculate about it, given that she had been living as a single woman ever since her husband abandoned her. These allegations of moral impropriety did not scare her since she was confident that Mariamman, to whom she prayed regularly, would protect her from such rumors. She also believed that Mariamman had every intention of curing her completely so that she could return home to her sons. She said it was because of this that the goddess had guided her to the Cancer Institute while the cancer was still at an early, curable stage. As a token of gratitude to the goddess, Kalaa had vowed to make offerings to Mariamman when she returned home from the hospital.

Kalaa also believed it was important to offer prayers during her long hospital stay. Since the hospital did not have a temple dedicated to Mariamman, Kalaa visited the small temple on the hospital grounds daily, where she worshipped Pillaiyar (the Tamil name for Ganesh) and Venkateswara. On Fridays, she did *puja* to Siva in the large Mahdhya Kailash temple across the road from the hospital. She also lit a lamp and offered flowers at the small altar on her hospital ward. This altar included pictures of Venkateswara, Lakshmi, Pillaiyar, Saraswati, and Murugan (Skanda)—five deities who are part of the pan-Indian Hindu pantheon and are associated particularly with middle- and upper-caste forms of Hindu worship.[18] Although the worship of Murugan has deep roots in pre-Vedic Hinduism in Tamil Nadu, he became incorporated into the Sanskritic pantheon as the South Indian version of Skanda (the son of Siva and Parvati and brother of Ganesh) as part of a process of "nationalist sanskritization."[19] Although Tamil forms of Murugan worship that include possession, religious body piercings, and fire-walking—akin to Mariamman worship—persist, when he is incorporated into the Sanskritic pantheon, as was the case in the hospital *puja* space, those forms of worship are not present.[20] Mariamman, the Tamil goddess associated with lower-caste and -class communities, was absent from the pantheon of deities at the altar in the hospital ward, and there were no Mariamman temples in the vicinity of the hospital, an absence that was conspicuous to many of the patients in the ward, the vast majority of whom came from rural Dalit communities.

While they regularly worshipped other gods at the hospital and in nearby temples, they deemed the protection of Mariamman as essential for a complete cure. While receiving treatment in the hospital, they made vows to Mariamman that if the doctors said they were free of cancer after their treatment, then once discharged from the hospital they would demonstrate their gratitude to the goddess by offering money or their hair to Mariamman at her temples. Others vowed to sacrifice chickens and goats to the goddess and to feed the entire village with the meat. Still others said they would wear flower garlands to go on pilgrimage to her temples and join devotees in fire-walking ceremonies to show their devotion and to demonstrate the protective powers of Mariamman. Kalaa and Parimala had vowed to do all of these things.

Although the public health discourse debunks supernatural understandings of the cause and cure for cancer, medical practitioners, counselors, and hospital administrators at government and NGO hospitals do acknowledge the significant role that patients and their families give to religion during the process of healing from cancer. These hospitals provide spaces where women can perform everyday religious rituals, such as a small Siva and Pillaiyar shrine at the entrance to the Government Cancer Hospital, the temple to Venkateswara and Pillaiyar at the entrance to the Cancer Institute, and the pictures of Venkateswara, Lakshmi, Pillaiyar, Saraswati, and Murugan hung on the walls of the hospital wards to allow patients to conduct daily *puja*. The Cancer Institute also provides yoga sessions for patients as a form of spiritual and physical healing.

The Hindu shrines and temples at these hospitals provide spaces for the worship of pan-Indian Sanskritic Hindu deities, which, like yoga, are deemed respectable to middle-class, upper-caste society. Lower-class and -caste women at these hospitals were grateful to be able to pray to these gods, but in many cases, these were not the deities with whom they had a personal relationship, as they did with Mariamman and other Tamil deities. Although *neem*-leaf-printed saris associated with Mariamman are for sale at the Government Cancer Hospital and most women patients there wore them, there were no shrines or spaces of worship for Mariamman (nor were there for other Tamil Ammans or popular male Tamil deities also worshipped among Dalit communities). Such forms of religious worship and responses to illness—which may include *samiyar* mediums, possession, and exorcisms—are popular among the marginalized, rural Dalit women who make up the majority of the patient populations in these hospitals. Yet they continue to be associated with backward, irrational, superstitious ways of thinking among the hospital staff.

Women like Parimala and Anjali explained that complete healing is possible only when they take steps to protect themselves against the ill wishes of jealous relatives and against the reprimanding moral blame of neighbors. They felt that Mariamman had the power to provide such protection and the power to help cure them of their disease. Yet apart from the saris and amulets that they wore, they found it difficult to seek assistance from Mariamman while they were patients in the hospital for several months. Their inability to openly worship Mariamman in the way they wanted to—more importantly, in the way they knew the *goddess* wanted them to—further added to their anxieties. Yet they were unable to publicly articulate these concerns, fearing that acknowledging such religious beliefs and practices linked to Dalit communities would heighten their social stigma. Since Mariamman holds the power both to cure and to harm depending on her judgement of people's devotion to her, women's perceptions of their inability to worship her in the hospital were no small matter.

## CHRISTIANITY AND CONVERSION

For some women, the devastating diagnosis of cancer made it more crucial to worship gods and goddesses; for others, the cancer diagnosis left them feeling disillusioned with the Hindu gods. Poongodai had always been devoted to Mariamman, but she felt betrayed by the goddess after both she and her husband were diagnosed with cancer. She reasoned that because they had fallen ill with this disease at the same time, it could have been caused by malicious sorcery. To understand her problem, she had consulted with two religious specialists with expertise in astrology—a Brahmin temple priest and a Muslim *imam* in a *dargah* (a shrine built at the grave of a Muslim Sufi saint). Both said her "time was not right" until the end of the Tamil month of Aadi. Having appeased the goddess Mariamman every day of her life by lighting a lamp in her temple, even when it meant forgoing her own evening meal to buy the oil for the lamp, Poongodai felt unjustly neglected by Mariamman. She was angry, thinking her time was not right because of the goddess's apathy or impotency, either of which was a sign of the Kali Yuga.

While battling the emotional pain of this betrayal, Poongodai met cancer survivors who visited the Cancer Institute from a Pentecostal church to speak to patients about the healing powers of Jesus Christ. When I met Poongodai, she had been discharged from the hospital for three months, but she was still undergoing cancer treatments on an outpatient basis. She decided she would wait until the end of Aadi to see if Mariamman would be able to turn her fortune to improve her health and end the moral condemnation she faced in her community. Poongodai had decided that if Mariamman was unable to do so by the end of the month of Aadi, she would convert to Christianity, even though her son was urging her not to because the whole family should be part of the same religion.

Like Poongodai, several women felt let down by their deities when they were diagnosed with cancer. Some teared up with sadness when they thought about being neglected by the gods and goddesses to whom they had been so devoted. Others spoke of this with bitterness and anger and viewed it as the ultimate sign that they were living in the Kali Yuga. Women who felt rejected by gods and goddesses often found it difficult to believe that their lives could have meaning going forward, even if doctors were to tell them that their bodies were clear of cancer. Saraswati, a therapist who counseled cancer patients, said that this sense of loss and betrayal could only be restored by reassuring patients that the gods and goddesses were still their allies and protectors. "Along with treatment, you need to believe in the power [*sakti*] of god," she said. She believed this gave patients a reason to stay alive, and this in turn gave them a reason to follow the biomedical advice they received at the hospitals.

Poongodai's son insisted that all members of a family should belong to the same religion and share religious practices. Yet cancer patients and survivors talked about the enormous fluidity in their allegiance to various religious traditions. Several mentioned visiting churches and *dargahs*, as well as *samiyars* and the temples of a wide range of Hindu deities, after their cancer diagnosis. They felt they might benefit from the interventions of any or all. Such religious syncretism is common in South India, even as Hindu nationalist movements that have a strong foothold in North India have sought to drive wedges between different religious communities and harden religious identities throughout India.

Sometimes a cancer diagnosis led women to reject the gods and goddesses with whom they had a personal relationship and to join new religious communities and practice new forms of worship. Several Dalit women had converted from Hinduism to Christianity to help them cope and find hope. They felt abandoned by their Hindu gods and were struggling to come to terms with the physical, social, and economic consequences of their cancer diagnosis.

Poongodai was contemplating converting to Christianity; Chitra, Devaki, and Chellamma had already done so. Those three were rural Dalit agricultural laborers like Poongodai and had joined Pentecostal churches near their homes. Their conversions to Christianity should be understood in the context of a history of Dalit Christian conversion in Tamil Nadu dating back to colonial times and recharged since the 1990s in the form of Pentecostal conversions, particularly among Dalit women.[21] The rising popularity of evangelical Pentecostalism has contributed to an anti-Christian backlash, especially with the rise of Hindu nationalism in India. Even in Tamil Nadu, a state seen as more immune to Hindu nationalists' overt attacks on the rights of religious minorities, Jayalalithaa passed statewide anti-conversion laws in 2002. Yet this did not put a stop to conversions, and when those laws met strong resistance, they were repealed in 2004.[22] During my previous research in early 2004, I met women living with HIV/AIDS who had converted from Hinduism to Christianity in the aftermath of their HIV-positive diagnosis because of the support they received from Pentecostal groups.[23] Similarly, women in 2015 and 2016 were converting to Christianity following their cancer diagnosis at the urging of members of the Pentecostal church.

I met both Chitra and Devaki at RUWSEC while they were attending a support group for cancer survivors. Both were in their mid-fifties and were friends from the same village. Chitra had been diagnosed with cervical cancer thirteen years before we met. She had suffered extreme pain in her pelvic area and had heavy white discharge for six months before her daughter finally insisted she see a doctor. She was shuttled around between four or five doctors, paying exorbitant out-of-pocket fees to private hospitals, before she was finally admitted to the Government Cancer Hospital, where she remained for three months. At her time of discharge, she was deemed free of the cancer. She felt she had received good medical treatment at the government hospital, yet she complained that the medical staff treated Dalit women like her with disdain, always keeping a distance between themselves and the patients. In the midst of her therapeutic ordeal, Chitra's brother had convinced her to convert to Christianity. He had become a Christian after staying in a hostel in Chennai run by Pentecostals. Chitra explained:

> I was worshipping Mariamman. I used to pray a lot. I became very frustrated with god when I was going around to all these hospitals. I thought, "This is truly the Kali Yuga when even the goddess doesn't care about people like me!" Then my brother came and gave me a picture of Jesus. He said, "You won't get comfort in anything other than the 'Lord.'" He said, "If you want comfort, you should consider this god." I thought, I have been praying to the Hindu gods, and I got this disease. I felt I must convert and take up this new god. Ever since, I have stuck to this. I go to church and I feel comforted. There is no segregation there. It doesn't matter if you are "SC" [Scheduled Caste] or something else. They don't separate you there like in the hospital. You are treated like an equal. You can tell them about this cancer and everyone will get together and pray for you. I whole-heartedly believe that this god cured me and set me free.

When Chitra learned that Devaki had been diagnosed with cancer, she went immediately to her home to give her support and advice. She told Devaki that when she went to church and prayed to Jesus, she started to feel better almost instantly; she urged Devaki to do the same. Devaki began accompanying Chitra to the church after she was discharged from the hospital. Devaki prayed to Yesappa (Jesus), offering him her nose-ring and promising to stop wearing nose-rings for as long as he could ensure that her cancer would not recur.[24] Still, she went once to a Mariamman temple, where she offered her *tali*, shaved her hair, and sacrificed a goat to fulfill a previously made vow to Mariamman for helping cure her cancer. After that, she did not pray to Mariamman again for a long time and continued to worship regularly in the church with Chitra. Her younger, unmarried daughter began accompanying her to church, and Devaki had started to look for a Christian groom for her daughter.

Four years later, before a wedding could be organized, Devaki's daughter committed suicide. The daughter was a teacher in a private school. She had been the bedrock of financial support for the family while also studying to be a lab technician. The day after she failed her exam for this certification she took her own life. Devaki said the "tension" that young Dalit women like her daughter endure to make ends meet "these days" was endemic in this Kali Yuga. The shock of her daughter's death was so profound for Devaki that she was compelled to return to Mariamman. She feared that this tragedy, which for her was exponentially more devastating than her own cancer diagnosis, might have been prevented if she had not forsaken her devotion to Mariamman while worshipping Jesus.

Similarly, when Chellamma returned home from the hospital after her breast cancer treatments, her brother's wife, who was Christian, came to her home, along with Christian relatives and their pastor to pray for her. They suggested that she go with them to church and said that Jesus would save her. She recalled, "They came home and they said, 'You should pray to the 'Lord.' He will save you. Don't deny this. Join us.' I said, 'I don't know how to pray to your god. How can I join?' She would say, 'Call out to Jesus and tell him what you feel.'" Her husband had died when her children were young, and given the travails of her life since then, Chellamma had lost confidence that Hindu deities could protect her. She showed me where she had hung a large photograph of her late husband in her home, explaining that instead of praying to the gods, she had lit a camphor flame and prayed to her husband's spirit every morning of her life since he died. This daily *puja* for her husband and the vision (*darsan*) of his face as she lit the camphor had been the center of her religious practice. In the aftermath of her cancer diagnosis, she felt that devotion to the spirit of her husband was insufficient:

> I was very frustrated. My husband was gone and now I thought I too will leave my children. I began hating my life when I got this *katti*. I think I got this [cancer] because I worked too hard to raise my children alone. I felt this was truly the Kali Yuga so I began to go with them to the church to see if it would help.

One day, on her way home from the church, she was bitten by a dog and needed to get a slew of anti-rabies shots. She took that to be a sign: "Then I thought, I have been going to church but still god is testing me so I stopped. I did not go back after that."

For Shantamani, it was her husband's suicide followed by her cancer diagnosis that led her to convert for the third time in her life. Shantamani was born into a Catholic family in a village near Tirunelveli. Her first conversion was to Hinduism when she married her Hindu husband and moved to Chennai.

After her husband died and she was diagnosed with cancer, she converted to Pentecostal Christianity. Members of the congregation at the Pentecostal church in her neighborhood convinced her that she had gotten cancer as punishment for abandoning Jesus and going to worship a Hindu god. She began to see Hindu gods as *pisasu* (malignant spirit/devils). She explained, "Jesus said to me that now that I was back to him, he would make sure I was not harmed. He will protect me."

Shantamani said that Jesus helped her heal from the double trauma of her husband's death followed by her diagnosis of cervical cancer at the age of thirty-three. She became a proselytizer for the Pentecostal church. When her husband killed himself, he left her with three young children, ranging in age from one to eight. As discussed earlier, she attributed her cancer in part to all of the hard labor, heat, and tension she had experienced in her life after her husband's death, when she became a "workaholic," juggling childcare with work over the hot smoky stove in her *idli* shop to make ends meet. Also, she thought she got cancer because she had stopped going to church and had been worshipping Hindu gods, whom she now considered to be demonic spirits: "I used to think about *kuri* and go to the *samiyar*. I used to go to Amman's temple. But those *pisasu* don't deliver or listen to you. They only cause the illness. But the minute you ask Jesus for something, he makes it happen."

A pastor from the Pentecostal church came to the Cancer Institute while Shantamani was an inpatient there and told patients that he could organize a prayer group for them after they returned home. Shantamani reached out to him after she left the hospital, and he organized a group prayer in her home. From that day onward, she became a devout believer in the powers of Jesus, whom she felt had saved her life while she was completing her cancer treatments on an outpatient basis. She became highly animated as she told us about her experiences with Jesus, who spoke to her directly. One day, after she returned home from an outpatient visit at the Cancer Institute, she suddenly had profuse vaginal bleeding, and her brother rushed her to the hospital closest to her home for a blood transfusion. She described her experience of receiving the transfusion:

> I prayed and said, "Oh Jesus, give me blood and give me life." I had been taught that by the pastor so I kept saying it. I thought about my children and my mother and I kept praying to Jesus to give me life. They were giving me units of blood in one arm and glucose in the other but I didn't feel anything. I couldn't feel those needles so I told Jesus, "Don't give my body the needles the way your body was given the

nails." I kept talking to him. Later that night, I got up to go to the bathroom. Once I was done in the bathroom, I died. I had died. They talk about "God's miracle," right? Because of that, I died. I was surrounded by doctors in the "ICU ward" and they all saw me and were writing down that I had died. My mother was also standing there and she started sobbing, saying, "Oh no, my daughter is dead!" and she started hitting my chest in mourning. Then I vomited and I jolted back to life. And the doctors all saw me come back to life. There was a Catholic nurse there from Kerala, and she asked me to read the Bible. I fell asleep reading it. I had a dream with my late husband in it along with my younger brother who had died years ago. I was reading a Bible and holding keys in my hand. My younger brother asked for the keys. I gave him the keys and he was dressed well and his face was beautiful. Then he turned into the ugliest and scariest face ever; he became bald! My husband's face was terrifying too! I set the Bible down and both of them—my husband and my brother—went back to looking normal and beautiful. If I picked up the Bible again, then they went back to looking scary. I called to Lord Jesus and showed his face in the Bible and the minute I showed his face, those two ran away. Then Jesus came to me and asked me what I wanted. I told him that the *pey pisasu* of my husband and brother were scaring me and calling me to join them. Immediately, my old dead grandmother, my late uncle, and my late husband showed up. Jesus made every person I mentioned show up and then made them go away. I told Jesus that my abdominal pains were unbearable. He put his hand there and you couldn't imagine how much my face lit up! He healed me!

Shantamani thought that the biomedical knowledge of the hospital's doctors and the treatment she had received there had been necessary to cure her cancer. Even so, she credited Jesus for saving her life by imbuing doctors with such knowledge in the first place:

> Without Jesus, you cannot do anything. Jesus is the one that gives the knowledge to the doctor, so Jesus is the principle person to give me my life. Only after him, I will thank the doctor. Jesus has done so much good for me so I will thank Jesus first.

Shantamani's commentary reveals several key elements of the Pentecostal faith, including the attentiveness to visionary experiences, rebirth through deliverance, the miraculous healing power of Jesus's touch, and having direct personal verbal communication with Jesus. We also see the emphasis on expelling demonic forces (here referred to as *pey pisasu*), which are understood to be the devil, through the force of the holy spirit. Furthermore, we see that after her conversion to Pentecostal Christianity, Shantamani came to see Hindu deities themselves as evil spirits (*pisasu*).

There is an interesting convergence between Tamil Hindu practices of possession and exorcism associated with *samiyars* on the one hand, and the Pentecostal emphasis on expelling demonic forces on the other. Neena Mahadev's study of Pentecostal movements in Sri Lanka demonstrates that Pentecostals recognize this convergence but claim that those who engage in Hindu and Buddhist forms of exorcism are only playing with the devil by offering food and other appealing things to lure spirits out of a person and that they only temporarily cast these forces out, whereas the holy spirit of Jesus has the power to vanquish the devil once and for all. Pentecostals view Hindu and Buddhist gods as diabolical and urge people to reject these forces forever.[25] Ellamma, the *samiyar*, claimed that the malevolent spirit is indeed destroyed when it is burned. Yet she did recognize that the destroyed malicious spirit is only one such spirit and that the afflicted person needs to remain vigilant and seek the assistance of the deities to protect against other such spirits in the future.

We see in many of these stories how catastrophic events—including but not limited to cancer—can shake people's faith and lead them to find succor from different gods and with different religious communities. In all of these conversion cases, members of the Pentecostal church approached women after their cancer diagnosis, at a time when they were vulnerable. While it is easy to view this as manipulative, it is important to understand what it is that women say they gain through embracing Jesus and these Pentecostal communities. Nathaniel Roberts's ethnography of urban Dalit Pentecostal conversion among women in Chennai demonstrates that Dalit women, who are thrice marginalized—by their caste, class, and gender status—are made to feel foreign in mainstream Hindu caste society. They may join the Pentecostal community in their moments of greatest need in order to feel cared for as well as to feel a sense of belonging.[26] He also suggests that women join the Pentecostal community and put their faith in Jesus because they perceive Jesus as fulfilling their prayer requests and providing them with salvation from suffering. As such, they do not view religion—whether Christianity or Hinduism—as a matter of identity or as tied to a spiritual teleology; rather they approach religion as fundamentally worldly and moral and seek gods that are best able to help them overcome their worldly suffering.[27] This rang true for the cancer patients in my study who were converting to Christianity and helps us understand the relative ease with which women move back and forth between Christian and Hindu gods in their search for care, belonging, and healing.

Jesus not only helped Shantamani heal from cancer but also provided her with a newfound sense of purpose in her life, and she became a proselytizer. She would go out in public to hand out pamphlets about Jesus in the streets and hostels surrounding the Pentecostal church in her neighborhood, spreading the word about Jesus's miracles. She said that as a cancer survivor, she was a living "witness of god's grace." In the past, she had never left her house unaccompanied by her husband or brother; now, she proudly said, she goes everywhere on her own to spread the word of god. Shantamani described a journey of self-discovery through novel forms of religious practice and a sense of newfound empowerment, forged from the agonizing struggles she had faced as cancer entered her life.

Padma, a middle-class Catholic, college-educated woman, similarly reported that in some respects her encounter with cancer had made her a better person and given her a sense of purpose as she had become a volunteer, providing support to women patients at the Cancer Institute. She was fifty-seven when I met her in her home in Chennai. She recalled [in English] what she was thinking when she was undergoing her treatments at the Cancer Institute:

> While I was there in the hospital and saw so many other women suffering with cancer, I decided to spend more time to help patients and to spread awareness about cancer screening. I said to god, "If you want me to spread awareness, you better keep me alive. That is not a prayer; it is an order! Keep me alive, and I will help someone overcome cancer." I was always a devout person, and today too I am the same. After cancer, I have become a more tolerant and a more passive person. Earlier, I would get angry, and overreact to things. Today I don't overreact; I am much calmer. Maybe it is the power of prayer. It is a miracle. I feel like I have had a better life after cancer. I have become more confident and done things I would not have done before. Sometimes I feel like I have to be thankful I had cancer. God wants me to do something. Why is someone born blind, and then why did Jesus cure that person? God wants to show power of healing to that person. Maybe I was supposed to show that cancer itself can be healing. It is amazing.

There is a genre of autobiographies of cancer in English, including autobiographies of people from India. This theme of being unexpectedly thankful for cancer because it helps those afflicted ultimately have a better life if they are lucky enough to survive it runs through many of these works.[28]

Karpagam, who had been raised as a Protestant and was widowed with small children, also found succor through the Pentecostal church during her cancer treatments. When her Pentecostal neighbors learned of her cancer, they started coming to her home with Bibles to pray for her and her children. They visited her in the hospital during her treatments and arranged for World

Vision to provide support to her and her children. Karpagam began attending Pentecostal services after she was discharged from the hospital. Like many women I met, whether they were Christian or Hindu, Karpagam believed that in order to survive this disease, she needed a combination of divine help and access to biomedical treatment:

> Treatment in the hospital is something god makes available for you. Doing nothing but praying is stupid. Even in the Bible, Jesus cures you using herbs and leaves. This means even Jesus believed that you need medicine. He uses fish and herbs to feed you, to cure you. He believes in gardens and in growing the plants that will cure you. Treatment is not antithetical to prayer. Some Pentecostal Christians say you don't need treatment, you just need prayer. But I think that is stupid. Jesus cures you, yes. His healing hand is important, but not everyone can touch you and heal it. We need doctors for that. Faith in god is important. Without faith, treatment won't work.

## CONCLUSION

Karpagam, who had joined the Pentecostal church, felt that prayer alone is stupid, but without it, treatment won't work. For Shantamani, also a converted Pentecostal, "Jesus is the one that gives the knowledge to the doctor, so Jesus is the principle person to give me my life, only after him I will thank the doctor." Similarly, Anjali explained that through the medium of a *samiyar*, Mariamman had directed her to seek treatment for her cancer in the hospital, assuring her that if she did so, Mariamman herself would make sure that Anjali was cured. And Rachana, a devotee of Ayappan and of Perunkootu Bhagavathi, explained, "It's partly in our hands; it's partly in the hands of the goddess. The treatment will work only if god wants us to survive." The majority of the women cancer patients and survivors in my study had a deep and abiding conviction in both the power of the supernatural emanating from varying deities and the power of biomedicine in the hands of qualified biomedical doctors. Both the gods and the doctors could fail them. For some, the worst part of their brush with cancer was that it led them to feel abandoned by their deities. For others, the worst part was feeling that the doctors were insensitive to their personal and emotional needs because of their marginalized class and caste social status. They considered both of these things to be signs of the Kali Yuga. But most agreed that both deities and doctors were essential and needed to work in tandem in order for them to survive the physical, social, and emotional hardships they faced after a cancer diagnosis. Listening to lower-class and -caste (and some middle-class) women's narratives about the role of religion in their quest for care in all its dimensions—medical, social, spiritual, emotional—as they struggled with the consequences of their reproductive cancers adds yet another dimension to our understanding of the lived experiences of the nexus of class, caste, and gender in twenty-first-century South India, particularly for rural Dalit women.

# CONCLUSION

Can I talk to you openly without offending you? You have traveled all the way here and you say you are only here to listen to us and to hear our stories. What is the point of that? How are the people in this area going to benefit from it? At least if you gave us information, the people would learn something, but all you are doing is listening to us, what is the point of that? Where is the benefit in this for us? There is no benefit for us and for the people who live here in this village. We have all been affected by it [cancer]. My older sister's twelve-year-old grandson died from it. In my own house, two people were affected by it. In the opposite house, their younger brother has been affected by it. They have spent lakhs for his treatments but he is dying. You have to find a cure for it; you absolutely must! They say there is no hope for this. Yet we spend so much money. We would spend that money even if we had no means to eat or had to sell our house, but there still is no cure for it. They have to find a cure for it. You have come from America; you have to bring all the medications for it here. Will you be able to make medications available here? Will you be able to help us in that way?

There was anger in the voice of this fifty-year-old woman. She challenged the value and premise of my research as we sat down to begin an intimate group meeting with eight women—her relatives and neighbors—in her home in an MBC section of her village in northeastern Tamil Nadu. Cancers of all kinds—blood cancer, stomach cancer, esophageal cancer, cervical cancer, and breast cancer—were rampant in her family and the whole village. Families that were already struggling to make ends meet from their agricultural labor were slipping into abject poverty as they spent all their savings and took high-interest loans from moneylenders in their desperate search for the best treatment possible for their loved ones, who, in the end, died. Close family relationships were fraying as people debated whether to spend scarce resources on treatments they increasingly deemed useless. People suffering from cancer felt ashamed for causing so much trouble. People caring for family members with cancer felt ashamed they could not save them. What good could possibly come from sharing these stories with me and having this pain and shame exposed?

Medical anthropologists are often confronted with these cold, hard questions, yet they rarely enter into the ethnographic record. This elision may be partly because we ourselves sometimes harbor these very same doubts about the value of our profession when confronted with the immediacy of dying and death in our research. How many times have I felt that my life would have been more impactful had I become a doctor or a nurse, tending to the immediate needs of the sick? How many times have I thought I could have contributed more to improving health outcomes had I been designing and implementing global and public health programs on the ground? In the face of such suffering, what is the value of ethnographic research and anthropological analysis?

How does one respond when confronted with the accusatory yet utterly appropriate questions this woman posed? How does one go on with this research in the face of such self-doubt? I reminded the woman, and others gathered with us, that I knew I was a guest in her home and in their community and that we did not need to continue with our discussion if they did not see any merit in it. I acknowledged that I was not a medical doctor, that I could not provide immediate cancer treatments, and that I was not a public health educator coming to give them information. I continued, "I am here to learn from you so that I can tell others what you know by writing a book and sharing your views. Cancer affects people all over the world but it does not affect all people in the same way. I think it is important for people in your country and in my country and around the world to know what you are going through and to know what you think needs to be done about the problem of cancer in your community. I cannot say this will benefit you directly, but perhaps it can make a difference for others like you in the future." After a long, tense silence, she nodded, and she and the other women told me they wanted to continue the conversation.

In this ethnography, I have tried to convey how women in one region of India experience and make sense of what they view as a mounting cancer crisis in their communities. I have paid particular attention to lower-class and -caste Tamil women's perceptions of and encounters with breast and cervical cancer in the midst of an emerging global public health campaign to increase screening and treatment for these cancers in low-income communities in India and throughout the global South.

These global public health campaigns emphasize educational programs to provide information about measures individuals should take to prevent and detect reproductive cancers. They also strive to provide more hospitals, medications, and technological interventions for cancer treatment. Educational programs and cancer treatments are crucial and help save lives. Lower-class and -caste women who are the targets of these campaigns in South India appreciate and value such information, and they want access to quality biomedical cancer care. In fact, they express their desire for more such educational programs in their communities and more access to oncological treatments, as is clear in the statement of the woman quoted above.

Even so, my research indicates that women have many concerns about cancer causality and cancer care that are not recognized or addressed by governmental and nongovernmental public health initiatives. These unacknowledged concerns reveal much about the ordinary living conditions of predominantly rural Dalit women who find themselves having to endure this extraordinary disease. My interlocutors saw cancer and its devastating effects as a sign that they were living in a time that resembled the Kali Yuga, an inhospitable era characterized by greed and devoid of dharmic justice. Their critiques, sometimes evoked in the idiom of the Kali Yuga, offer a glimpse of how they understand their social marginalization in early twenty-first-century India and give us insight into what they deem necessary for a better future. Although they did not engage in overt public protest to address their concerns about cancer in their communities, their ethnographic engagements with me and with my research assistants, Shweta and Shibani, created a space for them to express their critiques. In writing this book, I am publicizing their views and experiences and calling upon global public health planners and public policymakers in general to listen, take heed, and work to redress the social problems articulated through these critiques.

The lower-class and -caste women whom I met in Tamil Nadu in 2015 and 2016 understood their vulnerability to cancer and its consequences in ways that differed significantly from public health professionals. Public health programs emphasized the need for education and individual behavior change. They presented ignorance, traditional cultural practices, poor moral judgement, and religious superstitions as primary obstacles to the prevention and treatment of cancer among lower-class and -caste communities in India. With better public health education, they expect to see improved health outcomes among these communities. Yet the participants in my study—women in the general public as well as breast and cervical cancer patients—pointed to factors beyond their control as the primary culprits for what they saw as rising rates of cancer in their communities and for the challenges they faced in receiving healthcare and maintaining a sense of dignity while they struggled to endure the ordeal of cancer and cancer treatments. They pointed to inequalities relating to the nexus of class, caste, and gender that compromised their health and their ability to receive quality healthcare in a timely and respectful fashion. Theoretical frameworks of structural vulnerability and structural violence were self-evident for them.

This was apparent in women's explanations of causality for cancer in general and for cervical and breast cancers specifically. They saw cancer in general as a symptom of their poverty, exacerbated by water shortages that were becoming more frequent due to natural and human-made causes (including chronic droughts and inter-state water feuds, as well as illegal sand-mining facilitated by the collusion of private enterprise and government corruption). They linked rising rates of cancer to a host of potentially carcinogenic agricultural chemicals increasingly used since India's Green Revolution for profit. They considered cancer to be a deadly side effect of chewing *paan* and tobacco to deal with excruciating toothaches in the absence of affordable dental care.

Public health campaigns suggested that women were at risk for cervical and breast cancer due mainly to individual lifestyle choices associated with marriage and reproductive and sexual practices; whereas the women in my study felt at risk due to constraints on their lives over which they had little or no control. They saw cervical cancer as resulting from increasingly excessive work that lower-class and -caste women have had to take on in the wake of India's economic liberalization, which has brought with it pressures to sell off land, the nuclearization of family units, and new demands for conspicuous consumption as a prerequisite for social prestige. They singled out particular kinds of unpaid and underpaid forms of labor that are relegated to lower-class women (and girls) as putting them at risk for cancer: cooking, childcare, transplanting paddy, breaking and carrying stones at construction sites, and collecting firewood. They noted that the imperative for them to take on more work was compounded by the lack of help from their husbands, many of whom had abandoned them through suicide, affairs, or alcohol, leaving them as the sole breadwinners for themselves and their children. All of these factors were forcing them to engage in excessive labor, compromising their ability to eat nutritious food, and adding to their mental stress. As a result, their bodies were becoming overheated, making them prone to vaginal discharge and bleeding and to cervical cancer. Similarly, women viewed rising rates of breast cancer as caused by increasing demands for women to work a double shift in the neoliberal era both outside the home for pay (whether as agricultural workers, domestic servants, or wage laborers for private companies) and inside the home without pay. This left them with little time and energy to breastfeed their infants and with weakened, anemic bodies and high levels of tension that made it impossible for them to produce breastmilk, all of which they thought heightened their risks for breast cancer.

Public health workers made efforts to dispel the belief that cancer is contagious. They viewed this as essential to overcome the problem of stigma and to convince women to undergo cervical and breast cancer screening, to see a doctor immediately if they had symptoms associated with these cancers, and to get treatment as soon as they received a cancer diagnosis. They presented ideas of contagion and stigmatization of cancer patients as problems of irrationality and ignorance to be rectified through education. However, my research suggests that ideas about cancer and contagion may in fact be inadvertently perpetuated by public health and medical practitioners through the language of cancer germs/worms ("cancer *kirumi*") and cancer bugs ("cancer *poochi*"). Moreover, educational explanations about the connection between infectious HPV and noninfectious cervical cancer are not being presented in a clear manner, which in turn reinforces the idea that cancer itself is contagious.

Many women said that although *they* did not believe that cancer was contagious, they knew others who did. So they felt it was their responsibility as women to mitigate the potential dangers of the stigma of a cancer diagnosis—particularly of reproductive cancers—in order to protect not only their own dignity but also the prestige and social standing of their extended families. They did not hold themselves individually responsible for their cancer, but they did feel that it was their responsibility as women—as mothers, wives, and sisters—to carefully manage the flow of information about cancer in order to mitigate the threat of stigma and the serious danger that all family members would become social outcasts. In particular, they worried that their cancer might compromise the marriage prospects of their daughters and other young women in their extended families.

Women pushed back against the notion that their ignorance and fears of stigma and death were leading to delays in their diagnoses and cancer treatments, resulting in advanced stage cancers that were harder to cure. Instead, they cited numerous examples of initial misdiagnoses by biomedical practitioners in public and private healthcare facilities, who repeatedly sent them home without recommending tests for cancer. They pointed to the high out-of-pocket costs they faced for diagnostic tests and for travel, which deterred them from seeking a medical doctor, even if their oncological treatments in public and NGO hospitals were subsidized. They felt that they could not sacrifice their daily wages and set aside their unpaid domestic work to go see a doctor. They also noted that because of sociocultural constructions of gender, the health of their husbands and children took priority over their own healthcare needs; that it was unacceptable for women to travel alone to see a doctor; and that because cervical and breast cancers are associated with reproductive parts of women's bodies and with moral impropriety, there is a taboo against discussing symptoms associated with these cancers with people who could help them access healthcare.

Following the mandate of international bioethics that has emerged in the West, global public health programs insist on the importance of full and confidential disclosure of cancer diagnoses to patients and on providing patients with information about their prognosis and treatment options so that they can make fully informed decisions about their medical care. In practice, though, it is common for doctors in India (and in many other parts of the world) to shield patients from that information and to provide it only to family members. Some of the women in my study appreciated the fact that information was intentionally and carefully withheld from them, interpreting it as gesture of care and love on the part of medical practitioners and family members.

Yet other women complained that medical staff at the public government hospital provided them with little to no information about their diagnosis, prognosis, and treatment options. They saw this as symptomatic of a public healthcare system that is structured in such a way that doctors prioritize the needs of the paying patients at their private clinics, whom they see in the afternoons and evenings, after they have completed their morning rotations in the government hospital. Those who were critical of the dearth of information provided to them felt that above all, it reflected an endemic lack of respect for patients in public hospitals arising from their class and caste status. They complained that doctors in government hospitals were aloof—that they kept patients at arm's length and did not care for them as human beings even if, in the end, they provided quality biomedical treatments. One Dalit woman wondered whether the doctors themselves thought her cancer was contagious, given that they were unwilling to come close to her. She also interpreted their distance as a form of caste discrimination. Central to the ideology of caste hierarchy is the concept of degrees of ritual purity and pollution, which results in practices of caste separation to prevent higher-caste people from becoming ritually polluted by lower-caste people. From the vantage point of Dalits, who have been relegated to the bottom of this discriminatory system, and who represent the majority of the patients in the public healthcare system, the lines between the castist concept of "untouchability" and contagion sometimes feel blurred when doctors are distant and uncaring.

Public health initiatives emphasize the need to provide access to reproductive cancer treatments to women in all sectors of society. That is indeed of paramount importance. But my interlocutors insisted that they also deserve respectful cancer care. Moreover, we need to understand how the sociocultural context impacts women's views of and experiences with oncological treatments. Public health messages aim to relieve people's fears that cancer is always fatal and stigmatizing. But it is not just cancer that people fear; they also dread the biomedical cancer treatments themselves. This is in part because of the extremely uncomfortable and sometimes harmful iatrogenic effects of the treatments. It is also because of the language used by medical practitioners themselves, such as when they describe radiation therapy as "current shock." Crucially, breast and cervical cancer patients express anxiety about oncological treatments that result in the loss of body parts such as uteri, ovaries, breasts, and hair, all of which are associated with women's reproductive capacity and their femininity. This is most threatening when the loss of a body part is publicly visible, as is the case to some extent with a missing breast but strikingly so with bald heads. The visible absence of breasts and hair may lead other people to speculate that they have cancer, which can result in extreme forms of social stigma because of ideas about cancer as contagious and hereditary or because it leads to speculations about a woman's morality. Understanding the stigmatizing effects of reproductive cancer treatments helps us appreciate that women's fears of and aversion to cancer treatments are far from irrational and are not a result of ignorance. On the contrary, they reflect a clear-eyed assessment of their social realities; the loss of breasts from a mastectomy can sometimes be grounds for a husband to leave his wife and find another, and the loss of hair may render a woman inauspicious, in much the same way that a widow may be shunned by others because of her association with death and her potential to cause infertility.

This ethnography has demonstrated that the nexus of class, caste, and gender plays a powerful role both in the experience of stigma resulting from reproductive cancer treatments and in the ways women act creatively to mitigate that stigma in Tamil Nadu. Middle- and upper-class women can use breast prostheses and wear wigs and modern short hairstyles to cover up the loss of these body parts. These options are not available to lower-income women, who cannot afford the cost of such items, cannot perform manual labor while wearing these things, and lack the social capital to perform modern, middle-class identities associated with women's short hairstyles. Instead, lower-class and -caste women creatively navigate the stigma of their missing breasts and hair by drawing on cultural and religious resources available to them, some of which—such as head shaving as a vow—are uniquely South Indian and are practiced primarily by members of lower-class and -caste communities.

In their attempts to educate the population about the etiology of reproductive cancers, the importance of early diagnosis from a biomedical professional, and the value of seeking biomedical treatment in hospitals, public health messengers criticize "irrational" supernatural beliefs and practices, which they view as harmful because they run counter to biomedical knowledge and practice. In the South Indian context this includes delegitimizing the claims of *samiyars* who act as mediums for Tamil deities such as Mariamman and debunking the notion that sorcery, spirits, *samiyars*, and deities play a direct role in causing and curing cancer.

Public health educators condemn the belief in sorcery and the idea that *samiyars* possessed by Tamil deities can diagnose the sources of misfortunes, including cancer, and can prescribe actions to help patients heal. Yet many of the lower-class Dalit women whom I met felt that given the poor track record in their communities of biomedical interventions to cure cancer, it made sense for those facing reproductive cancers to cover their bases and seek therapeutic reprieve from any and all sources available. Furthermore, in a social context in which a reproductive cancer diagnosis opens women up to suspicions about her morality, women and their family members sometimes pursue a diagnosis from a *samiyar* in order to deflect blame from themselves and as a shield against accusations of sexual impropriety or other moral transgressions. Given that public health messages about cervical and breast cancers emphasize women's marriage, reproductive, and sexual practices as the primary causal factors for these reproductive cancers and promote normative ideas about women's morality in the process, it is not surprising that many women and their families turn to other culturally available frameworks of cancer causality in their efforts to maintain their dignity and the good name of their families.

Many of the women in my study who came from Dalit caste communities were devotees of Tamil deities who inhabit and speak through *samiyars*. Most worshipped the goddess Mariamman and believed she had the power to protect them and to help them recover from a calamity such as cancer. Administrators and healthcare providers at the Government Cancer Hospital and the NGO Cancer Institute were aware of the importance of religion for their patients. Echoing neoliberal assumptions about individual responsibility, some of the public health workers and oncologists whom I met mentioned that patients' religious beliefs can give them the hope and will to live that is necessary to get them to be compliant patients and follow doctors' advice. Indeed, these hospitals had Hindu temples on their grounds and provided small *puja* spaces for prayer in the hospital wards. But it was the Sanskritic deities who were present. The Tamil deities—the ones worshipped most often in Dalit communities—were noticeably unavailable to the patients who received subsidized cancer care at these hospitals. This was existentially unnerving to some patients, who could not properly propitiate their preferred deities, sometimes for as long as four months, while they were staying in the hospital wards—a time when they most needed their protective healing powers. For them, it was another reminder of their social marginalization.

Some lower-class and -caste cancer patients interpreted their cancer as a sign that their Hindu deities were impotent or had unfairly abandoned them. They felt they could no longer rely on these goddesses and gods for protection or healing from their cancer. As a result, some converted to Christianity after their cancer diagnosis, joining the increasingly popular Pentecostal churches. They were compelled by the promise of the Pentecostal faith healing, by the church's welfare programs for women and children, and by the ability of the Pentecostal congregations to provide a sense of belonging to Dalit women who felt marginalized within the caste system associated with Brahminical Hinduism.

Public health messages suggest that the superstitious and backward religious beliefs and practices of lower-class people with little formal education discourage these people from seeking biomedical treatment for cancer as modern, rational subjects should. Yet for the women in my study—Hindus and Christians alike—religion and biomedicine were not antithetical. In fact, they reinforced each another. Women placed faith in deities and doctors alike. Doctors themselves were sometimes said to be "like gods" because of the efficacy of their treatments. At the same time, though, they claimed that such treatments would not exist were it not for the creative power of Hindu and Christian gods. Hindu goddesses, speaking through possessed *samiyars*, referred women to hospitals for cancer care, and Pentacostal Christians asserted that Jesus believed people needed to seek medical care. The Hindu and Christian religious beliefs and practices of rural Dalit women in Tamil Nadu did not deter them from seeking biomedical care.

Throughout this book, we have seen that rural Dalit women in Tamil Nadu were conscious of their marginalized social position and the ways in which it made them vulnerable to cancer and precluded them from receiving respectful medical care that more privileged members of society would receive. It is also apparent that their sense of precarity due to their lack of economic, social, and cultural capital could silence their protest. We saw this in the brief but dramatic encounter with the woman who spoke out at the educational screening camp. She publicly criticized the public health worker who was telling the women gathered to practice yoga and other forms of exercise to avoid cancer. In her mind, it was the excessive physical labor of women like her and like those attending the meeting, not lack of exercise, that was leading to more cancer and other health problems in her community. Most of my interlocutors from across the state shared this woman's assessment. Yet women attending these public health educational programs rarely voiced such views in these forums because they felt they had to show respect for the educated "big people" (*periyavanga*); as well, they questioned what good could come from speaking up when they were receiving free cancer screenings. Indeed, when this one woman broke her silence and stood up to complain, her perspective was not taken seriously by the woman in charge, who continued to extol the values of regular exercise and yoga. The woman who had complained felt compelled to leave the session and did not receive cancer screening. None of the others present said a word.

We saw the impulse for Dalit women to censor their protest on vivid display when they suddenly and frantically sought to erase any trace of their complaint about the potential carcinogenic toxicity of the rice that was being provided free through the government subsidy for people living below the poverty line. Their fear was that the government—even Chief Minister Jayalalithaa herself—might take revenge on them and deny them this life-saving subsidy for publicizing their criticism. When I asked lower-class and -caste women if there were avenues for them to raise their concerns about the relationship between the heavy use of agricultural chemicals and what they perceived to be rising rates of cancer in their communities, they were sober about their power to do so. They explained that to make a difference, they would need to take their complaints to "big people" (*periya manushanga*)—the large landowners, people in the agricultural and agrochemical sectors, and "high level" people in the government. They said that as people from "lower humble families" (*thazhntha kudumbangal*) and self-described *kuli* workers, they would not be taken seriously. Some even feared that publicly voicing such complaints could result in having their MGNREGA right-to-work scheme revoked.

Women complained among themselves on the hospital wards and to me in our conversations about the lack of information and the disrespectful care that they received from doctors in government hospitals and their inability to properly worship Mariamman during their prolonged stays in these cancer hospitals. But they said they could not speak up to their doctors about these concerns while they were receiving free medical treatment. They explained that when patients ask for more information about what to expect in terms of their medical care in the government hospital or about when they may be able to go home to their families, they were often met with gruff and disparaging remarks. Most had learned to hold their tongues rather than experience such degradation. As one woman put it, "When they respond like that, we think, 'How can we ask them anything when they speak to us like that?' So we just don't ask." They felt powerless as simply "individual people" (*thaniarunga*) interacting with these "government people" (government *aalunga*), particularly when they were most vulnerable and dependent on the free, subsidized medical care for their cancer treatments. They did not want to compromise their access to their treatments. They praised the government for the quality of biomedical treatment they were receiving at little or no cost. They felt entitled to compassionate care but sensed they were being denied that because of their marginalized social status.

Despite their comments about their inability to speak out and protest publicly, lower-class and -caste women clearly articulated their criticisms and concerns to me through our ethnographic encounter. And they articulated these critiques to one another in instances when I was interacting with more than one person at a time. My interlocutors saw me as a potential conduit for them to express these complaints in part because I had framed my research project that way. Through our conversations, they explained to me—and by extension to a broader public—how the nexus of class, caste, and gender rendered them vulnerable to getting reproductive cancers and limited their ability to access healthcare, to receive respectful healthcare, and to manage the stigma associated with cancer and with the effects of cancer treatments within their communities. As they shared their views on cancer causality and cancer care, they painted a grim picture of the sociocultural and political-economic contours of their lives, evoking the Kali Yuga to underscore the magnitude and injustice of their daily struggles. These were struggles they faced every day even without cancer. They felt these challenging conditions were leading to rising rates of cancer in their communities and that reproductive cancers were further compromising their ability to survive and to live with dignity. At the same time, the stories they told revealed how creative and resourceful they could be—indeed, *had* to be—in order to persevere in the face of the rising threats and realities of cancer in their bodies, in their families, and in their communities. Their stories expressed a clear-eyed understanding of the effects of social inequality on their lives and on their bodies, leading them to conclude that they were living in the unjust era of the Kali Yuga.

As an ethnographer, I have listened to, collected, analyzed, contextualized, and presented these stories. I hope I have done justice to the views and experiences of the women at the heart of this book. Critical medical anthropology has a crucial role to play by presenting information and analysis that can help improve global and public health programs in order to improve health outcomes. As part of the broader field of sociocultural anthropology, medical anthropological ethnography also helps explain social and cultural phenomena and diversity in our interconnected world and has the capacity to remind us of our shared humanity. This insistence on the value of a shared sense of humanity was, I believe, the crux of the matter for women who framed cancer and its consequences as an indication that we are living in an inhumane time that has all of the characteristics of the Kali Yuga.

# NOTES

1. Lévi-Strauss 1969: 162.

2. Balshem 1993; McMullin and Weiner, eds. 2008.

3. Tamil speakers sometimes refer to this as *kaliyugam*. In North India, it may be referred to as *kaliyug*.

4. Unless otherwise noted, all of the names of research participants are pseudonyms to protect their confidentiality.

5. Breman and Daniel 1992.

6. During my research in 2016 the exchange rate for 1 US dollar was 67 Indian rupees.

7. South Indian sarongs.

8. Livingston 2012.

9. There is no comprehensive national registry to provide accurate epidemiological data on cancer incidence and mortality as a whole. The National Cancer Registry Programme established by the Indian Council of Medical Research in 1981 provides population-based data from a network of cancer registries across the country. The estimates, therefore, have limitations. They may underreport cancer deaths among the elderly. And they may be more representative of urban and South Indian contexts. Nevertheless, they are considered to be relatively accurate reflections of the general cancer epidemiological scenario in India (Mallath et al. 2014: e206).

10. Mallath et al. 2014: e205. According to the United States' National Cancer Institute, in 2015 every thirteenth new cancer patient in the world was Indian (*Times of India* 2015).

11. There are several reasons for probable underreporting: lack of requirement to report cancer deaths to a national, centralized body (as with some other diseases);

people may die of cancer without ever getting a proper diagnosis; doctors and families may attribute cancer deaths to some other cause due to the stigma of cancer.

12. Banerjee (2020) reports that although India is a major exporter of morphine, this drug is highly regulated in India due to concerns that patients will become addicted.

13. Mallath et al. 2014: e207. Mallath and colleagues also report that the cancer mortality rate in India is 68% of annual incidence. The mortality burden is high, with an estimated 600,000 to 700,000 deaths due to cancer in India in 2012.

14. National Cancer Registry Programme 2011; Sundar et al. 2018.

15. Although the incidence of cervical cancer is higher than breast cancer in some rural areas of India, breast cancer is more prevalent than cervical cancer in most metropolitan areas and in some states, including Tamil Nadu (Shetty 2012; Shanta, Swaminathan, and Rama 2013; Cancer Institute 2014; Agarwal and Ramkant 2008; Kannan 2013).

16. This report was also sponsored by the consulting firm Ernst & Young.

17. FICCI-FLO 2017.

18. The full name for the Pap smear is the cytology-based Babes-Papanicolaou test. It has been hailed as one of the top ten public health achievements of the twentieth century (Brownson and Bright 2004) and is widely used for early detection of cervical cancer in the global North along with mammograms for breast cancer prevention. These require technical skills, laboratory facilities, and machinery that are considered by some to be too costly for public health services in low- and middle-income countries.

19. Farmer et al. 2010; Mallath et al. 2014.

20. Davies 2013; Pamposh 2013; Mallath et al. 2014.

21. FICCI-FLO 2017; Mallath et al. 2014: e206.

22. FICCI-FLO 2017.

23. *The Hindu* 2013.

24. Muraleedharan, Dash, and Gilson 2011.

25. Government of Tamil Nadu, *Chief Minister's Comprehensive Health Insurance Scheme*, http://www.cmchistn.com/eligibility_en.php.

26. Pramesh et al. 2014. The Government of India spent 1.4% of the GDP on health care in 2014 compared to 3.1% in China and 8.3% in the United States in the same year (Goel and Kumar 2018).

27. *The Hindu*, "Government increases health insurance coverage," https://www.thehindu.com/news/national/tamil-nadu/government-increases-health-insurance-coverage/article25637859.ece.

28. Caduff et al. 2018: 2

29. Broom and Doron 2011: 250.

30. Dimmitt and van Buitenen 1978: 39.

31. Dimmitt and van Buitenen 1978: 40–41.

32. Allocco and Ponniah 2014: ii.

33. Halperin 2014:48–49. Citing Hudson (2013), Halperin writes that according to legend, "the Kaliyug is believed to have begun around the time of the Mahabharata

war, and dated by astronomers to 3102 BCE" (Halperin 2014:50). Others have written that people say the Kali Yuga began approximately 5,000 years ago, following the death of Krishna in the Mahabharata war (Allocco and Ponniah 2014: iv).

34. Dimmitt and van Buitenen 1978:21.

35. Allocco 2014; Halperin 2014; Lamb 2000; Pinney 1999; Cohen 1998; Gold 1998.

36. Pandian 2007.

37. Pooniah 2014.

38. This project was approved by the Syracuse University IRB. I received informed consent for all interviews, group meetings, recordings, and observations.

39. This is sometimes spelled Kancheepuram.

40. Van Hollen 2003; 2013.

41. Tharamangalam 2012, as cited in Kapadia 2017: 5.

42. Teltumbde 2017.

43. Kapadia 2017.

44. Hansen 1999.

45. Kapadia 2017; Sadanathan 2018.

46. Kapadia 2017: 22.

47. Kapadia 2017.

48. Kapadia 2017: 23.

49. Still 2017.

50. Anandhi 2017.

51. 2011 Census data on Tamil Nadu: http://www.census2011.co.in/data/religion /state/33-tamil-nadu.html; 2011 Census data for India: https://www.census2011.co .in/religion.php.

52. Roberts 2016.

53. Klawiter 2008.

54. Balshem 1993; Gregg 2003; Stoller 2004; McMullin and Weiner, eds. 2008; Livingston 2012; Jain 2013; Lora-Wainwright 2013; Mathews, Burke, and Kampriani, eds. 2015; Martinez 2018; Armin, Burke and Eichelberger, eds. 2019; Caduff and Van Hollen, eds. 2019; Banerjee 2020.

55. MacDonald 2015, 2016; Bright 2015; Banerjee 2020.

56. Kapadia 2017: 14.

57. Banerjee 2020: 173, 181.


CHAPTER I. HISTORY AND HOSPITALS

1. Banerjee 2020: 22.

2. Personal communication, April 1, 2018.

3. Trawick 1992a: 217. Siddha is a traditional system of medicine that has much in common with Ayurveda but is indigenous to and mostly practiced within Tamil Nadu.

4. Langford 2002: 184–85.

5. Banerjee 2014: 41.

6. Bhore, J. et al., *Report of the Health Survey and Development Committee*, vol. 2 (New Delhi: Government of India Press, 1946) (as cited by Mallath et al. 2014: e210).

7. All-India Institute of Medical Sciences, "Dr. B.R.A Institute-Rotary Cancer Hospital," https://www.aiims.edu/en/departments-and-centers/specialty-centers.ht ml?id=415.

8. Chittaranjan National Cancer Institute, "Welcome," http://cnci.org.in.

9. Cancer Institute 2015.

10. "Devadasi" is a term derived from Sanskrit that means a servant of god. Devadasis were women who had been dedicated to temples during puberty. They were ritually married to the god or goddess whom they served and they performed dances and other services for the temple. The devadasi practice was condemned and banned by British colonizers (who labelled devadasis as prostitutes) and subsequently by other Indian social reform movements, though a few devadasi communities continue some of their ritual practices under the radar.

11. Basu, ed. 1986.

12. Basu, ed. 1986: 11.

13. Basu, ed. 1986.

14. Basu, ed. 1986.

15. Sivaramakrishnan 2019.

16. Trawick 1992a: 217.

17. Sivaramakrishnan 2019: 539.

18. Trawick 1992a.

19. Sivaramakrishnan 2019: 532.

20. Dr. Shanta died in January 2021. I have dedicated this book to her and to my mother.

21. Ganesh 2017: 116.

22. Ganesh 2017.

23. Cancer Institute 2015.

24. Cancer Institute 2015.

25. Cancer Institute 2015.

26. Ganesh 2017: 95.

27. Cancer Institute (WIA), "With humanity and wisdom," http://cancerinsti tutewia.in/CIWIA/about%20the%20institute.html.

28. Shanta, Swaminathan, and Rama 2013.

29. "Dravidian" refers to a South Indian language family comprising of four linguistically related languages: Tamil, Malayalam, Kannada, and Telegu. Dravidian politics refers to political movements in the Tamil Nadu region. These political movements began with the Justice Party in 1916 and have continued to frame politics in Tamil Nadu ever since with a proliferation of Dravidian political parties.

30. Govt. Arignar Anna Memorial Cancer Hospital, "Institution history," http://www.aamci.ac.in/aamci/content_page.jsp?sq1=insthisty&sqf=1.

31. Govt. Arignar Anna Memorial Cancer Hospital, "Institution history."

32. Govt. Arignar Anna Memorial Cancer Hospital, "Institution history."

33. Govt. Arignar Anna Memorial Cancer Hospital, "Institution history."

34. Personal communication with Resident Medical Officer, Government Cancer Hospital, July 15, 2015.

35. 28,226 were outpatients and 4,860 were inpatients. 5,476 of the outpatients were registered at the hospital for the first time ("new patients") in 2014, whereas 22,750 had already been registered in previous years. 1,301 of the inpatients were new patients, whereas 3,559 were old patients.

36. 69% (261 out of 378).

37. Sankaranarayanan et al. 2007: 398.

38. *The Hindu* 2013.

39. Ortega 2013.

40. Petryna 2006: 36.

41. Colposcopy is a procedure that uses a colposcope to closely examine the cervix, vagina, and vulva for signs of disease.

42. Jayashree 2010.

43. The Tamil Nadu Health Systems Project was established with World Bank funding in 2006 to strengthen health care systems, including health care for non-communicable diseases.

44. Subha Sri and Ravindran 2017.

45. Subha Sri and Ravindran 2017: 317.

46. Subha Sri and Ravindran 2017: 324.

47. The National Rural Health Mission is a program of the Government of India's Ministry of Health and Family Welfare launched in 2005 to provide accessible, affordable, and quality health care to the rural population, especially vulnerable groups.

48. Van Hollen 2003.

49. Muraleedharan, Dash, and Gilson 2011; Smith 2009.

## CHAPTER 2. POVERTY AND CHEMICALS

1. The exchange rate was 63 Indian rupees to 1 US dollar in July 2015. Women reported a range between 50 and 150 rupees per day for agricultural *kuli* work.

2. People reported a range between 300 and 450 rupees for men's daily agricultural *kuli* work.

3. IndianJobTalks Forum, http://www.indianjobtalks.com/forum/showthread .php?t=67110.

4. IndianJobTalks Forum, http://www.indianjobtalks.com/forum/showthread .php?t=67110.

5. *Deccan Chronicle*, "Tamil Nadu moves Supreme Court against Andhra Pradesh dams," http://www.deccanchronicle.com/nation/current-affairs/190716/tamil-nadu -moves-supreme-court-against-andhra-pradesh-dams.html.

6. Arasu 2017.

7. Srinivasan 2008.

8. Arasu 2017.

9. Gupta 1998: 261–64.

10. Kumar 2017.

11. Gupta 1998.

12. Jayalalithaa, who was the Chief Minister during the periods of this ethnographic research project, died in December 2016.

13. Dravida Munnetra Kazhagam.

14. Madhav 2017.

15. *India Today*, "Tamil Nadu: Food minister Kamaraj blames Panneerselvam for ration shortage," http://indiatoday.intoday.in/story/tamil-nadu-panneerselvam-jaya lalithaa-ration-kamaraj/1/903744.html.

16. Jayashree and Vasudevan 2007.

17. Subramanian 2015: 41.

18. Ward 2009.

19. Harvey 2018.

20. Holmes 2013.

21. Bourdieu 1972.

22. Gupta 1998: 236.

23. Frankel 1971.

24. Subramanian 2015: 41.

25. Frankel 1971.

26. Pandian 2009; Jayashree and Vasudevan 2007.

27. Mint, "Women at the forefront of anti-Sterlite protests," https://www.live mint.com/Politics/X1YOly1SX4UKHN8XOM3ifN/Women-at-the-forefront-of -antiSterlite-protests.html.

28. Mohanty 1991.

29. Abu-Lughod 1990: 53.

30. Associated Press 2013.

31. Ramesh 2004.

32. *The Economic Times*, "Punjab plans to cut pesticides use in basmati rice," https://economictimes.indiatimes.com/news/economy/agriculture/punjab-plans-to -cut-pesticides-use-in-basmati-rice/articleshow/65604479.cms?from=mdr. See also *Hindustan Times*, "After EU, Saudi Arabia raises red flag over cancerous fungicide presence in basmati rice," https://www.hindustantimes.com/punjab/after-eu-saudi -arabia-raises-red-flag-over-cancerous-fungicide-presence-in-basmati-rice/story-TkN g6ygUeqYIyDDQ0HuGMK.html.

33. Carson 1962.

34. Livingston 2012: 48.

35. Smoke Free Media, "What is Hollywood hiding? Smoking on screen kills in real life," https://smokefreemovies.ucsf.edu/blog/india%E2%80%99s-strong-policy -protect-public-onscreen-smoking-under-attack.

36. Gajalakshmi, Whitlock, and Peto 2012.
37. *Kirumi* means "worms" but is commonly used to refer to the concept of "germs."
38. Nichter 2016.
39. Raskin 2015.
40. Sered and Fernandopulle 2006.
41. Singer 1986: 128.
42. Farmer 2001: 79.
43. Holmes 2011.
44. Quesada, Hart, and Bourgois 2011: 340.
45. Armin, Burke, and Eichelberger eds. 2019.
46. Sargent and Benson 2019: 25.

## CHAPTER 3. WOMEN AND WORK

1. Lora-Wainwright 2013.
2. Hunt 1998: 303.
3. Daniel 1984; Marriott 1990.
4. Lamb 2000; Van Hollen 2003.
5. Lamb 2000: 188.
6. Daniel 1984; Lamb 2000.
7. Daniel 1984: 187.
8. World Health Organization 2016.
9. Weaver 2018.
10. Sontag 1978.
11. Gregg 2003; Martínez 2018.
12. Pandian 2009.
13. Van Hollen 2011, 2013.
14. Trawick 1992b.
15. Ramaswamy 1997.
16. Hochschild 1989.
17. Rai et al. 2018.
18. American Cancer Society, "Mastitis," https://www.cancer.org/cancer/breast
-cancer/non-cancerous-breast-conditions/mastitis.html.
19. Moran-Thomas 2019: 489.
20. Cre-A 1992.
21. Winslow 1991 [1862].
22. Mukherjee 2010: 47.
23. Mukherjee 2010: 47.
24. Nichter and Nichter 1989.
25. Lamb 2000.
26. Lamb 2000: 183; Dumont 1970a; Marriott 1976.
27. Van Hollen 2013: 204.

CHAPTER 4. SCREENING AND MORALITY

1. A version of this chapter is forthcoming (Van Hollen forthcoming 2023).

2. Foucault 1978.

3. Martin 1987; Comaroff 1993; Lock 1995; Ram and Jolly, eds. 1998; Rapp 2000.

4. Arnold 1993, 2006; Harrison 1994; Levine 1994; Whitehead 1995; Hodges 2006.

5. Van Hollen 2003, 2013; Ram 1991, 2013; Ramberg 2014.

6. Sontag 1978.

7. Douglas 1992.

8. Balshem 1993; Jain 2013.

9. Hunt 1998; Lora-Wainwright 2013; Gregg 2003; Martínez 2018.

10. The Noble Foundation was founded in 2002. Its original mission was to increase voluntary blood donations for transfusions. During the time of my research it was also providing cancer education camps for women in underserved communities.

11. The Cancer Institute and RUWSEC camps were all run by women. The Noble camp had male and female presenters.

12. Fuller and Narasimhan 2008: 740.

13. The News Minute, "In three charts: Brides in Kerala and TN have gotten younger in nine years," https://www.thenewsminute.com/article/three-charts-brides-kerala-and-tn-have-gotten-younger-nine-years-44797#:~:text=While%20women%20in%20Kerala%20were,to%2021.2%20years%20in%202014.

14. UNICEF, "UNFPA-UNICEF Global Programme to End Child Marriage," https://www.unicef.org/protection/unfpa-unicef-global-programme-end-child-marriage.

15. Nag 1995.

16. Van Hollen 2013.

17. American Cancer Society, "Risk factors for cervical cancer," https://www.cancer.org/cancer/cervical-cancer/causes-risks-prevention/risk-factors.html.

18. Van Hollen 2003.

19. Whitehead 1995.

20. Government of India, "Swatchh Bharat challenges," https://swachhbharat.mygov.in/sb-challenges.

21. Garg, Goyal, and Gupta 2012.

22. Coffey and Spears 2017.

23. Visaria and Ramachandran, eds. 2007. Unnithan-Kumar (2010) found that some women in Rajasthan, North India, have positive attitudes toward abortion not only as a preferred form of birth control, but also because of perceptions that an abortion is a process of "cleaning" that relieves women of the burden of childbearing and paves the way for stronger, better-quality children in the future. I have not come across this discourse on abortion in Tamil Nadu.

24. Anandhi 2007.

25. Remennick 1990: 59.

26. Remennick 1990: 263.

27. Van Hollen 2013.
28. Sarojini, Anjali, and Ashalata 2010; Sunder Rajan 2017.
29. Mattheij, Pollock, and Brhlikova 2012.
30. Fuller and Narasimhan 2008.
31. Banerjee 2020.

## CHAPTER 5. DISCLOSURE AND CARE

1. A version of this chapter was previously published (Van Hollen 2018).
2. Gorringe 2017.
3. Held 2005: 15.
4. Held 2005: 13.
5. Held 2005: 12.
6. Mol 2006; Mulla 2014; Stevenson 2014.
7. Stevenson 2014: 3.
8. Stevenson 2014: 174.
9. Stevenson 2014: 174.
10. Sontag 1978; Taylor 1988.
11. Taylor 1988: 441.
12. Crane 2013; Petryna 2009.
13. Finkler 2008: 158.
14. Good et al. 1990.
15. Rabinow and Rose 2006.
16. National Institutes of Health 2015.
17. Alexander, Narayanakurup, and Vidyasagar 1993; Banerjee 2020; Khanna and Singh 1988; Miyata et al. 2005; Montazer et al. 2009; Seo et al. 2000.
18. Jain 2013: 182–83; Lupton 1997; Taylor 1998.
19. Khanna and Singh 1988.
20. Crigger, Holcomb, and Weiss 2001: 464.
21. National Institutes of Health 2015.
22. Good et al. 1990; Kleinman 1997.
23. Kleinman 1997: 47–48.
24. Das 1999.
25. Gammeltoft 2014.
26. Good et al. 1990: 61.
27. Jain 2013: 54.
28. Bright 2015: 147.
29. Hunt 2000.
30. Gregg 2003, 2011.
31. Kangas 2002; Sargent and Benson 2019.
32. Banerjee 2020.
33. Khanna and Singh 1988.
34. Taylor 1998: 458.

35. *Eri-pori* is literally a fuel-burning engine. The term is used to convey a stern demeanor of talk.

36. *Nerum vandhuruchu* literally means "time has come" but is an expression that means fate, like the Tamil word "*vidi.*"

37. *Nalla paathukuvanga* means "they look after [you] well" or "they take good care [of you]."

38. Lupton 1997: 379–80.

39. Muraleedharan et al. 2011.

40. Livingston 2012: 101.

41. Held 2006: 15.

42. Held 2006: 16.

43. Gupta 1995: 376.

44. Gregg 2003: 142.

45. George 2009; Killmer 2014.

46. Kleinman 1997: 67.

## CHAPTER 6. BIOMEDICINE AND BODIES

1. Sontag 1978: 3.

2. Klawiter 2008; Hansen 2007; Aureliano 2015.

3. Pinto 2014; Halliburton 2009.

4. Van Hollen 1998, 2003.

5. Cohen 1999.

6. Moniruzzaman 2012.

7. Mamidi and Pulla 2013; Desai et al. 2017; Prusty, Choithani, and Gupta 2018.

8. Jadhav 2019.

9. Klawiter 2008: 105.

10. Klawiter borrows this term from Chapter 11, "Breasted Experience: The Look and the Feeling," in Young (1990).

11. Klawiter 2008: 118.

12. Klawiter 2008: 121.

13. Klawiter 2008: 134.

14. Look Good Feel Better, "About," http://lookgoodfeelbetter.org/about.

15. Lorde 1980; Cartwright 1998; Klawiter 2008.

16. Jain 2013; Klawiter 2008.

17. Rabin 2016.

18. Manderson 2001; Aureliano 2015.

19. Manderson 2001, 2011; Klawiter 2008.

20. Quoted in Puri 1999: 88–89.

21. Klawiter 2008: 233.

22. Banerjee 2020.

23. Van Hollen 2011, 2013.

24. Klawiter 2008.
25. Typically associated with North Indian women's clothing, these are long tunics worn over loose-fitting pants. Younger, urban women in Tamil Nadu began wearing these in the late twentieth century.
26. Aureliano 2015.
27. Hart 1973: 250.
28. Lamb 2000.
29. Olivelle 1998.
30. Leach 1958.
31. Leach 1958; Hershman 1974; Obeyesekere 1981; Olivelle 1998; Ramberg 2014.
32. Van Hollen 2003.
33. Lamb 2000.
34. Olivelle 1998: 23, 39.
35. Miller 1998: 264.
36. Hansen 2007: 22.
37. MacDonald 2015.
38. Fuller 1992.
39. Fuller 1992: 72–73.
40. Fuller 1992: 72.
41. Olivelle 1998: 20.

## CHAPTER 7. SORCERY AND RELIGION

1. Portions of this chapter were previously published (Van Hollen, Krishnan, Rathnam 2019).
2. Parry 1994.
3. Van Hollen 2019.
4. Hunt 1998.
5. Evans-Pritchard 1937; Farmer 1992; Stoller 2004; Rödlach 2006.
6. Lévi-Strauss 1963; Csordas 1997.
7. Kakar 1982; Daniel and Pugh, eds. 1984; Halliburton 2009; Flueckiger 2006.
8. In the Winslow (1862) and Cre-A (1992) Tamil–English dictionaries, each of these words is translated as sorcery. *Seyvinai* is also translated as witchcraft; *suniyam* is also translated as witchcraft and black magic; *manthirivaatham* is also translated as magic.
9. Winslow 1991 [1862]; Cre-A 1992.
10. Nabokov 2000: 31.
11. Nabokov 2000: 20.
12. Romanucci-Ross 1969.
13. Farmer 1992.
14. Van Hollen 1987.
15. Nabokov 2000.

16. Obeyesekere 1991; Ramberg 2014.

17. Nabokov 2000: 81.

18. Dumont 1970b; Fuller 1992; Mines 2005.

19. Hansen 1999: 107.

20. Chella Meenakshi Centre for Educational Research and Service 2015.

21. Roberts 2016.

22. Baptist Press, "Anti-conversion law repeal announced in Indian state," https://www.baptistpress.com/resource-library/news/anti-conversion-law-repeal-announced-in-indian-state.

23. Van Hollen 2013.

24. Roberts (2016: 234–35) describes newly converted Dalit Pentecostal women in Chennai removing jewelry because "women must come to see themselves as Christ sees them" and must feel comfortable with their "true beauty and inner goodness."

25. Mahadev 2014.

26. Roberts 2016.

27. Roberts 2016: 9.

28. Banerjee 2020.

# BIBLIOGRAPHY

Abu-Lughod, Lila. 1990. "The Romance of Resistance: Tracing Transformations of Power through Bedouin Women." *American Ethnologist* 17(1): 41–55.

Agarwal, G., and P. Ramakant. 2008. "Breast Cancer Care in India: The Current Scenario and the Challenges for the Future." *Breast Care Journal* 3(1): 21–27.

Alexander, John P., Dinesh Narayanakurup, and M.S. Vidyasagar. 1993. "Psychiatric Morbidity among Cancer Patients and Its Relationship with Awareness of Illness and Expectations about Treatment Outcome." *Acta Oncologica* 32(6): 623–26.

Allocco, Amy L. 2014. "The Blemish of 'Modern Times': Snakes, Planets, and the Kaliyugam." *Nidān* 26(1): 1–21.

Allocco, Amy L., and James Ponniah. 2014. "Introduction." *Nidān* 26(1): i–vi.

Anandhi, S. 2007. "Women, Work, and Abortion Practices in Tamil Nadu." In *Abortion in India: Ground Realities*, edited by L. Visaria and V. Ramachandran, 62–99. New York: Routledge.

———. 2017. "Gendered Negotiations of Caste Identity: Dalit Women's Activism in Rural Tamil Nadu." In *Dalit Women: Vanguard of an Alternative Politics in India*, edited by S. Anandhi and Karin Kapadia, 98–130. New York: Routledge.

Arasu, Sibi. 2017. "Miners Plunder Tamil Nadu's Sands, Dropping Some Rivers by 50 Feet." *New Security Beat, Woodrow Wilson Center for International Scholars*, May. https://www.newsecuritybeat.org/2017/05/miners-plunder-tamil-nadus-sands -dropping-rivers-50-feet.

Armin, Julie, Nancy Burke, and Laura Eichelberger, eds. 2019. *Negotiating Structural Vulnerability in Cancer Control*. Albuquerque: University of New Mexico Press.

Arnold, David. 1993. *Colonizing the Body: State Medicine and Epidemic Disease in Nineteenth-Century India*. Berkeley: University of California Press.

———. 2006. "Official Attitudes to Population, Birth Control, and Reproductive Health in India, 1921–1946." In *Reproductive Health in India: History, Politics, Controversies*, edited by S. Hodges. Delhi: Orient Longman.

Associated Press. 2013 (July 20). "'Very Toxic' Levels of Pesticides in Lunch That Killed 23 Kids: Indian Police." http://www.ctvnews.ca/world/very-toxic-levels-of -pesticide-in-lunch-that-killed-23-kids-indian-police-1.1375754.

Aureliano, Waleska De Araújo. 2015. "From Part to Whole: Gender Roles and Health Practices in the Experience of Breast Cancer in Northeast Brazil." In *Anthropologies of Cancer in Transnational Worlds*, edited by H. Matthews, N. Burke, and E. Kampiriani, 177–92. New York: Routledge.

Balshem, Martha. 1993. *Cancer in the Community: Class and Medical Authority*. Washington, D.C.: Smithsonian Institution Press.

Banerjee, Dwaipayan. 2014. *Concealments and Conciliations: The Emergent Politics of Cancer in India*. Ph.D. diss., NYU.

———. 2020. *Enduring Cancer: Life, Death, and Diagnosis in Delhi*. Durham: Duke University Press.

Basu, Aparna, ed. 1986. *The Pathfinder: Dr. Muthulakshmi Reddi*. Delhi: All India Women's Conference.

Bourdieu, Pierre. 1972. *Outline of a Theory of Practice*. Cambridge: Cambridge University Press.

Breman, Jan, and E. Valentine Daniel. 1992. "Conclusion: The Making of a Coolie." *Journal of Peasant Studies* 19(3–4): 268–95.

Bright, Kristen. 2015. "Love in the Time of Cancer." In *Anthropologies of Cancer in Transnational Worlds*, edited by H. Matthews, N. Burke, and E. Kampiriani, 135–55. New York: Routledge.

Broom, Alex, and Assa Doron. 2011. "The Rise of Cancer in Urban India: Cultural Understandings, Structural Inequalities, and the Emergence of the Clinic." *Health* 16(3): 250–66.

Brownson, R.C., and F.S. Bright. 2004. "Chronic Disease Control in Public Health Practice: Looking Back and Moving Forward." *Public Health Report* 119(3): 230.

Caduff, Carlo, Mac Skelton, Dwaipayan Banerjee, Darja Djordjevic, Marissa Mika, Lucas Mueller, Kavita Sivaramakrishnan, and Cecilia Van Hollen. 2018. "Analysis of Social Science Research into Cancer Care in Low- and Middle-Income Countries: Improving Global Cancer Control through Greater Interdisciplinary Research." *Journal of Global Oncology* 18.00045, published online June 15, 2018: 1–9.

Caduff, Carlo, and Cecilia Van Hollen. 2019. "Cancer and the Global South." *Cancer and the Global South: Special Issue of BioSocieties* 14(4): 489–95.

Cancer Institute (WIA). 2014. "Cancer Registration in Chennai, India: Incidence, Pattern, and Trend, 1982–2011." Chennai: Madras Metropolitan Tumour Registry (MMTR) of the National Cancer Registry Program, Indian Council of Medical Research (ICMR) at the Cancer Institute (WIA).

———. 2015. "Cancer Institute (WIA): 60 Years, 1954–2014." Commemorative publication. Chennai: Cancer Institute.

Carson, Rachel. 1962. *Silent Spring*. New York: Houghton Mifflin.

Cartwright, Lisa. 1998. "Community and the Public Body in Breast Cancer Media Activism." *Cultural Studies* 12(2): 117–38.

Chella Meenakshi Centre for Educational Research and Service. 2015. *Lord Murugan and South Indian Hinduism*. Documentary film. Center for South Asia, University of Wisconsin.

Coffey, Diane, and Dean E. Spears. 2017. *Where India Goes: Abandoned Toilets, Stunted Development, and the Costs of Caste*. New York: HarperCollins.

Cohen, Lawrence. 1998. *No Aging in India: Alzheimer's, the Bad Family, and Other Modern Things*. Berkeley: University of California Press.

———. 1999. "Where It Hurts: Indian Materials for an Ethics of Organ Transplantation." *Daedalus* 128: 135–65.

Comaroff, Jean. 1993. "The Diseased Heart of Africa: Medicine, Colonialism, and the Black Body." In *Knowledge, Power, and Practice: The Anthropology of Medicine and Everyday Life*, edited by Shirley Lindenbaum and Margaret Lock, 305–29. Berkeley: University of California Press.

Crane, Johanna Taylor. 2013. *Scrambling for Africa: AIDS, Expertise, and the Rise of American Global Health Science*. Ithaca: Cornell University Press.

Cre-A. 1992. *Cre-A Tamil English Dictionary*. Madras.

Crigger, N.J., L. Holcomb, and J. Weiss. 2001. "Fundamentalism, Multiculturalism, and Problems of Conducting Research with Populations in Developing Nations." *Nursing Ethics* 8(5): 459–68.

Csordas, Thomas J. 1997. *The Sacred Self: A Cultural Phenomenology of Charismatic Healing*. Berkeley: University of California Press.

Daniel, E. Valentine. 1984. *Fluid Signs: Being a Person the Tamil Way*. Berkeley: University of California Press.

Daniel, E. Valentine, and Judy F. Pugh, eds. 1984. *South Asian Systems of Healing*. [*Contributions to Asian Studies*, vol. 18]. Leiden: E.J. Brill.

Das, Veena. 1999. "Public Good, Ethics, and Everyday Life: Beyond the Boundaries of Bioethics." *Daedalus* 128 (4): 99–133.

Davies, Will. 2013. "India Has Most Cervical Cancer Deaths." *Wall Street Journal*, May 10, 2013. http://blogs.wsj.com/indiarealtime/2013/05/10/india-has-highest-number-of-cervical-cancer-deaths.

Desai, Sapna, Oona Campbell, Tara Sinha, Ajay Mahal, and Simon Cousens. 2017. "Incidence and Determinants of Hysterectomy in Low-Income Setting in Gujarat, India." *Health Policy Planning* 21(1): 68–78.

Dimmitt, Cornelia, and J.A.B. van Buitenen, eds. 1978. *Classical Hindu Mythology: A Reader in the Sanskrit Purāṇas*. Philadelphia: Temple University Press.

Douglas, Mary. 1992. *Risk and Blame: Essays in Cultural Theory*. New York: Routledge.

Dumont, Louis. 1970a. *Homo Hierachicus: The Caste System and Its Implications*. Chicago: University of Chicago Press.

———. 1970b. "A Structural Definition of a Folk Deity of Tamil Nadu: Aiyanar, the Lord." *Contributions to Indian Sociology* 3: 75–87.

Evans-Pritchard, E.E. 1937. *Witchcraft, Oracles, and Magic among the Azande*. Oxford: Oxford University Press.

Farmer, Paul. 1992. *AIDS and Accusation: Haiti and the Geography of Blame.* Berkeley: University of California Press.

———. 2001. *Infections and Inequalities: The Modern Plagues.* Berkeley: University of California Press.

Farmer, Paul, Julio Frenk, Felicia M. Knaul, Lawrence N. Shulman, George Alleyne, Lance Armstrong, Rifat Atun, et al. 2010. "Expansion of Cancer Care and Control in Countries of Low and Middle Income: A Call to Action." *Lancet* 376(9747): 1186–93.

FICCI-FLO (Federation of Indian Chambers of Commerce). 2017 (September 21). "Call for Action: Expanding Cancer Care for Women in India." file:///C:/Users/yncvhcc/Documents/nBox/Cancer%20Research-%20India/Articles/Reports-Statistics/Expanding-cancer-care-for-women-in-India.pdf.

Finkler, Kaja. 2008. "Can Bioethics Be Global and Local, or Must It Be Both?" *Journal of Contemporary Ethnography* 37(2): 155–79.

Flueckiger, Joyce. 2006. *In Amma's Healing Room: Gender and Vernacular Islam in South India.* Bloomington: Indiana University Press.

Foucault, Michel. 1978. *The History of Sexuality*, vol. 1. New York: Vintage Books.

Frankel, Francine. 1971. *India's Green Revolution: Economic Gains and Political Costs.* Princeton: Princeton University Press.

Fuller, C.J. 1992. *The Camphor Flame: Popular Hinduism and Society in India.* Princeton: Princeton University Press.

Fuller, C.J., and Haripriya Narasimhan. 2008. "Companionate Marriage in India: The Changing Marriage System in a Middle-Class Brahman Subcaste." *Journal of the Royal Anthropological Institute* 14(4): 736–54.

Gajalakshmi, Vendhan, Gary Whitlock, and Richard Peto. 2012. "Social Inequalities, Tobacco Chewing, and Cancer Mortality in South India: A Case-Control Analysis of 2,580 Cancer Deaths among Non-Smoking Non-Drinkers." *Cancer Causes and Control* 23(S1): 91–98.

Gammeltoft, Tine. 2014. *Haunting Images: A Cultural Account of Selective Reproduction in Vietnam.* Berkeley: University of California Press.

Ganesh, K. 2017. "Healing Touch: Dr. V. Shanta's Journeys in Cancer Treatment and Care." In *Feminists and Science: Critiques and Changing Practices in India*, edited by S. Krishna and G. Chadha, 2: 93–120. New Delhi: Sage.

Garg, Rajesh, Shobha Goyal, and Sanjeev Gupta. 2012. "India Moves towards Menstrual Hygiene: Subsidized Sanitary Napkins for Rural Adolescent Girls—Issues and Challenges." *Maternal and Child Health Journal* 16(4): 767–74.

George, Asha. 2009. "'By Papers and Pens, You Can Only Do So Much': Views about Accountability and Human Resource Management from Indian Government Health Administrators and Workers." *International Journal of Health Planning and Management* 24(3): 205–24.

Goel, Vindu, and Hari Kumar. 2018. "India Wants to Give Half a Billion People Free Health Care." *New York Times*, February 1, 2018.

Gold, Ann Grodzins. 1998. "Sin and Rain: Moral Ecology in Rural North India." In

*Purifying the Earthly Body: Religion and Ecology in Hindu India*, edited by Lance E. Nelson, 165–95. Albany: SUNY Press.

Good, Mary-Jo del Vecchio, Byron J. Good, Cynthia Schaffer, and Stuart E. Lind. 1990. "American Oncology and the Discourse on Hope." *Culture, Medicine and Psychiatry* 14: 59–79.

Gorringe, Hugo. 2017. "Liberation Panthers and Pantheresses? Gender and Dalit Party Politics in South India." In *Dalit Women: Vanguard of an Alternative Politics in India*, edited by S. Anandhi and Karin Kapadia, 131–57. New York: Routledge.

Gregg, Jessica. 2003. *Virtually Virgins: Sexual Strategies and Cervical Cancer in Recife, Brazil*. Stanford: Stanford University Press.

———. 2011. "An Unanticipated Source of Hope: Stigma and Cervical Cancer in Brazil." *Medical Anthropology Quarterly* 25(1): 70–84.

Gupta, Akhil. 1995. "Blurred Boundaries: The Discourse of Corruption, the Culture of Politics, and the Imagined State." *American Ethnologist* 22(2): 375–402.

———. 1998. *Postcolonial Developments: Agriculture in the Making of Modern India*. Durham: Duke University Press.

Halliburton, Murphy. 2009. *Mudpacks and Prozac: Experiencing Ayurvedic, Biomedical, and Religious Healing*. Walnut Creek: Left Coast Press.

Halperin, Ehud. 2014. "The Age of Kālī: Contemporary Iterations of the Kaliyug in the Kullu Valley of the Western Himalayas." *Nidān* 26: 42–64.

Hansen, Helle. 2007. "Hair Loss Induced by Chemotherapy: An Anthropological Study of Women, Cancer, and Rehabilitation." *Anthropology and Medicine* 14(1): 15–26.

Hansen, Thomas Blom. 1999. *The Saffron Wave: Democracy and Hindu Nationalism in Modern India*. Princeton: Princeton University Press.

Harrison, Mark. 1994. *Public Health in British India: Anglo-Indian Preventive Medicine 1859–1914*. Cambridge: Cambridge University Press.

Hart, George. 1973. "Woman and the Sacred in Tamilnad." *Journal of Asian Studies* 32 (2): 233–50.

Harvey, Fiona. 2018. "India's Farmed Chickens Dosed with World's Strongest Antibiotics, Study Finds." *The Guardian*, February 10, 2018.

Held, Virginia. 2005. *The Ethics of Care: Personal, Political, and Global*. Oxford: Oxford University Press.

Hershman, P. 1974. "Hair, Sex, and Dirt." *Man* 9(2): 274.

*The Hindu*. 2013 (June 3). "India Doctors Develop Low-Cost Screening for Cervical Cancer." http://www.thehindu.com/sci-tech/health/indian-doctors-develop-low cost-screening-for-cervical-cancer/article4778565.ece.

Hochschild, Arlie. 1989. *The Second Shift*. New York: Penguin Books.

Hodges, Sarah. 2006. "Indian Eugenics in an Age of Reform." In *Reproductive Health in India: History, Politics, Controversies*, edited by S. Hodges, 115–38. Delhi: Orient Longman.

Holmes, Seth. 2011. "Structural Vulnerabilities and Hierarchies of Ethnicity and Citizenship on the Farm." *Medical Anthropology* 30(4): 425–49.

———. 2013. *Fresh Fruit, Broken Bodies: Migrant Farmworkers in the United States.* Berkeley: University of California Press.

Hudson, Emily T. 2013. *Disorienting Dharma: Ethics and the Aesthetics of Suffering in the Mahābhārata.* Oxford: Oxford University Press.

Hunt, Linda M. 1998. "Moral Reasoning and the Meaning of Cancer: Causal Explanations of Oncologists and Patients in Southern Mexico." *Medical Anthropology Quarterly* 12(3): 298–318.

———. 2000. "Strategic Suffering: Illness Narratives as Social Empowerment among Mexican Cancer Patients." In *Narrative and the Cultural Construction of Illness and Healing,* edited by Cheryl Mattingly and Linda Garro, 88–107. Berkeley: University of California Press.

Jadhav, Radeshyam. 2019. "Why Many Women in Maharashtra's Beed District Have No Wombs." *The Hindu: Business Line,* April 11, 2019. https://www.thehindu businessline.com/economy/agri-business/why-half-the-women-in-maharashtras -beed-district-have-no-wombs/article26773974.ece.

Jain, S. Lochlann. 2013. *Malignant: How Cancer Becomes Us.* Berkeley: University of California Press.

Jayashree, B. 2010. "Tamil Nadu Pioneers Easy Cervical Cancer Screening." *Infochange News and Features: Public Health,* June 2010.

Jayashree, R., and N. Vasudevan. 2007. "Organochlorine Pesticide Residues in Ground Water of Thiruvallur District, India." *Environmental Monitoring Assessment* 128: 209–15.

Kakar, Sudhir. 1982. *Shamans, Mystics, and Doctors: A Psychological Inquiry into India and Its Healing Traditions.* Chicago: University of Chicago Press.

Kangas, Beth. 2002. "Therapeutic Itineraries in a Global World: Yemenis and Their Search for Medical Treatment Abroad." *Medical Anthropology* 21(1): 35–78.

Kannan, Ramya. 2013. "Breast Cancer Incidence Growing at Higher Rate Than Cervical Cancer." *The Hindu,* June 5, 3013. http://www.thehindu.com/todays-paper/ tp-national/tp-tamilnadu/breast-cancer-incidence-growing-at-higher-rate-than -cervical-cancer/article4783101.ece.

Kapadia, Karin. 2017. "Introduction." In *Dalit Women: Vanguard of an Alternative Politics in India,* edited by S. Anandhi and Karin Kapadia, 1–50. New York: Routledge.

Khanna, R., and R.P.N. Singh. 1988. "Terminal Illness in an Indian Setting: Problems of Communication." *Indian Journal of Psychiatry* 30(3): 257–61.

Killmer, Jocelyn. 2014. "Improvising the 'Up-Down' Life: Young Women Doctors in Rural Rajasthan." Paper presented at the Annual Conference on South Asia, University of Wisconsin–Madison, October 2014.

Klawiter, Maren. 2008. *The Biopolitics of Breast Cancer: Changing Cultures of Disease and Activism.* Minneapolis: University of Minnesota Press.

Kleinman, Arthur. 1997. *Writing at the Margin: Discourse between Anthropology and Medicine.* Berkeley: University of California Press.

Kumar, Nilotpal. 2017. *Unravelling Farmer Suicides in India: Egoism and Masculinity in Peasant Life.* Oxford: Oxford University Press.

Lamb, Sarah. 2000. *White Saris and Sweet Mangoes: Aging, Gender, and Body in North India*. Berkeley: University of California Press.

Langford, Jean. 2002. *Ayurvedic Remedies for Postcolonial Imbalance*. Durham: Duke University Press.

Leach, E.R. 1958. "Magical Hair." *Journal of the Royal Anthropological Institute*. 88(2): 147–64.

Levine, Philippa. 1994. "Venereal Disease, Prostitution, and the Politics of Empire: The Case of British India." *Journal of the History of Sexuality* 4(4): 579–602.

Lévi-Strauss, Claude. 1963. "The Sorcerer and His Magic." In *Structural Anthropology*, 167–85. New York: Basic Books.

———. 1969. *Totemism*. New York: Penguin Press.

Livingston, Julie. 2012. *Improvising Medicine: An African Oncology Ward in an Emerging Cancer Epidemic*. Durham: Duke University Press.

Lock, Margaret. 1995. *Encounters with Aging: Mythologies of Menopause in Japan and North America*. Berkeley: University of California Press.

Lora-Wainwright, Anna. 2013. *Fighting for Breath: Living Morally and Dying of Cancer in a Chinese Village*. Honolulu: University of Hawai'i Press.

Lorde, Audre. 1980. *The Cancer Journals*. San Francisco: Aunt Lute Books.

Lupton, Deborah. 1997. "Consumerism, Reflexivity, and the Medical Encounter." *Social Science and Medicine* 45(3): 373–81.

MacDonald, A. 2015. "Revealing Hope in Urban India: Vision and Survivorship among Breast Cancer Charity Volunteers." In *Anthropologies of Cancer in Transnational Worlds*, edited by H. Matthews, N. Burke, and E. Kampiriani, 119–32. New York: Routledge.

———. 2016. "Delivering Breast Cancer Care in Urban India: Heterotopia, Hospital Ethnography, and Voluntarism." *Health and Place* 39: 226–32.

Madhav, Pramod. 2017. "Tamil Nadu: Government Issues Guidelines for Ration Supply, Excludes Many." *India Today*, August 3, 2017. http://indiatoday.intoday .in/story/tamil-nadu-government-issues-guidelines-for-public-distribution-system -excludes-many/1/1017675.html.

Mahadev, Neena. 2014. "Conversion and Anti-Conversion in Contemporary Sri Lanka: Pentecostal Christian Evangelism and Theravada Buddhist Views on the Ethics of Religious Attraction." In *Proselytizing and the Limits of Religious Pluralism in Contemporary Asia*, edited by J. Finucane and R.M. Feener, 211–35. Singapore: ARI–Springer Asia Series.

Mallath, Mohandas, David Taylor, Rajendra Badwe, Goura Rath, V. Shanta, C.S. Pramesh, Raghunadharao Digumarti, et al. 2014. "The Growing Burden of Cancer in India: Epidemiology and Social Context." *The Lancet Oncology* 15(6): e205–12.

Mamidi, Bharat, and Venkat Pulla. 2013. "Hysterectomies and Violation of Human Rights: Case Study from India." *International Journal of Social Work and Human Services Practice* 1(1): 64–75.

Manderson, Lenore. 2001. *Surface Tensions: Surgery, Bodily Boundaries, and the Social Self*. New York: Routledge.

———. 2011. "Anthropologies of Cancer and Risk: Uncertainty and Disruption." In *A Companion to Medical Anthropology*, edited by Merrill Singer and Pamela Erickson, 323–38. West Sussex: Wiley-Blackwell.

Marriot, McKim. 1976. Hindu Transactions: Diversity without Dualism. In *Transaction and Meaning: Directions in the Anthropology of Exchange and Symbolic Behavior*, edited by Bruce Kapfrerer, 109–42. Philadelphia: Institute for the Study of Human Issues.

———. 1990. "Constructing an Indian Ethnosociology." In *India through Hindu Categories*, 1–39. New Delhi: Sage.

Martin, Emily. 1987. *The Woman in the Body: A Cultural Analysis of Reproduction*. Boston: Beacon Press.

Martínez, Rebecca G. 2018. *Marked Women: The Cultural Politics of Cervical Cancer in Venezuela*. Stanford: Stanford University Press.

Mathews, Holly, Nancy Burke, and Eirini Kampriani, eds. 2015. *Anthropologies of Cancer in Transnational Worlds*. New York: Routledge.

Mattheij, I., A. Pollock, and P. Brhlikova. 2012. "Do Cervical Cancer Data Justify HPV Vaccination in India? Epidemiological Data Sources and Comprehensiveness." *Journal of the Royal Society of Medicine* 105(6): 250–62.

McMullin, Juliet, and Diane Weiner, eds. 2008. *Confronting Cancer: Metaphors, Advocacy, and Anthropology*. Santa Fe: School for Advanced Research Advanced Seminar Series.

Miller, Barbara. 1998. "The Disappearance of the Oiled Braid: Indian Adolescent Female Hairstyles in North America." In *Hair: Its Power and Meaning in Asian Cultures*, edited by Alf Hiltebeitel and Barbara Miller, 259–80. Albany: SUNY Press.

Mines, Diane. 2005. *Fierce Gods: Inequality, Ritual, and the Politics of Dignity in a South Indian Village*. Bloomington: Indiana University Press.

Miyata, H., M. Takahashi, T. Saito, H. Tachimori, and I. Kai, 2005. "Disclosure Preferences Regarding Cancer Diagnosis and Prognosis: To Tell or Not to Tell?" *Journal of Medical Ethics* 31(8): 447–51.

Mohanty, Chandra Talpade. 1991. "Under Western Eyes: Feminist Scholarship and Colonial Discourses." In *Third World Women and the Politics of Feminism*, edited by C.T. Mohanty et al., 51–80. Bloomington: Indiana University Press.

Mol, Annemarie. 2006. *The Logic of Care: Health and the Problem of Patient Choice*. New York: Routledge.

Moniruzzaman, Monir. 2012. "'Living Cadavers' in Bangladesh: Bioviolence in the Human Organ Bazaar." *Medical Anthropology Quarterly* 26(1): 69–91.

Montazer, A., A. Tavoli, M. Mohagheghi, R. Roshan, and Z. Tavoli. 2009. "Disclosure of Cancer Diagnosis and Quality of Life in Cancer Patients: Should It Be the Same Everywhere?" *BMC Cancer* 9(39).

Moran-Thomas, Amy. 2019. "What Is Communicable? Unaccounted Injuries and 'Catching' Diabetes in an Illegible Epidemic." *Cultural Anthropology* 34(4): 471–502.

Mukherjee, Siddhartha. 2010. *The Emperor of All Maladies: A Biography of Cancer*. New York: Scribner.

Mulla, Sameena. 2014. *The Violence of Care: Rape Victims, Forensic Nurses, and Sexual Assault Intervention*. New York: NYU Press.

Muraleedharan, V., Umakant Dash, and Lucy Gilson. 2011. "Tamil Nadu 1980s–2005: A Success Story in India." In *"Good Health at Low Cost" 25 Years on: What Makes a Successful Health System?*, edited by D. Balabanova, M. McKee, and A. Mills, 159–92. London: London School of Hygiene and Tropical Medicine.

Nabokov, Isabelle. 2000. *Religion against the Self: An Ethnography of Tamil Rituals*. Oxford: Oxford University Press.

Nag, M. 1995. "Sexual Behaviour in India with Risk of HIV/AIDS Transmission." *Health Transition Review* 5, Supplement: 293–305.

National Cancer Registry Programme, Indian Council of Medical Research (NCRP/ICMR). 2011. "Source of Cancer Incidence Data. Report." [Data from this report came from the WHO International Agency for Research on Cancer Globocan Project.]

National Institutes of Health (National Cancer Institute). 2015. Communication in Cancer-Care for Health Professionals: Unique Aspects of Communication with Cancer Patients. https://www.cancer.gov/about-cancer/coping/adjusting-to-cancer/communication-hp-pdq#section/_9.

Nichter, Mark. 2016. "Comorbidity: Reconsidering the Unit of Analysis: Comorbidity Reconsidered." *Medical Anthropology Quarterly* 30(4): 536–44.

Nichter, Mark, and Mimi Nichter. 1989. "Cultural Notions of Fertility in South Asia and Their Impact on Sri Lankan Family Planning Practices." In *Anthropology and International Health: Asian Health Studies*, edited by Mark Nichter and Mimi Nichter, 3–34. Dordrecht: Kluwer Academic.

Obeyesekere, Gananath. 1981. *Medusa's Hair: An Essay on Personal Symbols and Religious Experience*. Chicago: University of Chicago Press.

Olivelle, Patrick. 1998. "Hair and Society: Social Significance of Hair in South Asian Traditions." In *Hair: Its Power and Meaning in Asian Cultures*, edited by Alf Hiltebeitel and Barbara Miller, 11–49. Albany: SUNY Press.

Ortega, Bob. 2013. "Ethical Questions Linger in Cervical Cancer Study." *USA Today*, August 31, 2013. https://www.usatoday.com/story/news/nation/2013/08/31/ethical-questions-linger-in-cervical-cancer-study/2751705.

Pamposh, Raina. 2013. "India Ranks No. 1 in Cervical Cancer Deaths." *India Ink: The New York Times*, May 10, 2013.

Pandian, Anand. 2009. *Crooked Stalks: Cultivating Virtue in South India*. Durham: Duke University Press.

Pandian, M.S.S. 2007. *Brahmin and Non-Brahmin: Genealogies of the Tamil Political Present*. Delhi: Permanent Black.

Parry, Jonathan. 1994. *Death in Banaras*. Cambridge: Cambridge University Press.

Petryna, Adriana. 2006. "Globalizing Human Subjects Research." In *Global Pharmaceuticals: Ethics, Markets, Practices*, edited by Adriana Petryna, Arthur Kleinman, and Andrew Lakoff, 33–60. Durham: Duke University Press.

———. 2009. *When Experiments Travel: Clinical Trials and the Global Search for Human Subjects*. Princeton: Princeton University Press.

Pinney, Christopher. 1999. "On Living in the Kal(i)Yug: Notes from Nagda, Madhya Pradesh." *Contributions to Indian Sociology* 33(1–2): 77–206.

Pinto, Sarah. 2014. *Daughters of Parvati: Women and Madness in Contemporary India*. Philadelphia: University of Pennsylvania Press.

Ponniah, James. 2014. "Alternative Discourses of Kali Yuga in Ayyā Valli." *Nidān* 26(1): 65–87.

Pramesh, C.S, Rajendra A. Badwe, Bibhuti B. Borthakur, Madhu Chandra, Elluswami Hemanth Raj, T. Kannan, Ashok Kalwar, et al. 2014. "Delivery of Affordable and Equitable Cancer Care in India." *The Lancet Oncology* 15(6): e223–33.

Prutsy, Ranjan K., Chetan Choithani, and Shiv D. Gupta. 2018. "Predictors of Hysterectomy among Married Women 15–49 Years in India." *Reproductive Health* 15(3) doi:10.1186/s12978-017-0445-8.

Puri, Jyoti. 1999. *Woman, Body, Desire in Post-Colonial India: Narratives of Gender and Sexuality*. New York: Routledge.

Queseda, James, Laurie Hart, and Philippe Bourgois. 2011. "Structural Vulnerability and Health: Latino Migrant Laborers in the United States." *Medical Anthropology* 30(4): 339–62.

Rabin, Roni Caryn. 2016. "'Going Flat' after Breast Cancer." *New York Times*, October 31, 2016.

Rabinow, Paul, and Nicholas Rose. 2006. "Biopower Today." *BioSocieties* 1: 195–217.

Rai, Rajesh Kumar, Wafaie W. Fawzi, Anamitra Barik, and Abhijit Chowdhury. 2018. "The Burden of Iron-Deficiency Anaemia among Women in India: How Have Iron and Folic Acid Interventions Fared?" *WHO South-East Asia Journal of Public Health* 7(1): 18–23.

Ram, Kalpana. 1991. *Mukkuvar Women: Gender, Hegemony, and Capitalist Transformation in a South Indian Fishing Community*. Delhi: Kali for Women.

———. 2013. *Fertile Disorder: Spirit Possession and Its Provocation of the Modern*. Honolulu: University of Hawai'i Press.

Ram, Kalpana, and Margaret Jolly, eds. 1998. *Maternities and Modernities: Colonial and Postcolonial Experiences in Asia and the Pacific*. Cambridge: Cambridge University Press.

Ramaswamy, Sumathi. 1997. *Passions of the Tongue: Language Devotion in Tamil India, 1891–1970*. Berkeley: University of California Press.

Ramberg, Lucinda. 2014. *Given to the Goddess: South Indian Devadasis and the Sexuality of Religion*. Durham: Duke University Press.

Ramesh, Ramdeep. 2004. "Soft Drink Giants Accused over Pesticides." *The Guardian*, February 5, 2004.

Rapp, Rayna. 2000. *Testing Women, Testing the Fetus: The Social Impact of Amniocentesis in America*. New York: Routledge.

Raskin, S. 2015. "Decayed, Missing, and Filled: Subjectivity and the Dental Safety Net in Central Appalachia." Ph.D. diss., University of Arizona.

Remennick, L.I. 1990. "Induced Abortion as Cancer Risk Factor: A Review of Epidemiological Evidence." *Journal of Epidemiology and Community Health* 44(4): 259–64.

Roberts, Nathaniel. 2016. *To Be Cared For: The Power of Conversion and Foreignness of Belonging in an Indian Slum*. Berkeley: University of California Press.

Rödlach, Alexander. 2006. *Witches, Westerners, and HIV: AIDS and Cultures of Blame in Africa*. Walnut Creek: Left Coast Press.

Romanucci-Ross, Lola. 1969. "The Hierarchy of Resort in Curative Practices: The Admiralty Islands, Melanesia." *Journal of Health and Social Behavior* 10(3): 201–9.

Sadanathan, Anoop. 2018. "What Lies Beneath the Alarming Rise of Violence against Dalits?" *The Wire*, June 15, 2018.

Sankaranarayanan, Rengaswamy, Pulikkottil Okkuru Esmy, Rajamanickam Rajkumar, Richard Muwonge, Rajaraman Swaminathan, Sivanandam Shanthakumari, Jean-Marie Fayette, and Jacob Cherian. 2007. "Effect of Visual Screening on Cervical Cancer Incidence and Mortality in Tamil Nadu, India: A Cluster-Randomised Trial." *The Lancet* 370(9585): 398–406.

Sargent, Carolyn, and Peter Benson. 2019. "Cancer and Precarity: Rights and Vulnerabilities of West African Immigrants in France." In *Negotiating Structural Vulnerability in Cancer Control*, edited by Julie Armin, Nancy Burke, and Laura Eichelberger, 21–46. Albuquerque: University of New Mexico Press.

Sarojini, N., S. Anjali, and S. Ashalata. 2010. "Findings from a Visit to Bhadrachalam: HPV Vaccine 'Demonstration Project' Site in Andhra Pradesh." Delhi: SAMA Resource Group for Women and Health.

Seo, Mitsuru, Kazuo Tamura, Hiroshi Shijo, Eiji Morioka, Chie Ikegame, and Keiko Hirasako. 2000. "Telling the Diagnosis to Cancer Patients in Japan: Attitude and Perception of Patients, Physicians, and Nurses." *Palliative Medicine* 14(2): 105–10.

Sered, Susan Starr, and Rushika J. Fernandopulle. 2006. *Uninsured in America: Life and Death in the Land of Opportunity*. Berkeley: University of California Press.

Shanta, V., R. Swaminathan, and R. Rama. 2013. "Cancer Prevention and Control in India: A Perspective from the Cancer Institute (WIA)." *Cancer Control (Regional Initiatives)*, 129–34.

Shetty, Priya. 2012. "India Faces Growing Breast Cancer Epidemic." *The Lancet* 379(9820): 992–93.

Singer, Merrill. 1986. "Developing a Critical Perspective in Medical Anthropology." *Medical Anthropology Quarterly* 17(5): 128–29.

Sivaramakrishnan, Kavitha. 2019. "An Irritable State: The Contingent Politics of Science and Suffering in Anti-Cancer Campaigns in South India (1940–1960)." *BioSocieties* 14(4): 529–52.

Smith, Stephanie. 2009 (May). *Public Health and Maternal Mortality in India*. Ph.D. diss., Syracuse University.

Sontag, Susan. 1978. *Illness as Metaphor*. New York: Random House.

Srinivasan, R.R. 2008. *En Peyar Palar ("My Name Is Palar")*. Documentary film. Social Action Movement and the Water Rights Protection Group, Chengalpattu, Tamil Nadu, India.

Stevenson, Lisa. 2014. *Life beside Itself: Imagining Care in the Canadian Arctic*. Berkeley: University of California Press.

Still, Clarinda. 2017. *Dalit Women: Honour and Patriarchy in South India*. New York: Routledge.

Stoller, Paul. 2004. *Stranger in the Village of the Sick: A Memoir of Cancer, Sorcery, and Healing*. Boston: Beacon Press.

Subha Sri, B., and T.K. Sundari. 2017. "RUWSEC: Challenges Faced by a Grassroots Feminist Clinic." In *Re-Presenting Feminist Methodologies: Interdisciplinary Explorations*, edited by Kalpana Kannabiran and Padmini Swaminathan, 329–31. New York: Routledge.

Subramanian, Meera. 2015. *A River Runs Again: India's Natural World in Crisis, from the Barren Cliffs of Rajasthan to the Farmlands of Karnataka*. New York: Perseus Books.

Sundar, Sudha, et al. 2018. "Harnessing Genomics to Improve Outcomes for Women with Cancer in India: Key Priorities for Research." *The Lancet Oncology* 19: e102–12.

Sunder Rajan, Kaushik. 2017. *Pharmocracy: Value, Politics, and Knowledge in Global Biomedicine*. Durham: Duke University Press.

Taylor, Kathryn. 1998. "Physicians and the Disclosure of Undesirable Information." In *Biomedicine Examined*, edited by Margaret Lock and Deborah Gordon, 441–64. Dordrecht: Springer.

Teltumbde, Anand. 2017. "Foreword." In *Dalit Women: Vanguard of an Alternative Politics in India*, edited by S. Anandhi and Karin Kapadia, 53–74. New York: Routledge.

*Times of India*, 2015 (October). "One in 13 World Cancer Patients Is Indian." http://timesofindia.indiatimes.com/india/One-in-13-world-cancer-patients-is-Indian-Study/articleshow/49330716.cms.

Trawick, Margaret. 1992a. "An Ayurvedic Theory of Cancer." In *Anthropological Approaches to the Study of Ethnomedicine*, edited by Mark Nichter, 207–222. Philadelphia: Gordon and Breach.

———. 1992b. *Notes on Love in a Tamil Family*. Berkeley: University of California Press.

Unnithan-Kumar, Maya. 2010. "Female Selective Abortion—beyond 'Culture': Family Making and Gender Inequality in a Globalising India." *Culture, Health, and Sexuality* 12(2): 153–66.

Van Hollen, Cecilia C. 1987. "Mariamman: A Festival in Madurai." Senior Thesis Fieldwork Project–Year in India Program, University of Wisconsin.

———. 1998. "Moving Targets: Routine IUD Insertion in Maternity Wards in Tamil Nadu, India." *Reproductive Health Matters* 6(11): 98–106.

———. 2003. *Birth on the Threshold: Childbirth and Modernity in South India*. Berkeley: University of California Press.

———. 2011. "Breast or Bottle? HIV-Positive Women's Responses to Global Health Policy on Infant Feeding in India." *Medical Anthropology Quarterly* 25(4): 499–518.

———. 2013. *Birth in the Age of AIDS: Women, Reproduction, and HIV/AIDS in India*. Stanford: Stanford University Press.

———. 2019. "May the Vital Force Be with You: An Indian Homeopathic Doctor's Approach to the Gendered Ills of Our Time." In *Local Health Traditions: Plural-*

*ism and Marginality in South Asia*, edited by Arima Mishra, 291–310. Delhi: Orient Blackswan.

———. Forthcoming 2023. "Morality Tales of Reproductive Cancer Screening Camps in South India." In *Cancer and the Politics of Care*, edited by Linda Bennett, Lenore Manderson, and Belinda Spagnoletti. London: UCL Press.

Van Hollen, Cecilia, Shweta Krishnan, and Shibani Rathnam. 2019. "'It's Partly in Our Hands; It's Partly in the Hands of the Goddess': Cancer Patients' Quest for Well-Being in India." *Purushartha: Sciences Sociales En Asie Du Sud (Social Science in South Asia)*. 36: 179–206.

Visaria, L., and V. Ramachandran, eds. 2007. *Abortion in India: Ground Realities*. New York: Routledge.

Ward, Mary. 2009. "Too Much of a Good Thing? Nitrate from Nitrogen Fertilizers and Cancer." *Reviews on Environmental Health* 24(4). https://doi.org/10.1515/REV EH.2009.24.4.357.

Weaver, Lesley Jo. 2018. *Sugar and Tension: Diabetes and Gender in Modern India*. New Brunswick: Rutgers University Press.

Whitehead, Judy. 1995. "Bodies Clean and Unclean: Prostitution, Sanitary Legislation, and Respectable Femininity in Colonial North India." *Gender and History* 7(1): 41–63.

Winslow, Miron. 1991 [1862]. *Winslow's: A Comprehensive Tamil and English Dictionary*. Madras: Asian Educational Services.

World Health Organization (WHO). 2016. "Media Centre: Household Air Pollution and Health. Fact Sheet no. 292," February. http://www.who.int/medicentre/fact sheets/fs292/en.

# INDEX

Note: page numbers in italics refer to maps. Those followed by n refer to notes, with note number.

Founded in 1893,
UNIVERSITY OF CALIFORNIA PRESS
publishes bold, progressive books and journals
on topics in the arts, humanities, social sciences,
and natural sciences—with a focus on social
justice issues—that inspire thought and action
among readers worldwide.

The UC PRESS FOUNDATION
raises funds to uphold the press's vital role
as an independent, nonprofit publisher, and
receives philanthropic support from a wide
range of individuals and institutions—and from
committed readers like you. To learn more, visit
ucpress.edu/supportus.

www.ingramcontent.com/pod-product-compliance
Lightning Source LLC
Chambersburg PA
CBHW020830270326
41928CB00006B/475